W9-CKQ-500

The Hitler Escape Trilogy

HITLER in ARGENTINA

The Escape of Adolf Hitler and Martin Bormann from the Führerbunker as Told by Nazi Spy Don Angel Alcazar de Velasco...and more!

IN A LETTER TO HARRY COOPER IN 1984

First released as *"Escape from the Bunker"*

First Printing July 2006   **Second Printing May 2010**
Revised January 2014

Edited by Harry Cooper

Cover art by David Dees at DDees.com

Sharkhunters International

P. O. Box 1539 Hernando, FL 34441

www.sharkhunters.com

Revised 2014

This book has been given a major revision in early 2014. The main text is not revised. It remains verbatim – exactly as **DON ANGEL ALCAZAR de VELASCO (158-1985)** told us in his letter sent to us in the mid-1980's.

That is unchanged because the facts are unchanged – so what is revised? We have added some personal letters from **DON ANGEL** to Sharkhunters around that same time **AND** many previously classified files from various sources.

DON ANGEL of course, got things started but recently other S.E.I.G. Agents have pulled classified files and sent them to us. This acronym is from **S**harkhunters **E**aglehunters **I**ntelligence **G**roup.

S.E.I.G. Agent **REMBRANDT** pulled files for us from the Dutch Secret Service. S.E.I.G. Agent **TAUCHER** pulled files of the FBI, OSS and CIA from dusty corridors in the National Archives. Top of the group is S.E.I.G. Agent **PIZZARRO** who pulled countless files from many sources including some forgotten STASI files from the collapsed DDR.

Enjoy this revised book with all the new solid proof that Adolf Hitler, Eva Braun, Martin Bormann and thousands of others of the collapsed Third Reich did not perish in the ashes of the ruined Germany but indeed, lived out their lives in safety and comfort in various South American countries, primarily in Argentina.

Fähnrich!

A Fähnrich is a midshipman, an officer in training. Contrary to popular propaganda, the German officer corps was held to an extremely high standard of honor as we see here in the Code of Conduct written by Vizeadmiral Lohmann, Commandant of the Naval Academy at Mürwick.

"The following professional and lifetime rules are valid in war and peace. I give them to you; put them to good use."

1. Be example setting in all situations of life, especially in critical hours. You must be an ideal for your soldiers.

2. Always assert the interior and exterior behavior of a soldier. The superior must be the best disciplined man if he demands each subordinate will obey him.

3. Keep your honor unblemished. It is lost when you tamper with it in thoughts, words and deeds.

4. Preserve your courage to the utmost truth. Stand by your words and actions.

5. Be open with your superior, but remain tactful. Observe the sharp border between 'on-duty' and 'off-duty'.

6. Learn from 'verbal corrections'; do not play the insulted.

7. Restrain your judgment on matters which you do not master. The right to critique is reserved for those who have proven that they can do it better.

8. Pay attention to your own posture and behavior on duty and off duty. Only he who masters the common forms of society possesses the image for an officer necessary for successes in presenting himself.

9. Keep your body under control. Strengthen it regularly and maintain it in action preparedness. Self-control and restraint are manly. Letting go of yourself is irresponsible.

10. Restrain yourself from excessive alcohol consumption. It is often the cause for derailments.

11. Do not incur debts. They diminish your joy of life and drive for action.

12. Take advantage of time in your youth to educate and further yourself.

13. Sharpen your mind through periodic intellectual work in all areas, especially in regards to your profession. Immerse yourself in matters of literature, culture and history.

14. Form your own personality on examples of great men.

15. Listen to experienced comrades. From listening and contemplating, you can draw great winners.

16. When you are entrusted with men, always remember how in the past you wanted to be treated in the same situation.

17. Have respect for your superior and subordinates. You protect yourself from troublesome circumstances.

18. Act with common sense and heart. Otherwise you run the danger of losing your authority.

19. Hold the honor feeling of your soldiers as sacred.

20. Avoid harsh language; usually the sign of insecurity.

21. Before giving orders, look very carefully at your people and try to identify the human beings in them.

22. Orders only make sense when they convince and are executable.

23. The language of orders must be plain and penetrate the heart.

24. Keep your crew tightly together.   Help each other in effective camaraderie.

25. Often read the book by Sorge, '***The Navy Officer as Leader and Teacher***'. It will give you guidance in all questions regarding daily duties.

26. Preserve your belief in your citizens, the German mission and God.   Your belief will give you energy for life, combat and victory.

(Sent by Sharkhunters Member **WALTER KERN (6345-2001)**, photo right as a young soldier during the '***Battle of the Bulge***')

EDITOR NOTE - When we can get our heads out of the wartime propaganda and more so out of the really intense post-war fiction, we see that the German officer corps was indeed, extremely honorable.

On the next pages you will read what various people, military and otherwise, thought of the Sharkhunters book series.

Explanation of Membership Numbers. You will note that a Member has two sections to his//her Membership Number. The first is their Member Number – in the case of **WALTER KERN**, it is #**6345**. The second number denotes the year is which they joined Sharkhunters and in his case, **KERN** joined in 2001.

TABLE OF CONTENTS

Escape from the Bunker

FOREWORD

My Friend, the Spy
Foreword by HARRY COOPER (1-LIFE-1983)

In this book, we examine probably the biggest mystery of the 20th Century and beyond.....did Adolf Hitler commit suicide in the Führerbunker or not? The world demanded to know the fate of the three leaders of the Axis powers when the war ended. There was no doubt about the fate of Italian leader '*Il Duce*' Benito Mussolini (below left). He and his mistress were caught by Italian communists, brutally butchered and their bodies hung by the heels in a gas station. The world also knew that Japanese war leader Hideki Tojo (below right) shot himself as the Americans closed in on him, but he failed in his suicide attempt. He was nursed back to health then tried, found guilty and hanged.

But Hitler – only the Soviets were on the scene and they were sadly lacking in the sciences and refused to communicate with the West. So what did happen to Hitler? This book will tell you exactly what happened.

Keep in mind that no one witnessed the alleged suicide of Adolf Hitler and his wife, Eva Braun-Hitler in the Führerbunker. The three men who told about the suicide claim that they heard shots but they did not witness any suicide – and their stories differed markedly in the description of vital details as you see here from the book *"The Secret Alliance"* written by S.E.I.G. Agent Michael Ivinheim. Ivinheim tells us:

1. Three SS officers entered Hitler's suite at the Reich Chancellery on the afternoon of 30 April 1945 and saw the bodies of Hitler and Eva Hitler.

2. The three officers all held the rank of SS-Sturmbannführer (Major). These persons were:
- (i)   Otto Günsche, Hitler's SS adjutant.
- (ii)   Heinz Linge, Hitler's valet.
- (iii) Erich Kempka, Hitler's driver and head of the motor pool.

Günsche   Linge   Kempka

3. These three officers subsequently made statements which do not coincide in the following:
- (i)   The time of the occurrence.
- (ii)   Who was where at the time.
- (iii) How the suicide was discovered.
- (iv)   Who entered the suite with whom.
- (v)   The position of Hitler's body.
- (vi)   The order in which the bodies were removed and by whom.

4. The source material appears in two books:
(i) Heinz Linge: *Bis zum Untergang*, Wilhelm Goldmann Verlag, 1980 at p.284-288.
(ii) Erich Kempka: *Die letzten Tage mit Adolf Hitler*, Deutsche Verlagsgesellschaft, Preussisch-Oldendorf, 1991 at p.89-96.
(iii) In Kempka's book at p.311-313 is the statement made by Günsche in a letter to Kempka dated 1 July 1975, the year in which Kempka died.

5. In *Kempka*, p.93, there appears the sketch of the room in which the alleged suicides occurred. The room was rectangular, approximately 3 x 2.5 metres. Entering by the double doors from the ante-room, the visitor faced the long wall against which the sofa was located. There was an armchair either side of the sofa. Before the sofa was a table with a vase of flowers. These details are important for understanding the major discrepancy.

It may be helpful to read the Conclusion at the foot of this article first and use the three statements to confirm what the Conclusion says. Some important areas of discrepancy between the accounts are highlighted in the primary account in block.

Statement of Kempka.
(The following is condensed from 4 pages of unimportant matter.)

Towards midday on 30 April 1945 I was in a little-damaged restroom in the subterranean garage. I had just come in from outside to oversee the change of shift. Half an hour later the phone rang. It was Günsche. He said he had to have 200 litres of petrol. He wanted it immediately at the entrance to the Führer-bunker. I had to stand the world on its head to get it.

I said I would have to go to the underground fuel store at the Zoo for that amount, and suggested that he wait until 1700 hrs when the Russian artillery would be quieter. Günsche said he had to have it now and hung up. I ordered my assistants to syphon out what they could find in the vehicles in the garage bunker and hurried over the rubble to the Führerbunker to find out what was going on.

I met Günsche in the annex to the situation room as he left the Führer-suite. I asked what was amiss and he said,
"The Chief is dead!"

Günsche gave me his story. He said that Bormann, Linge and he, Günsche, had heard the shot and rushed into the suite at once. The Chief had shot himself in the head with his pistol and had inclined forward over the table top. Eva Hitler had taken poison and lay at an angle against the right arm of the sofa beside him. Her right arm hung over the sofa arm and her revolver (elsewhere he says "pistol") was on the floor near her. Dr Stumpfegger had certified death. Goebbels and Axmann were also in attendance.

Stumpfegger   Axmann

Immediately after this conversation Linge came out of the Führer-suite and asked where the petrol was. I had just been told by one of my staff that we had up to 180 litres ready, and so replied,
"The petrol is here!"

Seconds later the door to the suite opened again. Dr Stumpfegger and Linge carried out the body of Adolf Hitler, wrapped in a dark field blanket, through the ante-room to the corridor. Behind them followed Martin Bormann with the dead Eva Hitler. She wore a black dress, her blonde head laid back. Eva had hated Bormann in life. I said to Günsche,
"Help them carry the Chief, I will take Eva."

Then I took her body from Bormann. Her side was wet. Later Günsche told me that as Hitler fell forward over the table he had upset the vase of flowers, and probably the water had splashed her.

Halfway up the twenty bunker steps my strength failed me and Günsche came back to share the load and help me bring her dead body into the open. In their haste Dr Stumpfegger and Linge had laid Hitler about 3 metres away from the bunker entrance. Günsche and I laid Eva Hitler beside her husband.

EDITOR NOTE – Günsche was a tall and powerful man.

It was getting on for two in the afternoon (p.95 *"Inzwischen war es gegen zwei Uhr nachmittags geworden"*). (This was not a typographical error, for Kempka repeats it):....The cremation lasted from two o'clock in the afternoon until about 7.30 in the evening. (p.99 *"Von mittags gegen 14 Uhr bus ungefähr 1930 Uhr abends dauerte die Verbrennung an."*)

Statement of Linge

After the midday meal, Eva Hitler took her leave of me. Then she spoke with Frau Goebbels while Hitler withdrew to the suite. Günsche had told me that Frau Goebbels wanted a personal interview with the Führer. I told Hitler, and he said she should come to the suite. They were alone for a while. When I entered, Hitler told me to fetch a gold Party badge from one of his uniforms and he presented it to Frau Goebbels.

Immediately after this, Hitler and I went to the waiting room where Dr Goebbels appeared and made an attempt to convince Hitler to leave Berlin. Hitler declined, shook Goebbels' hand and then returned to the suite with me. Now came the last goodbyes, with Flugkapitän Baur and Otto Günsche. Finally Hitler gave me a tired look and indicated that he was retiring for the last time. It was 1515 hrs."

He told me, ***"Linge, now I am going to shoot myself,"*** and gave me instructions on how I was to break out of Berlin. Once he went inside, I shut the door behind him.

I walked to the bunker exit, where the SS bodyguard was sitting around. As I assumed that Hitler would very soon put an end to his life, I did not stay there long, but went back to the ante-room adjacent to the suite. **There I smelt the smoke from a gun having been discharged.**

I did not feel I could face opening the suite door and going in alone. I went to the situation room where a group had gathered around Martin Bormann. They were unaware of what had happened. I gave Bormann a sign and asked him to accompany me to Hitler's suite. Once there I opened the door and entered, Bormann following...

Adolf and Eva Hitler were seated on the sofa. Both were dead. He had shot himself in the right temple with his 7.65 mm pistol. This, and the reserve 6.35mm pistol lay on the floor near his feet. His head was inclined a little to the wall; blood had sprayed on the carpet near the sofa. His wife sat at his right, her legs drawn up under her. She had taken cyanide. The ampoule lay on the table.

I pushed him to one side to make room to work. Bormann went out to find helpers to carry the bodies. I spread out the blankets, laid the bodies on them and wrapped them over. I did not look at Hitler's head and so I cannot say what damage the bullet inflicted.

Eva Hitler was carried out first. Kempka carried her in his arms.

I took hold below Hitler's head, two officers of the escort lifted up the body in its grey blanket. Like that we carried him out.

Outside the bunker entrance in the Reich Chancellery Park we laid him next to Eva's body in a small depression and poured petrol over them. (*Describes the difficulty in lighting the pyre*). The last witnesses, Bormann, Goebbels, Stumpfeger, Günsche, Kempka and I made a last Hitler salute and returned inside. I had work to do and so did not see the bodies again. I understand they were still burning at around 1930 hrs.

Statement of Günsche

At about nine in the morning of 30 April 1945, I saw Martin Bormann who informed me that Hitler and his wife intended to commit suicide that day. The Führer had ordered that their bodies be incinerated immediately after death. I was to make the arrangements.

A little later I was summoned by the Führer. He repeated what Bormann had said, but made me responsible personally for the bodies of himself and his wife being burnt beyond recognition.

Earlier photo of Günsche with Hitler

After arranging for all available petrol supplies to be brought from the garage complex in the Hermann Goering Strasse, I posted sentries of the Führer's SS-bodyguard at the entrance to the ante-room. Only Goebbels, Bormann, Burgdorf, Krebs, Rattenhuber, Mohnke, Linge, Kempka and myself had access to this ante-room immediately in front of the Führer's suite.

Adolf Hitler and his wife took their leave of various close colleagues between 1430 and 1500 hrs including Goebbels, Frau Goebbels, Bormann and Burgdorf in a room adjacent to the ante-room. Then they returned to the Führer-suite.

I stationed myself in immediate proximity to the door to Adolf Hitler's suite. A short while later the sentry at the ante-room doorway informed me that Frau Goebbels was waiting at the door and had asked to speak privately again with the Führer at once. I knocked at the inner door of the suite - (there was an outer door and inner door) - and Adolf Hitler opened it himself and said brusquely,
    "What is it, Günsche?"

I told him the reason and, apparently annoyed, he went past me to where she stood in the ante-room. She begged him to leave Berlin. Hitler gave her a dismissive answer and returned at once to the suite. I closed the double doors behind him. After that nobody could, or did, enter the private suite of Adolf Hitler and his wife before their suicide.

When Bormann, Linge and I opened the double doors to Hitler's suite at 1530 hrs we saw Adolf Hitler sitting in the armchair near the divan on the left wall in front of us ("...*sahen wir Adolf Hitler auf dem an der linken Wand vor uns, neben dem Divan stehenden Sessel sitzen*"). He had slumped and hung over the right arm of the armchair. His head was inclined to the side. Blood was dripping from the right temple. One could see immediately that he had shot himself in the right temple with his PPK 7.65."

(*This Statement, made in 1975 thirty years after the event, differs substantially from what Günsche told Kempka immediately after the event in 1945. Neither statement by Günsche concurs with what Linge stated. In this later statement, Eva Hitler was alone on the divan, and Hitler was seated in the armchair between the right side of the divan and the central heating cover with the photograph of Hitler's mother.*)

You see the dilemma here. **HARRY COOPER (1-LIFE-1983)** is absolutely certain that Adolf Hitler did NOT die in Berlin but lived out his normal life in Argentina. On the other hand, here we have testimony of three SS officers who were in the bunker and say they saw Adolf and Eva Hitler's dead bodies.

It's all clear in the conclusions of S.E.I.G. Agent Michael Ivinheim which you will read on the next page.

Did Adolf Hitler and Eva Braun-Hitler die in the bunker as accepted history tells us – or is **COOPER**'s research accurate?

In his extensive research, interviewing people, gathering facts from S.E.I.G. Agents **PIZZARRO, TIGER, SECOND SON** and many others plus using the thousands of pages of documents gathered by S.E.I.G. Agent **TAUCHER** there can be no doubt that Adolf Hitler and Eva Braun-Hitler did not die in the Führerbunker. **DON ANGEL ALCAZAR de VELASCO (158-1985)** told this story and he was backed up by US Naval Intelligence Captain **ROBERT THEW (333-1987)**. But now we look at the testimonies of three honorable SS officers and they tell that they are eye witnesses to the death of Adolf Hitler and Eva Braun-Hitler in the bunker. But were they really?

Michael Ivinheim removes the riddle and again, proves that the story of the suicide in the bunker is a false trail. He tells us the following:

Here we have a charade in which three SS-officers even long after the war fail to collaborate to get their story straight regarding the events of the afternoon of 30 April 1945 in the Berlin bunker.

All three men held equal rank - SS-*Sturmbannführer*. Linge (left) was Hitler's valet, Günsche was Hitler's SS adjutant and Kempka Hitler's personal driver and head of the motor pool. The statements of Linge and Kempka appear in their own books listed above; Günsche's 1975 statement appears in Kempka's book. Kempka also reports what Günsche told him immediately after "*Hitler shot himself*".

Kemka driving Hitler and Mussolini   Günsche

The account of Linge is so worded as to eliminate Günsche from the scene as from 1515 hrs. when Hitler said his last goodbye to Günsche, i.e. a quarter of an hour before he alleges that he (Linge) and Bormann entered the Führer-suite. According to Linge there was no guard posted at the doors to the Führer's suite or ante-room.

The area was deserted. At the critical time, he had absented himself and gone to the entrance to the Führer bunker for an unspecified reason. He returned to the suite area and became aware, from the odour of the burnt powder passing through the double doors to the suite that a gun had been discharged inside. He alerted Bormann in the situation room, and both men entered the Führer suite together. They saw the couple dead on the sofa. Linge says that the body of Eva Braun was carried out first. The porters were Linge and two officers of the escort, although the other accounts say Linge and Dr Stumpfegger. They laid Hitler's body next to his wife outside the bunker entrance, i.e her body was already there when Hitler's body was brought out.

In his account, Günsche reports that he posted sentries of the SS bodyguard at the entrance to the ante-room before 1430 hrs, and he stationed himself in immediate proximity to the doors to Hitler's suite, and was there at all times prior to the event. He had told Kempka in 1945 that he, Bormann and Linge all heard the shot, and this was the reason why they entered the suite together.

Linge states that he did not hear the shot, he smelled gunsmoke. He saw no SS bodyguards, nor Günsche, outside the Führer's suite and the ante-room. That was why he went to fetch Bormann.

Günsche told Kempka originally in 1945 that Hitler and Eva Hitler had died on the sofa together, and Hitler must have overturned the vase of flowers when he collapsed over the table top. By Günsche's 1975 statement, Hitler could not have overturned the vase if he had been in the armchair to the right of the divan - but even if Hitler had slumped over the tabletop from the sofa to knock over the vase, how did he get back from the tabletop to the left hand side of the sofa after he shot himself?

Kempka's account begins by saying that the body of Hitler was brought out first by Linge and Dr Stumpfegger, then came the body of Eva Hitler which he carried himself with the aid of Bormann and later Günsche. They laid the body of Eva Hitler beside her husband, whereas Linge says that he laid the body of Adolf Hitler beside his wife, and they cannot both have been right. Moreover, Kempka says that the suicides occurred before two o'clock whereas Linge and Günsche, and Bormann in a later signal to Dönitz, all have the "*time of death*" as being later than 3.30.

In my opinion (Ivinheim's), these officers were all stupid, or this is an SS charade which contains a message. And that message says; you cannot believe what we say about the suicide of Adolf Hitler and his wife.

The Very Strange Death of Otto Günsche

According to S.E.I.G. Agent **NIGHTINGALE**, Otto Günsche (previous page) was in perfect health when he celebrated his 88th birthday. About ten days later, his housekeeper found him dead in the sauna at 9am and he had been there since the previous afternoon with the temperature set at 85° Celsius! That is about 185° Fahrenheit! Meat isn't cooked at that high temperature. Perhaps he was ready to reveal the truth to the world. Of course, it could simply have been a heart attack as reported.........

Sharkhunters was only two years old when **DON ANGEL ALCAZAR de VELASCO** joined as a new Member in 1985. Over the next few years, we became friendly and he became more trusting, and he told us his story.

His background has been thoroughly checked and he was indeed, who he said he was – he was a spy for the Axis; first for Japan then for Germany. In addition to various confirmations, two highly trained agents, both Members of Sharkhunters, confirmed he was genuine. One of these agents was Captain **ROBERT THEW (333-1987)**, retired as a full captain in Naval Intelligence then for many years well placed in the NSA. The other was German Abwehr agent **PETER HANSEN (251-1987)** photo left, who personally knew both Großadmiral Karl Dönitz and Admiral Wilhelm Canaris, the German spy chief who was executed with piano wire after the failed attempt on Hitler's life at the Wolfsschanze.

Here at Sharkhunters in the middle to late 1980's, we were digging deeply into the rumors of the '*Black Boats*' that were taking escaping Germans to Argentina. We learned that the little town of Villa Garcia seen on this chart, about thirty kilometers from the port city of Vigo, Spain was a main

jumping off point for former Abwehr and Party officials as well as high ranking SS officers and German scientists. The existence of the '*Black Boats*' was confirmed early by two other Sharkhunters Members. One was an officer and

the other an enlisted man. Both served on '*Black Boats*' that went to Argentina well after the reported suicide of Adolf Hitler in late April 1945 and the German surrender in May 1945.

We were asked not to reveal their names while they were living. They have departed on their *"Eternal Patrol"* and we can report that they were **PAUL BOCHEN (5051-1996)** and **KARL WALDECK (6167-2000)**.

BOCHEN emigrated to the United States in the 1950's where he lived the normal American lifestyle – got a job, worked hard, was married, bought a home and lived out his life as a normal, hard working guy with a family.

WALDECK and his wife Anni moved to England where they managed large hotels for their working life. Once retired, they moved back to Austria where they lived out their retirement.

BOCHEN (seen here in 1943 – photo right) rode the *"Black Boats"* from late in the war until a year after the end of the war. **WALDECK** was attached to German destroyers at the end of the war but that was only on paper as the Kriegsmarine had no more destroyers at that time. In fact he rode a *"Black Boat"* on three separate patrols after the end of the war to the central Atlantic. There they met steamers and transferred their passengers to the ships. **WALDECK** was quick to add that he could not remember the names of any of the passengers aboard his submarine.

Our extensive research showed that at least three German U-Boats were on the high seas in the central Atlantic at the time of the surrender. First was *U-530*, commanded by Sharkhunters Member **OTTO WERMUTH (1344-1990),** surrendered at the Argentine Navy submarine base at Mar del Platte in July 1945, more than two months after the surrender order was given. Then in August 1945, about two weeks later, *U-977* under command of Heinz Schäffer, surrendered at the same submarine base at the other end of the world. Both commanders said they had no knowledge that the other boat was at sea or that they were going to surrender at the very same far flung South American port. When each Skipper was asked, separately and in private, why they chose to surrender at Mar del Platte, their replies were exactly the same. They said they wanted to surrender their men at a place where they would be treated with dignity – and each claimed that they knew nothing of the other boat's plans.

OTTO WERMUTH in Mar del plate, Argentina where he surrendered *U-530* two months **AFTER** the German surrender.

While *U-530*, a long range Type IX-C submarine, had the *'legs'* to reach Argentina, the Type VII-C submarine *U-977* poses a real enigma. According to Commander Schäffer's own report, they departed their base in Norway with only ¾ of a fuel load and went to their assigned patrol station off the British Isles. Then came the surrender order and Schäffer, according to his own book, headed back to their Norwegian base to offload the married men and with short-handed crew of the unmarried men but no additional fuel (according to his book), set out for Argentina, arriving there nearly three months later.

Even if she had full fuel load, a Type VII-C would have a tough time making that vast distance as their range is but 6,500 miles. However, despite Schaeffer's own reports of short fuel, *U-977* made it to Mar del

Platte. It was Schäffer's claim that he was able to make this long distance by remaining submerged and running on just one diesel while snorkeling. That makes no sense. I would be far more difficult to push the submerged boat with the angular structures above the deck through the water as opposed to running surfaced, thereby they would be using more fuel.

In the book *"The Secret Alliance"* S.E.I.G. Agent Michael Ivinheim debunks the claim of the sixty-six days running submerged.

U-977 in Mar del Plata, 3 months after the German surrender

Both **WERMUTH** and Schäffer claimed that they had jettisoned all forms of paperwork at sea prior to arriving Mar del Plate. However, former Abwehr agent **PETER HANSEN (251-1987)** was brought to Buenos Aires in 1947 to translate all the papers – that *"were not aboard"* these boats. And when **HARRY COOPER (1-LIFE-1983)** visited the submarine base at Mar del Plate in 2008, the boxes of these papers were shown to him and **COOPER** was told he could return any time and read these documents.

On the next page we see some of the documents that *"were not aboard"* either *U-530* or *U-977*. Fortunately we have an excellent rapport with the Argentine Navy and can return if we want to.

These are just some of the documents we saw at Mar del Plate. **PETER HANSEN (251-1987)** tells us there is nothing earth-shattering here; that they were merely operational manuals for the various pieces of equipment aboard the submarines. That really does make sense, as we believe that any and all orders pertaining to the escape of anyone of significant rank would all be verbal.

Hitler's Suicide A Hoax? Government Said It's True.

When we received this very long story from Don Angel, I just couldn't believe it. Hitler died by his own hand – that was published and accepted history and I told him so, but he insisted that his story was true. Some of his claims were easy to verify while others remained only shadows. Then the unimaginable happened – the Soviet Union evaporated! When that happened, we were able to get into the many small archives that were previously behind the '*Iron Curtain*'; the pieces began to fall into place.

Secret Bases? Secret Suicides? Too Many Secrets.

We learned about such places as '*Basis Nord*' and '*Feuerland*'!

'*Basis Nord*' (Northern Bases) refers to an agreement between Germany and the Soviet Union for the German Navy (Kriegsmarine) to use secret bases on Russia's northern coast. This included maintenance, repair and fuel facilities of the most rudimentary kind and the fuel was more or less unsuitable for the Kriegsmarine ships. It was a short-lived operation anyhow and once Germany invaded the Soviet Union with *Operation BARBAROSSA*, all agreements between the two nations ceased to exist.

'*Feuerland*' was an entirely different situation. That German word means '*Land of fire*' and in Spanish, it is known as Tierra del Fuego and refers to the southernmost part of South America. In 1915, the German light cruiser **DRESDEN** made her way through the Straits of Magellan at the southern tip of South America after the cruiser squadron of Admiral Graf von Spee was wiped out in the Battle of the Falkland Islands.

On board was a young Leutnant named Wilhelm Canaris and it was his job to scout out '*U-Plätze*' or hidden places. He was looking for hidden harbors where ships could safely anchor and not be seen by enemy ships. In 1938, the aging battleship **SCHLESWIG HOLSTEIN** (photo below) retraced the route, making more detailed notes to those of Canaris in 1915. By the time of World War Two, young Leutnant Canaris was Admiral Canaris in command of the Abwehr, Germany's Secret Service.

These harbors, these '*U-Plätze*' had no facilities at all; they were merely places to hide a ship and personnel aboard the old battleship produced some extremely detailed specifications on each hidden harbor including the proximity to steamer lanes, to civilization and gave the prevailing wind directions, bottom characteristics, how many ships could remain in each harbor, maximum height of the masts to be concealed by the trees and much more. An example is on the next page.

Island Clarence 54° 103'S x 71° 45'W A long channel begin after Dunellon. Bay is 20 miles from Cockburn Channel, then a great bay thirty meters deep.

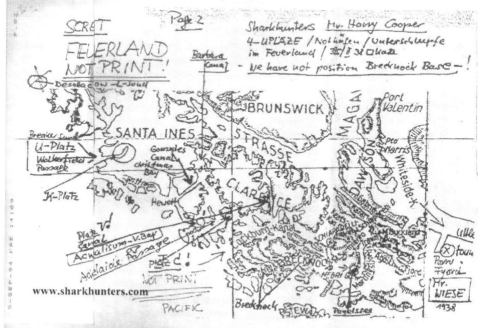

This chart and many other secret charts and photos appeared in the **KTB** Magazine that Sharkhunters publishes ten times annually.

Back to the Führerbunker. The bloodstains on the sofa where Hitler was said to have shot himself were not the same blood type as Hitler. The only person of that inner circle still living into the 21st Century was Hitler's aide, Otto Günsche (right). He poured gasoline on the bodies – but whose bodies? He steadfastly refused to talk about that incident, and his silence speaks volumes; and his strange death also poses more questions.

Hitler was not a coward nor did he believe in giving in. Suicide was completely out of character. After he learned of the suicide of the mayor of Leipzig with his entire family, he condemned suicide as cowardly and unbecoming to a National Socialist.

His personal pilot initially stated that on the first of May 1945, he flew Hitler and Bormann to an airfield in Norway where they transferred to another aircraft and flew onward. He later  retracted this story and backed the suicide story. German forces in Norway held out longer than anywhere else and we know that **LEON deGRELLE (1835-1991)**, a Sharkhunters Member until his death, did indeed arrive in Norway aboard a minesweeper out of Copenhagen thanks to **GÜNTER DIETRICH (339-1987)**, another Member of Sharkhunters thence aboard a plane to Spain where he lived out his life at Malaga. Norway was indeed a key.

Another glaring source is from 1959. This comes to us from S.E.I.G. Agent **PIZZARRO** and he tells us that after prison camp in Russia, General Hans Bauer in 1955 is back to Western Germany. Hans Bauer was chief of all airplanes of Hitler and his Staff. Bauer told in 1959 that on airfield Rechlin-Lärz on 28 to 29 April 1945 was one big airplane for long range to Argentina or Japan. He did not tell the type but the six engine JU 390-V2 had this kind of range. There were several long-range JU 290 four engine transports there as well. So in 1957 General Bauer has written one book and in this book is the same information but Bauer did not give information about the pilot and crew of this last big airplane and he never told the type of this long range airplane.

Russian troops were on 2 May 1945 on the airfield Rechlin-Lärz but these troops did not find any JU 290 and no JU 390. Possibly the JU 390-V2 was on airfield Rechlin-Lärz the last day on 30 April 1945; it is possible this big airplane was on 1 May 1945 on the German airfield in northern Norway.

EDITOR NOTE – Several charts, hand drawn by S.E.I.G. Agent **PIZZARRO** are found at the end of this book.

The body was found by the Soviets and the West was not allowed to inspect the body. Their level of forensic science at that time was sorely lacking indeed and the body they found was badly burned. Stalin wanted Hitler dead in the worst way, so God help the poor Soviet officer who had to tell '*Uncle Joe*' that Hitler had given them the slip. It was in the best interest for long life that Soviet officers tell Stalin that Hitler was dead.

Marshall Zhukov did however, inform Stalin that they could find no corpse in Berlin that could be that of Adolf Hitler.

However, mere hours after the discovery of the body, one sharp eyed Soviet officer noticed that the body was wearing socks that had been mended. It was decided that surely the real Hitler would wear only new socks – socks without holes in them. Many years after the war, some Soviet officer based in Magdeburg in what was then East Germany, laughingly reported that they had Hitler's body buried at their headquarters. Impossible! If they really did have the body of Hitler, Stalin would have been using his skull as an ash tray. The hatred between these two men was that intense.

Further proof – as late as July 1945, two months after the German surrender and finding what was claimed to be Hitler's body in the Chancellery garden, Stalin publicly stated that Hitler was still alive and he demanded that the Americans and the British find him and turn him over. For years Stalin was afraid that the specter of Hitler would appear again at the gates of Moscow with more legions.

Shortly after we received the file from **DON ANGEL**, we received a visit from another Sharkhunters Member, Captain **ROBERT THEW**, USN (Retired). **BOB** was a graduate of the Naval Academy and spent his Navy career in Naval Intelligence. After he retired from the Navy, he went into America's most secret agency, the NSA which refers to the National Security Agency rather than '*No Such Agency*' as is jokingly stated. **BOB** stopped in for a visit in 1988 and we asked him if he had ever heard of **DON ANGEL ALCAZAR de VELASCO**. He smiled and confirmed that **DON ANGEL** certainly was the spy he claimed to be; but that he was such a bad spy that everyone in the spook world knew that he was a spy.

I told **BOB** about the file that **DON ANGEL** had sent to us and said that this guy must be nuts! **DON ANGEL** said that Martin Bormann and also Hitler did not die in Berlin. I said that everyone knows that Hitler killed himself in the bunker. I remember **BOB**'s reply as if it were yesterday. He sat on our sofa and as calmly as if he were asking for another cup of coffee, he said;

"We knew Hitler wasn't dead in Berlin."

This was a shock, so I asked him who he meant when he said '*we*' knew that Hitler wasn't dead, and he said;

"The Intelligence agencies. Every time we tracked down a high ranking Party official, an SS officer or Abwehr agent in the 1940's or early 1950's, the first thing we grilled him on was – where is Hitler?"

If Adolf Hitler killed himself in Berlin as the official history tells us, then why were the world's spy services still looking for him into the middle 1950's? Why did Stalin continue to claim that Hitler did not die in Berlin? Could it be that the story of the suicide was made up to cover the failure of the Soviets to find Hitler? There is another possibility why this was kept from the public. Now in the early 21st Century we are finding hints of possibilities that a trade off was made to allow Hitler to escape in exchange for a huge amount of German technology, including nuclear weapons, that would otherwise been lost or worse yet, gone to the Soviets. At this point, this merely was theory, but a lot of Intel was pointing in that direction and we were digging.

We must remember that official government sources state definitely that Hitler committed suicide in the Führerbunker and that the body found not far from the Chancellery some years later was indeed Martin Bormann.

One must wonder that with the tens of thousands of skeletal remains still in Berlin, why anyone would even think to check if that body or any other body in Berlin, was that of Martin Bormann – unless they needed to put an end to any speculation. The bodies were all skeletons and all looked alike by the time the one alleged to be that of Bormann was "*found*", so why would this one particular body be suspected as that of the Party Secretary unless it was necessary to put an end to some stories of the Reich?

Naturally, we must believe what the governments tell us, right? We must believe that John F. Kennedy was shot by a single madman using a worthless rifle and a '*magic bullet*'. Nobody with any sense believes that story but the Warren Commission tells us that this is the truth. Former President Gerald Ford was on that Commission, and someone once said of Ford that he could not chew gum and urinate at the same time – but this was the official government finding. We must believe it because the government says we must. Let us not forget the Gulf of Tonkin incident in which an American warship was fired upon by two gunboats, thereby sending the United States into the Vietnam War only to learn years later that this was a contrived fictional event that didn't happen. The list of lies by the world's governments could fill a massive book – actually an entire library of books………….but you already know that.

Did Hitler die in the Führerbunker? Did he escape to South America? After you read this book, your questions will be answered.

Sharkhunters' Credits

Founded in 1983, Sharkhunters International is recognized as the only official worldwide publication source of information on German U-Boat history. The U-Boat Skippers, officers and many crewmen worked with Sharkhunters to give their knowledge and their memories so that the real history will continue. Sharkhunters has done productions for various television shows including the History Channel as well as assisting many authors write highly accurate and well acclaimed books.

Aside from the U-Boat Archive in Germany, the Sharkhunters U-Boat Archive is the world's largest.

BBC reporter Graham Pound stated that Sharkhunters are:
"The most respected and most authoritative source in the world for U-Boat history."

Reporter Adam Harcourt-Webster said that;
"Sharkhunters are <u>*THE*</u> *experts on the U-Boats."*

In addition, Sharkhunters has helped many authors with their works:
  "Operation Drumbeat" by Professor Michael Gannon
  "Torpedoes in the Gulf" by Melanie Wiggins
  "Critical Mass" by Carter Hydrick
  "Hitler's Ashes" by Col. Howard Buechner
…..to name just a few. These authors were all Sharkhunters Members.

Sharkhunters has also assisted in productions for:
  The History Channel
  Ghost Hunters International

DEDICATION – and THANKS

A work of this magnitude cannot possibly be accomplished by one man. It takes a great team who constantly dig for hidden files and personal memories of a time most only know from history books and movies, most not even close to historical truths.

Naturally, I must make a large dedication to my wife and kids, Kay, Meaghan and Sean. They didn't see much of me while I was putting this work together. Another sincere thanks goes to the veterans who helped with their input. But we have other '*spooks*' to thank:

PAUL BOCHEN (5051-1996), seen here in 1943, was a radioman in the U-Bootwaffe from 1941 until 1945. In 1943, he was in Vigo, Spain and in 1945 was aboard his "*Black Boat*" in South America.

ERICH GIMPEL (884-1988) (photo right) was Abwehr Agent #146 out of more than 20,000 agents. He was caught, tried and sentenced to death by hanging. Roosevelt's death just three days before his date with death saved him. In March 2010, he celebrated his 100th birthday.

KARL WALDECK (6167-2000) was a petty officer aboard a boat that made three trips after the end of the war with '*special*' passengers from Villa Garcia to the Sargasso Sea where they put these passengers aboard steamers for the rest of the journey to Argentina.

S.E.I.G. Agent **SECOND SON,** best on the 3rd Reich in Argentina.

S.EIG. Agent **TIGER**, liaison with Second Son and a good researcher.

S.E.I.G. Agent **REMBRANDT**, retired '*spook*' from the Netherlands who turned up a great deal for us from the Dutch archives.

S.E.I.G. Agent **TAUCHER**, a tireless researcher who has uncovered a lot.

S.E.I.G. Agent **PIZZARRO** – without question, the most prolific and valuable of our agents who has found and contributed an incredible amount of data.

We also remember S.E.I.G. Agent **NIGHTENGALE** who personally knew so many of the men of the old Reich and gave us much inside information. She was **INGRID SCHARFELBERG (3308-1993)** who sadly was killed 17 February 2013 in a suspicious fall in her hotel.

Without our S.E.I.G. Agents, including Captain **BOB THEW** and **PETER HANSEN**, our research would be incredibly more difficult.

There is another S.E.I.G. Agent who does not figure into this book but in the follow up book, "***The Secret Alliance***", **MICHAEL IVINHEIM** sent some critically important information.

The 2nd of the Hitler Escape trilogy, this book lays the groundwork that made such escapes possible.

A MAJOR THANK YOU!

A huge **THANK YOU** to Sharkhunters Members **JACK GOODIER (127-LIFE-1985)** and **CHARLES ENTENMANN (3331-LIFE-1993)** for their generous financial support! If not for them and their critically needed help, we could not have gone to Argentina (four times) and to Brazil (once so far) and therefore, none of this would have been accomplished. **JACK** and **CHARLIE**; thank you to the max!

Argentina Influence

Before getting into the meat of this story, look at these WW II photos, taken in 1941. Good looking German troops, right?

But these were not German Wehrmacht – these were Argentina Army troops with uniforms, equipment and training from the German military; in 1941. Maybe there really IS more to this story.......read on.

Now turn the page and we begin reading the report from **DON ANGEL**.

PART I

Waltzing Matilda

January 1945, Germany was crumbling and the brains guiding this floundering Nazi war machine were flocking to Hitler's side in the

subterranean stronghold under the Reich Chancellery in battle scarred Berlin. I was one of those summoned to the German capital to serve on Hitler's staff in the terrible spring of 1945, and became the only non-German to actually work within the Führer's personal headquarters in the bunker.

Exit from the Führerbunker

I will describe for you the incredible days I spent in the Führerbunker, cut off from the outside world, as Adolf Hitler raved against his Generals, his armies, his own people - and the enemy who was then preparing the death thrust into the heart of the much-vaunted Thousand Year Reich.

We lived in the constant shadow of a deranged genius in a chaotic world of our own, out of which has grown a thousand theories and a mass of conflicting stories telling the fate of Hitler and the elite of the Nazi Party. I was there and I can tell you the truth as I lived it, of those fantastic days.

I know the truth about the reported suicide of Hitler and Eva Braun. I shall tell you of my flight from Berlin under fire from the Russians and my final escape from Germany. And how, after my return to Spain, I assisted in the flight of Adolf Eichmann from Europe after finding him in a Swiss monastery two years after the war ended. Perhaps most important of all, I can now reveal the fate of Martin Bormann, that shadowy eminence who was Hitler's top Lieutenant in the halcyon days of the Nazi regime.

How do I know these things? Because I was chosen by the underground Party movement to escort Hitler's top deputy when he made his dramatic dash for freedom beneath the Atlantic in a U-Boat in May, 1946. Many years have passed since I first entered the service of the Nazis. They considered me one of their most trusted agents with access to their closely guarded plans for re-emergence as a world power.

I know the power of these men and their underground organization. I have seen the determination with which they plot their return to power, and have helped with the formation of secret action groups on two continents. They are well organized. The High Command still exists and meets each year in Western Germany, where they do not lack support.

This then, is my story. I had been head of the Nazi espionage ring in Spain throughout the War and as such, was one of their most trusted agents, but it was not until January of 1945 when British, American and Russian armies were smashing their way across the borders of the Fatherland, that I was called to the Führer's side.

On January 15th, Hitler returned to Berlin from Bad Nauheim, where he had been directing the ill-fated Ardennes Offensive, the last drive of the smashed and demoralized Wehrmacht. After gambling away the remains of the once-invincible Panzer armies, the Führer retreated in a towering rage to the Führerbunker beneath the Reich Chancellery. It was in almost total defeat that Hitler, his enemies closing in from all sides, his defenses overrun, his armies outnumbered, returned to his blitzed & ruined capital.

On the day he returned, I had been working in SS Intelligence Headquarters, close to the old Reichstag. I had then been in Germany for seven months, directing the activities of certain foreign agents abroad.

The following day I was informed by SS Commander Willie Oberbeil - at that time, my immediate superior in the Intelligence Service - that we had been ordered to Hitler's bunker where we would be responsible for passing our agents' reports directly to the Führer himself.

That night, Berlin was subjected to a heavy air raid, and smoke hung over the city as Oberbeil and myself picked our way through streets littered with rubble and broken glass to the Reich Chancellery.

This vast mausoleum-like building, which Hitler had designed himself with the purpose of overawing ambassadors and foreign heads of state who came to pay homage to him in his days of power, was now almost

completely destroyed. All that remained was a blackened shell. The great marble walls had collapsed and the heavily carved doors and costly fittings were scattered about the floors in crazy disorder. At the head of the steps leading into the building, our passes were inspected by a steel-helmeted SS guard, who directed us to a part of the building that was still intact. Another guard ushered us down a narrow staircase leading to a small pantry. We found ourselves led down a second, steeper flight of steps at the bottom of which was a thick steel door. This was the entrance to the bunker.

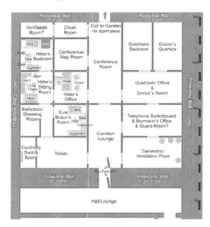

It was part of a steel and concrete bulkhead airtight, watertight, and blast proof which when closed, effectively shut off the fifty-foot deep underground shelter from the outside world. Our passes were again inspected by a black uniformed SS Sergeant before we were allowed to pass through. The doorway was so narrow we were forced to pass through sideways.

We entered into a brightly lit, low roofed corridor with a second larger bulkhead midway along on our left. This door opened into the upper bunker which contained kitchens and servant's quarters. A central corridor, twelve feet wide, was furnished with tables and chairs, and was used as a dining room by the Führer's staff. At the far end of this corridor, a curved concrete stair descended to a second and larger bunker, where Hitler had his offices and command headquarters.

Oberbeil and I followed the armed guard to the foot of the stairs, which opened into another wide corridor, at the far right of which was a wooden partition and a door guarded by two more SS men. Beyond the door, I discovered, were Hitler's private apartments. As we entered the Führerbunker, a slim, gray-suited man rose from the armchairs lining the walls of the corridor and came towards us.

'Good morning, gentlemen.'
He said, in a piping, well-educated voice. I assumed Willie Oberbeil already knew him for, turning to me he continued,

'I am Colonel Wagner. I am in charge of SS Intelligence down here.'
He clicked his heels, bowed, and with a thin smile said,

'You gentlemen are my staff.'

He led us through one of two doors leading off to the right into a small room, where two secretaries were busy typing. On the right, behind the door, a third typist was working in a small partitioned cubicle.

Finally, Wagner ushered us into our own office. This room had been ordered created by erecting a floor to ceiling partition at the far end of the typist's room. It had been put up following Hitler's decision to have a permanent intelligence staff operating within his defense headquarters. The concrete walls of the office had been sprayed with a watery gray paint which did nothing to lessen the dismal appearance of the room, which was cramped and airless. A brand new radio transmitter and receiver, and a decoding machine had been set against the wall to the right and there was barely room to move between the desk, filing cabinets and chairs which had been crammed into the eight foot by ten foot cubicle.

I didn't relish the idea of spending long in this place. It was clear that, should we ever become shut up for any length of time that the lack of space, the stuffy atmosphere, and the strain of working on top of one another would be intolerable. On top of this was the maddening throb which penetrated to every corner of the bunker. I had become aware of it the moment I had entered, but now, in this office it was so intense that the wooden partition actually vibrated.

Wagner sensed my discomfort.
"Do not let the noise upset you. What you hear is the diesel engine in the next room, on which we depend for lights and air.'

In time, I got used to the noise and the cramped conditions and the ever-burning lights, but never the lack of fresh air.

There were at least two other large bunkers beneath the Chancellery and a series of smaller ancillary shelters, used as dormitories by the bunker personnel. Willie Oberbeil and myself were assigned to one of these cement-walled dormitories, which we shared with sixteen others. It was about fifteen feet below the Chancellery cellars, immediately above the main bunker. We nick-named this depressing tomb the *'LAGER'*, the German word for camp. The lager was badly ventilated and all eighteen of us who slept there were constantly complaining about the claustrophobic effect it had on us.

This unnatural life would have been unbearable had we not been occupied by working 16 hours a day. Living like moles, not knowing day from night and in the bunker itself, subjected twenty four hours a day, to the unblinking glare of harsh electric lights - one lived an automatic routine. The absurdity of this existence was illustrated by a little pantomime devised by Hitler to regiment our lives. Each day at noon, a uniformed guard would enter our office, snap to attention and formally announce:

'Today is the 23rd of February.'

or whatever the date happened to be. Then he would salute, turn sharply around and stamp out. It was laughable - or would have been if laughter, like every other normal show of emotion were not a stranger in that place.

The bunker resembled a giant ant-heap and at times, the hurried coming and going of messengers, officials, officers and their staffs made it difficult to move about inside. There was a universal lack of space. The High Command, with its staff of many hundreds pressed together in this labyrinth of burrows had, with the usual lack of foresight, failed to provide adequately for such elementary human needs as space to move and breath.

Many nights I woke on my bunk bed in the lager, half suffocating, and groping my way, afraid, to the roofless Chancellery above. I sucked in great lungfulls of cold night air and longed for the cool breezes of my native Spain. It seemed a lifetime ago that I had last seen my home.

It had been six months since I had left Madrid where, for four years, I had organized the activities of a German espionage ring, unhindered either by the Spanish government or the many Allied agents operating in my neutral country.

But in June of 1944, I narrowly escaped death at the hands of British and American secret service agents in Madrid, who were attempting to abduct me to England for interrogation.

I had been betrayed by a certain Conrado Blanco, a man whom I had called my friend. He telephoned me in the middle of the night and said that he had a group of highly important men waiting for me at his house.

..... Waiting for me was the right expression!

The door of Blanco's house was ajar when I arrived, and all was silent. I found him in his study. He seemed slightly embarrassed. In that instant, my long experience made me sense that something was wrong. My fears were confirmed by a quiet English voice from behind me.

'How good of you to come, Mr. Velasco.'

I spun around and there behind me, with a smile on his face, was my old foe, the English secret service agent John Fulton. He was joined by two other men I knew to be Allied agents - one American and the other Canadian. Outwardly friendly, they offered me a glass of whiskey which I took. It was while we stood drinking that Fulton announced that he would be taking me back to England. My only comfort was the .32 revolver I had slipped into my jacket pocket before leaving my home. Now was the time to use it!

I pulled the pistol from my pocket and fired two shots blindly as I dived for the French windows. I heard them stumbling after me in the darkness as I raced down the garden and scaled the rear wall. I was lucky and found a taxi a few streets away.

Although outwardly friendly, I knew Fulton was deadly serious in his plan to abduct me. Every moment I stayed in Madrid, I knew my life would be in danger. I might not be so lucky the next time. I paused at my home long enough to snatch up a few clothes and papers, and put a call through to my Second-in-Command in Madrid.

Explanations weren't necessary. I merely mentioned the code name *'MATILDA'*. He knew what to do. *'MATILDA'* was a code word in our ring for an emergency exit from Spain.

Within an hour after leaving Blanco's house in the Colonia del Viso district of Madrid, I was being driven in a fast car towards the northwest coast of Spain. Throughout the war, German U-Boats had been patrolling the Gallegan coast. Now members of my organization had sent a radio message and arranged a rendezvous.

After a twenty hour journey, I arrived exhausted in the fishing village of Villagarcia. Waiting for me was a powerful diesel launch. I tumbled from the car and jumped aboard, and immediately I was being taken out to sea. A few minutes after 0400, the conning tower hatch on the U-Boat clanged shut behind me. I was on my way to Germany. Our destination was Hamburg. During our trip past England, we dived deeply with the crew at battle stations. The U-Boat Captain explained that the area was alive with ships and we guessed that this must be the assembly point for a huge Atlantic convoy.

I experienced the usual depression which grips me on a U-Boat. It was forbidden for men of my profession to mix with members of the armed forces under all but the most exceptional circumstances. And so on a submarine, it was customary for an agent to eat alone, sleep alone and avoid all contact with the officers and crew.

It was therefore with a feeling of great relief that I stepped onto the jetty of one of the huge U-Boat pens in Hamburg docks - a feeling which soon evaporated when I saw the shattered state of the city. The night and day pounding by Allied bombers had taken its toll. I saw signs of their marksmanship along every street. That is, where it was still possible to make out where streets had been. For in places, whole blocks had been flattened, roads obliterated and all that remained were piles of rubble where once had been houses, shops, churches.

News of my arrival was radioed ahead. I was contacted by local intelligence and ordered to report to Berlin. I arrived in the capital, having ridden in the guard's van of a troop train, packed with soldiers heading for the Eastern Front.

In Berlin, I was driven to the old Reichstag in a staff car. My orders had been to report to an SS Intelligence unit stationed there. But when I arrived, the whole place was in pandemonium! The officer who was to deal with my case was in a state of great agitation.

'What is all the panic?' I asked him.

He looked at me incredulously,

'Haven't you heard?' He said, shaking his head in wonder. *'The Allies have landed in Normandy.'*

I thought immediately of the huge armada of ships was passed during the journey from Spain.

Within a couple of days - when I was set to work with SS Intelligence, I was to handle hundreds of top secret telegrams from the front, it became clear to me that our Armies in France had been taken completely by surprise. Despite that, Field Marshall von Rundstedt (photo left), Commander-in-Chief in the West, reported the landings were not of major importance. Our Intelligence Service were hourly receiving what claimed to be authentic reports that he was powerless to prevent the full-scale invasion which would surely take place in the next few days. If the much-praised Atlantic Wall had collapsed so easily, it boded ill for Germany's more pregnable fronts further east.

EDITOR NOTE - if the handwriting was already on the wall at this stage of the War, do you think it just possible that some of those in positions of great power just might think about putting an escape route into effect?

About the middle of June, I was directed to München where I was to work in the Foreign section of SS Intelligence and so; equipped with a new passport proclaiming me to be *Dr. Juan Gomez*, a Spanish doctor of medicine, I caught the train south.

Unfortunately, my stay in München was curtailed as the Royal Air Force started to devote their attentions to that city.

Every morning, I noticed a change in the skyline as seen from my hotel window. I was therefore not surprised one morning to learn that a blockbuster had demolished the Intelligence Department offices and, after two days of confusion, I was ordered to Köln; our Central Headquarters.

I was met in Köln by SS Commander Willy Oberbeil. He was a man in his early forties, of medium height and with a short crop of receding brown hair. He wore thick, steel rimmed glasses. He took me into his office on the fifth floor of the headquarters building and he told me something of what had been decided for my future. The Nazi Party he said, were satisfied with the work I had been doing and now that it was no longer possible for me personally to supervise my organization in Spain, I had been chosen to assist him in his work at Intelligence HQ. I was to work in his office and be responsible for editing a mass of reports that came in daily from agents throughout the world. From me, these reports would be wired direct to the Führer. As Oberbeil outlined my duties, I grasped the significance of what he was saying. I was soon to be given a complete panorama of the work of the Nazi espionage service.

Perhaps had I then known what effect this was going to have on my later life, I would have refused this job and walked out on my Nazi masters there and then. But I was flattered by Oberbeil's verbal pat on the back and by the knowledge that the Nazi High Command considered me valuable enough to be entrusted with a position of such responsibility.

PART II

Nazi Espionage

My work in Germany showed me the tremendous complexity of their intelligence service, with its spies in every corner of the world. It also showed me for the first time, some of its appalling inefficiencies. I must explain that at this time, the Nazi espionage service was in the process of reorganization. Formerly under the direction of Admiral Wilhelm Canaris, the service had become so hopelessly unreliable that the whole works was taken over by the SS.

EDITOR NOTE - After the bomb attempt on Hitler's life in **WOLF'S LAIR**, Canaris (photo left) was arrested and held in Flossenberg Prisoner Camp until just before the camp was taken by Allied troops. Canaris was hanged by a thin piece of piano wire, actually strangling to death.

It was generally accepted that Canaris was anti-Nazi and anti-Hitler, but it remains to be learned if he was also a traitor to Germany and in the pocket of the Soviets, as some rumors states.

A laughable instance of the unreliability of the Intelligence Service under the Abwehr, I discovered for myself, when checking a file referring to Casablanca in Africa, which is the most top secret category. I had been looking for information on President Roosevelt's residence in Washington and was amazed to find several handfuls of papers reporting the activities of Arab sympathizers. The mix-up was obvious. Reports on both subjects had come in Spanish, and Casablanca literally translated means *'WHITE HOUSE'* but no one had troubled to question that there might not be Arabs on Roosevelt's Washington staff!

I settled down to work in Köln but before long, 'round the clock air raids made it almost impossible to carry on. In fact, there wasn't a window left in our office when Willy Oberbeil told me

'Good news, Juan. We're getting out of this hell-hole. We've both been ordered to Berlin.'
and he waved a coded telegram jubilantly in front of my face.

But I did not share Willy's joy. From what I had seen of the capital a couple of months earlier, I fancied that Berlin would be no more pleasant than Köln - and I was right. I worked out the last months of 1944 in a draughty, comfortless room behind the old Reichstag in Berlin. I cannot remember clearly Christmas day 1944; except that everyone drank a little too much. The Führer's name was toasted in a wave of optimism, following the early success of the Ardennes offensive, which he promised would drive the Allies back to the sea.

Instead, it drove him back to Berlin, and Oberbeil and myself found ourselves summoned back to the Bunker.

Within a few days of arriving in the Bunker with Oberbeil, I was to be called into that *HOLY OF HOLIES*, Hitler's private office, to be questioned by the Führer himself. All through my stay in Germany, I had been receiving a trickle of reports from our men in the United States and South America of a new American secret weapon. Although no details were forthcoming, the reports hinted at an entirely new type of bomb of devastating destructive power. At the same time, I understood that the Nazi scientists were working desperately to design a workable nuclear warhead for our *V-2* rockets. However, our hopes were crushed after Allied bombers totally destroyed German atomic research laboratories in Norway and Prussia. It was becoming obvious that the Americans would win the race to perfect this hideous weapon; the first Atomic Bomb. It was in connection with one of our reports from the United States that the Führer sent for me.

One morning in the last week of January, Oberbeil burst into our office, highly excited and spoke to me so rapidly in German that I had difficulty catching what he said. When he finally ran out of breath, I asked him to repeat his message.

'You are ordered to report to Hitler immediately"

He said;
'He wishes to question you personally regarding the reliability of one of our agents. Now come and follow me, quickly.'

This was not the first time I had seen Hitler face to face. Eighteen months earlier I had stood at rigid attention while he decorated me, a Spanish subject, with the *IRON CROSS* for my services to the NAZI cause. Yet, as I followed Oberbeil in the direction of Hitler's office, I found myself unconsciously straightening my tie and smoothing my hair into place.

Entering this inner sanctum (Hitler's private office and apartments in the Führerbunker) was a complicated business. One had to have an express order, signed by the Führer himself personally to get in. This was examined by an SS Sergeant of the Führer's personal body guard before one could be admitted beyond the partitioned wall of the main conference corridor.

The fact that Oberbeil was an officer of the SS made no difference; only someone personally referred to in the Führer's signed order could pass. Having satisfied this guard, we went through into a passage where there was a large wooden table with some 15 or 18 chairs arranged around its sides. To the left, three doors opened off the corridor.

The middle one was blocked by a huge SS guard. He too scrutinized our passes. He told us to sit down and wait, and disappeared into the room at his back. He came back a moment later and announced:
"The Führer will see you immediately."

When I crossed the threshold of his map room, Adolf Hitler was sitting at his desk. He looked shrunken and indescribably aged. His light brown uniform jacket - the Nazi party dress he almost always wore - hung from his shoulders like a shroud. Such was the power and personality of this man that one always expected to see someone of giant proportions, but in this setting his smallness was emphasized by the size of the desk at which he sat. It was an enormous piece of furniture, littered with trays, each stacked with bundles of papers. Four telephones, all of them black, clustered within easy reach of his right hand. The walls to the left and right of the door were lined by slanting tables covered with maps.

Three high-ranking Wehrmacht officers were working on them, fixing brightly colored pins according to the instructions contained in military directives to which they referred from time to time. These men did not even glance up as Oberbeil and myself entered. Two chairs had been placed facing Hitler's desk and the Führer motioned me to sit down while Oberbeil remained standing just inside the door.

I studied Hitler - fascinated. His head did not seem to be fixed firmly on his shoulders but wobbled alarmingly as he talked. He appeared to have little control over its movement. His left arm, which rested on the side of his leather chair throughout the interview, did not move once the whole time I was there. His right hand and arm trembled violently as he spoke of our new weapons, flying bombs and rockets, seem like nursery toys.

Hitler revealed no clue to his thoughts, but he studied the report again for a full minute before he asked:

"You are quite sure that if this information had not been correct, then our agent would not have transmitted?"

"Yes, absolutely, my Führer." I replied.

Until that moment, his speech had been slow and without emotion; the hesitant throaty voice of an exhausted man. But now, having thought a few moments longer, he seemed to come to a decision. His manner changed abruptly. Staring wildly at me, his eyes bulging horribly from their sockets, he rasped:

"You will contact this man immediately. Find out the date of the first full scale tests and the place where they will occur."

His voice rising with each word he went on:
"I want to know how many of these devices the enemy possesses.   How am I expected to make decisions without knowing the facts?"

As he spoke, the fingers of his right hand beat a sharp tattoo on the desk top. I tried to answer calmly, but my heart was beating so hard against my ribs that I thought he must surely detect my fear of him.

"I am not sure how soon I can get this information." I told him.

"I realize the urgency, my Führer, but even so it might take our agent several weeks to procure this kind of information."

Even as I spoke, I wondered if I might have provoked him into one of his fits of screaming and abuse, which were the horror of anyone called in to see him. But I was fortunate. Hitler stopped his finger tapping abruptly as if making an effort to control himself. When he answered, his voice had sunk to its former low pitched level.
"I appreciate the difficulties in carrying out my order, Herr Gomez," He said flatly, *"but I cannot stress too highly the importance of receiving this information quickly. I am sure our friends in America will realize this too."*

He nodded and became absorbed in other documents on his deck. I felt a tap on my shoulder and half turning in my chair, saw Oberbeil standing beside me. He beckoned and walked towards the door. I stood up, saluted the bowed figure behind the desk, received a slight jerk of his right hand in acknowledgment - the interview was over. I turned on my heel and followed Oberbeil into the corridor.

I left that office with mixed emotions; frightened and for the first time, unsure of my leader. I was at the same time, filled with such a great feeling of affection and loyalty as not to know which of my emotions to trust. What was it about this man, I thought, which made otherwise strong willed men follow him blindly? I think it was the power of his eyes.

There was something uncanny about them. He could inspire confidence in his followers and turn enemies into friends merely it seemed, by looking at them.

He was not tall, of muscular build, or even handsome. Although he could, when he chose, be charming, he was for the most part unnecessarily rude to those around him and was possessed of a cruel streak and delighted in wanton destruction when he thought it necessary - which was often. Yet when it came to his own self-destruction, Hitler failed, as only a handful of people, including myself, know.

I was glad to get out of his office without inadvertently rousing him to one of his screaming tantrums, which was always liable to erupt - with little provocation. I have known brave men utterly demolished by one of these maniac diatribes, though I have never witnessed one myself.

But I shall never forget the day when Colonel SS Rudolf Wagner, my Intelligence Chief in the Bunker, staggered into our office, pale and shaking, after attending one of the Führer's stormy conferences.

Wagner's face was grey with shock. He leaned on the half open door, his eyes closed;
   'God help us all.'   He gasped.   *'Hitler is mad. We are in the hands of a homicidal maniac.'*

The man standing before me sobbed out the words over and over again and then sank, tears streaming down his cheeks, into a chair in front of my desk. Colonel SS Wagner, Chief of the Intelligence Department in the Berlin Bunker, had just returned from one of Hitler's daily conferences.

It was March, 1945. I had been in the Führerbunker beneath the Berlin Reich Chancellery for just eight weeks, having been forced to flee my native Spain. In my own country, I had been Chief of the Nazi espionage ring, but left hurriedly when enemy agents tried to kidnap me. In the eight weeks I'd been in the Reich Capital, I had been reduced to a shadow of my former self, my nerves in shreds, irritable and jumpy. The ceaseless pounding of bombs on the city fifty feet above our heads, the fear that the rapidly advancing Russian Army might, at any moment, over-run us, and the knowledge that I was closeted in the bunker with a madman had undermined my physical and mental health to such an extent that I was no longer able even to sleep.

Wagner was in even worse shape. Looking at him now, slumped across my desk with his head buried in his hands; I knew that he had reached his limit. I glanced across at Willy Oberbeil, the SS Commander who was the third member of our team. The sight of Wagner had obviously upset him, and he crouched over his desk, nervously biting the backs of his knuckles. Our eyes met for a moment before he glanced away.

I waited, sick and embarrassed, until Wagner pulled himself together sufficiently to tell us what had happened in the Führer's conference. Puffing nervously on the cigarette I had lit for him, Wagner told us simply, *'Hitler has ordered the complete destruction of Germany and the German people. He claims the nation has proved itself weak and therefore does not deserve to survive.'*

So this was it. Hitler had finally recognized that our position was hopeless. He had accepted defeat. And now, with this *'scorched earth'* policy, meant to ensure that nothing of any value would be left to the armies now gathering for their final thrusts into the Third Reich.

'There is no need,' the Führer had said, *'to consider the basis of even a most primitive existence any longer.'*

I could not believe that any German would take this spiteful, lunatic order seriously. To me, as to Wagner, it seemed like the final proof that Hitler was mad.

In fact, this order was never totally carried out, thanks to the sanity of men like Albert Speer, the Reich Industrial Minister. Even though he had served the Nazi cause since the beginnings of their power, he clearly saw the catastrophic possibilities of *'scorched earth'*.

But from the babble of orders and counter-orders which flowed in and out of the bunker in those last desperate days, it was clear that there was one man at least who was determined to put the Führer's policy into action; Martin Bormann!

Early in my days in the bunker, I'd become fascinated by this man. He seemed to move almost unnoticed among the strutting Nazi hierarchy. He was a quiet man, not given to powerful speeches or death-defying slogans like the bunker's other powerful occupant, Josef Goebbels. And yet, there was no doubting his tremendous power. Here was Hitler's most faithful

 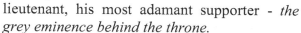

lieutenant, his most adamant supporter - *the grey eminence behind the throne.*

His quietness was deceptive. Although almost unknown outside the immediate circle of Nazi rule, he had succeeded in usurping the influence of men like Himmler and even Göring, now a discredited and untrusted buffoon. Bormann's secret of success seemed to be his constant presence. Hitler could hardly have turned around in those days without finding the attentive Bormann at his elbow. And such ready attention was to pay off for Martin Bormann. Before the end, he was to take charge, even over his old master.

When Hitler unleashed his *'scorched earth'* policy, it was Bormann who reinforced it with a series of dreadful orders.

On March 23, he decreed that the whole population of Germany; men, women, children, slave laborers and prisoners of war were to be rounded up and force-marched to Berlin.

Had that order been carried out, the result would have been mass starvation. He must have been aware that millions would have died. But knowing Martin Bormann as I do, I doubt whether any such appeals on the grounds of humanity would have affected him.

I came into contact with this shadowy man only rarely while in the bunker. Yet on the few occasions when I did see him, I was struck by his apparent determination, his power and his dedication to the Führer. Even then it crossed my mind that if there was one man who might keep the flag of Nazism flying even after defeat in war, that man would be Martin Bormann. And events proved me right.

Now, as March slipped by, the military situation grew more and more desperate. The Red Army had smashed its way through Prussia, the British were thrusting into Northern Germany and the American armies were gathering for their thrust deep into the heart of the Reich. The messages we handled were a catalogue of gloom, with only the occasional local success to revive our sinking spirits. Days and nights became meaningless, the atmosphere among the staff in the bunker alternated between resignation and fear, and visitors to the bunker dwindled to four or five a day.

Always there was Bormann, with his own quarters and his own staff in a separate bunker under the Chancellery, but the impression I got was that fewer and fewer Nazi officials and Generals were risking a trip to Berlin and the ominous threat of the advancing Russians. They knew that above all, the Russians would exact awful retribution from the Nazis they so bitterly hated. And the hope that the remnants of our best Panzer Divisions would be able to hold off the Red Army seizing Berlin were now crumbling.

One morning, I was sitting at my overcrowded desk talking to Wagner and Oberbeil when the teleprinter began to click. Wagner rose and went over to the machine. He ripped out a two-line message, which was in code and had to be fed into the deciphering unit. Then Wagner read it. He froze for a moment, then with a sudden burst of fury, he screwed the paper into a ball and threw it into the corner.

'Oh the bastards!' He snarled, smashing his fist down on the table. *'The lousy bastards!'*

Oberbeil went over and picked the ball of paper off the floor and smoothed it out.
'We shall have to communicate this to the Führer, whatever it is.' He said as he did so.

Wagner rounded on him.

'What do we communicate?" Everything is lost, you fool!'

and he collapsed into a chair. Oberbeil showed me the message. It told us that our defenses had been smashed and the Red Army was fighting its way into Berlin. The news, although it had been expected, stunned the bunker. We could do little - except pray that the Russians did not take us prisoner. It was like living in a mad-house. By now I was thoroughly frightened. But it was nothing to be ashamed of; everyone else around me was frightened too

Since the heavy bombardment of Berlin had begun in March, morale had sunk almost to zero. The whole bunker trembled continually. Bombing by aircraft was going on around the clock and had been for six weeks and now, as the Russians closed in, the perceptibly different noise of artillery shelling added to the general din. We could definitely tell the difference between the explosions of shells and bombs.

The shells we heard - but the bombs we could feel. During really heavy raids, it became necessary when drinking coffee to hold the cup firmly with both hands to prevent its spilling. Now and again even our emergency supply of electricity would be cut, plunging us into total darkness. It was then the urge to scream out loud became really terrible. I can think of only one reason, in fact, why I didn't go raving mad in that bombarded rat hole. It was that we were all encouraged, often instructed, to take drugs in the form of pills which, it was claimed, would make us feel optimistic. No drug could have done that but the stimulant we took might have been the reason we carried on.

They certainly worked on Wagner for short spells, but he took them in handfuls. Willy Oberbeil and myself were more wary. Even so, when I had to do without them after being interned in a Swiss refugee camp, I found my nerves in shreds and I quickly became depressed to the point of suicide.

Perhaps the only message which brought any consolation to those in the bunker the last days, was the startling news we received on April 13. We learned that President Franklin Roosevelt had died.

Oddly enough, Wagner was instructed to contact Intelligence headquarters in the stronghold of Rottach am Egern in southern Germany, to ask if we had any hand in it. The answer came back:
   'No, it was a normal death.'

The news of the American leader's death was seized on in the bunker both as a sign of a change in our fortunes and as an event which would lead to our salvation, even at this eleventh hour. I heard that Dr. Goebbels confidently predicted that, with Roosevelt out of the way, the Allies would

now wake up to the threat of Russia dominating Europe and would quickly end hostilities against Germany and join us in the fight against the Red hordes. According to reports which had come into the bunker earlier in the year from our agents in the United States, it was Roosevelt who snuffed any hopes the Nazis had that the Russians would be kept out of Berlin. Even then it was quite clear that, had they wanted to, the Americans and British could easily have won the race to the Reich capitol.

But Roosevelt, we were told, had already had secret talks with Stalin without the knowledge or approval of the British and French in which the Americans had agreed that the Russians take the capitol. We were informed that, privately, the President regarded the Russians as the only people fit to do the dirty job of taking Berlin. The Russians, he said, were savages and he was perfectly happy to let them take Berlin. The Americans wanted no part of it. And as he further agreed with the Russians, our agents said, just how Germany would be partitioned when hostilities ended.

Accordingly, instructions were issued to the Allied Commander, General Eisenhower direct from the White House, ordering him to slow the advance of the British and American armies into Germany. The Russians must be given time to take Berlin and do their *'dirty work'*. Therefore, in contradiction of his Field Generals Patton and Montgomery, Eisenhower put on the brakes on the drive for Berlin. But now, with Roosevelt dead, Nazi hopes were rising that the Allies in the west would resume their push to the capitol. Regrettably for Germany - and as it turned out, for the rest of the world - this never happened. One effect of this American failure was to make it easier for me to escape Germany. And not only for me, but for many Nazi leaders who fled across the borders to Switzerland.

EDITOR NOTE – Thanks to critical help from the Vatican, most went to Spain then to Argentina.

Had they seized their opportunities, the Allies might well have captured the man who was destined to continue preaching our Nazi creed long after the war was over- Martin Bormann himself! But these considerations hardly worried us as we waited there in the besieged bunker in April 1945. On the 15th of that month, the bunker received one of its most interesting visitors......Eva Braun.

Eva Braun arrived the Führerbunker coming up from Bavaria.

(above) Eva and her Scotty at the Eagle's Nest, Bavaria

(below) Eva at Hitler's Berghof on the Obersalzberg, Bavaria

PART III

Hitler's Mistress

Eva Braun was as different from the popular image of a dictator's mistress as one could imagine. She came from a simple middle-class family . . . and she was a simple, middle-class person. This woman, pretty rather than beautiful, had in her twelve years courtship spent little more than a few weeks alone with Hitler since their first meetings in a photographer's studio in 1933.

And now, with the Führer alternately raving at the break-up of his empire and directing impossible orders at the badly mauled armies, she found it no less difficult to have him to herself. It is difficult to say what she did with herself in the Führerbunker. She came in with no luggage but carrying a fur coat, and disappeared beyond the door to Hitler's personal quarters. I saw her only once more.

On April 16, Wagner ordered Oberbeil and myself to remove all the office records from their files. Box by box, was carried them into an adjoining room where they were burned in a boiler. Even then, those reports which arrived during the following few days were destroyed as soon as they had been read by Hitler. On the 21st, we were ordered to evacuate the bunker.

An hour before we were told, I had gone upstairs to the upper level of the bunker and I saw Martin Bormann arrive. His face was stern, his uniform had been torn and spattered with mud - which gave support to a rumor in the bunker that he had been personally directing rear guard action of our troops in Berlin. He entered the bunker in a hurry, ignoring the greetings of those Party officials standing, waiting for him in the entrance corridor. I followed downstairs and, as I stopped to enter my own office, I saw him brush aside the SS guard outside the door to Hitler's quarters and stride in.

From the look of unsmiling resolve on his face, I got the impression that he had arrived at some important decision. But even this did nothing to sweeten the air of defeat which hung like a shroud around the bunker. A state of mind which was summed up in a phrase which I heard more and more often:

"ALL IS LOST EXCEPT HONOR."

Bormann was closeted with the Führer when Wagner joined Oberbeil and myself in our office and announced:
'Today will be our last day in the bunker, gentlemen.'

He sat on his deck and handed 'round cigarettes. Then, in a steady voice, more composed than he'd been for many weeks, he went on:
'Our work here is finished. There is nothing left for us to do.'

'Nothing?' I queried.

'No. At least, not here. I have been told that we are leaving for another part of the Reich. I imagine we shall continue our work there.' Wagner replied.

Then he strode out of the office and left us to our own thoughts. Mine turned around the problem of how we would ever get out of Berlin alive. I was technically a neutral citizen - but I had a strong suspicion that Russian shells did not respect neutrality and that if I were captured by Soviet troops, I would be shot anyway. But, however great the odds against living in that battleground upstairs, I was perfectly willing to take them; anything rather than die in this hole in the ground.

I must have been in my office for some two hours after Wagner's announcement when I heard the sounds of unusual activity in the central corridor of the bunker. I went out and looked. I was in time to see Martin Bormann leaving Hitler's quarters in company with General Zimmermann and half a dozen other men, most of them out of uniform. Bormann seemed much more relaxed than he had on entering, and I even saw him smile weakly at some remark of Zimmermann's.

From the other end of the corridor, a group of officers had entered and now stood in groups along both sides of the corridor. One group stood within a yard of me and it was in front of these officers that Zimmermann stopped and spoke. He told them:

"The war is not lost. Although the situation is both heavy and dangerous, I am convinced that the faith and courage of the Wehrmacht will enable us to make a last stand which will, I am sure, oblige the Allies to await negotiations."

Despite the Patriotic assurances of this SS General, the officers near me received his words with little enthusiasm. I could see from their faces they quite plainly did not believe a word he said. But Bormann seemed in a hurry to get away and took the General by the arm to lead him toward the stairs and the exit from the bunker.

Another two hours passed - though to me, anxious to leave, it seemed like two years - before anything more happened.

There was another commotion in the corridor outside and once more I went to investigate. This time I counted about thirty officers and officials standing in small groups along the corridor. Now and again, they glanced towards the door leading to Hitler's quarters, outside which the SS guard still stood, impassively, to attention.

Somewhere, an unseen radio crackled an announcement. I caught only these words: *'The Führer ...'* before someone switched it off. I sensed that something big was about to happen.

Moments later, the door of the Führer's quarters opened and Eva Braun appeared. A fur coat was folded over her arm and in her right hand, she was holding a black vanity case. Behind her came two young girls in civilian clothes, and an elderly woman followed by three uniformed SS officers carrying cases.

Eva Braun had changed terribly in the few days since I had seen her. She seemed to be sleep-walking. Her hair was tangled and uncombed, and the rings beneath her eyes were dark and startling as if she had not slept for days. Her eyes lifeless, as if all life had been drained from her. She walked slowly along the corridor, turning to murmur a vague *'Goodbye'* to some of the men who now lined the corridor and were looking at her incredulously. Her feet appeared to drag and scuff along the floor, as if walking was an effort. After nerve-wracking minutes, she reached the foot of the stairs where a young Colonel stepped forward and took her arm. She gave him a quick, weak smile and leaning heavily on him, disappeared from sight.

The last of my courage seemed to go with her and at that moment, I felt the greatest coward in the world. To me, this tragic figure was a living symbol of our defeat.

Hardly had she disappeared when the door of the conference room opened again and Hitler himself appeared in the doorway. A group of Generals; Keitel and Jodl among them, and Grossadmiral Dönitz followed close behind him. The Führer shuffled down the corridor, his left leg dragging slightly, shaking hands with every one of us assembled there.

EDITOR NOTE - At this point in Don Angel's letter, it appeared that we had caught him in a lie. We did not think that Admiral Dönitz could be in Berlin at that late stage of the War. I telephoned immediately to Sharkhunters Member **PETER-ERICH CREMER (114-1985)**, nicknamed *"Ali"*. He was head of the personal guard of Dönitz at Flensburg and so should have personal knowledge.

I did not give him any specific date - I only asked if Admiral Dönitz was in Berlin anytime in March or April of 1945. He said very quickly that it was not possible for Dönitz to be in Berlin in those months because he was in Flensburg, commanding the Navy and Berlin was under constant siege and nearly encircled by the Red Army. At this point, I believed that **DON ANGEL** was lying. I put his letter into a file and went on about my work.

Two days later, *'Ali'* **CREMER** called me back from his home in Germany. He said that he had looked at his personal notebook of the War years and he told me that Grossadmiral Dönitz **WAS** in the Führerbunker over 21st April. I had not given him a date in my earlier question, only *"March or April"* and he told this precise date, the same as claimed by **DON ANGEL**.

I realized that the letter from **DON ANGEL** was not a lie, and I pulled it again from its dusty file.

Three U-Boat Skippers at our 1988 Sharkhunters Convention in Hamburg. **CREMER** is on the right.

Hitler's complete degeneration was there in every movement he made. He was like a puppet without strings, an empty shell of a man whose power alone prevented his complete collapse. Step by step he moved nearer, pausing in front of each of my companions for a handshake and a mumbled word. My eyes were glued on him; fascinated. I who had thrilled to his stirring oratory and responded to his call to war could hardly believe that this hobbling creature had come so close to ruling the world.

Yet when he came to me and I held his limp, thin hand in mine, I felt a great force - like an electric shock in my arm. It was as if all his distress and sickness were being passed into me. His eyes were down cast and when he spoke, his voice was so low I could hardly catch his words. I craned forward lest he had some vital message of hope and encouragement. But all he said was:

'Where goes this man without a motive?'

To this day, I don't know what he meant but considering the situation then, he could hardly have muttered more apt words. He turned away from me. He stumbled, and Keitel and Admiral Dönitz leapt forward and took him under the armpits to stop him falling. But with a tremendous effort, Hitler shrugged them away and continued down the corridor without assistance. Throughout this funereal walk, he waved his right hand aimlessly. It was as if he was trying to say:

'My dear friends, excuse me.'

I, and I imagine everyone else, had been expecting some kind of excuse or explanation.....some word to tell us what was to happen now. But there was nothing.

Bormann had promised that the Führer would find some way of pulling through, but now it was plain to us all that neither Hitler; a finished and broken old man on the evidence of my own eyes; not Bormann; nor anyone else believed this promise any longer. Indeed Bormann, who for so long had diligently worked in Hitler's shadow night and day, was conspicuous by his absence.

It was believed by some of the bunker staff that Bormann, in collusion with Dönitz, was attempting to negotiate with the Russians. Wagner himself told me this, adding:

'It is probably the only way of getting free of this cemetery in which we are living.'

He did not seem to question the rights and wrongs of it. Survival was all that mattered. But I, who later heard Bormann condemn the Communists and all they stood for, could not accept that this fervent Nazi could betray us so easily to the enemy. As he told me himself, eight months after the War ended:

'I was not concerned that day with making excuses for Adolf Hitler. I was only concerned with saving his life.'

And he told me then:

'Our Führer can still unify Germany and make it free from spiritual and geographical division.'

From what Bormann told me and from what I saw in those last hours in the bunker I have almost satisfied myself as to what actually happened to Hitler. I know that many people who remained in the bunker after I have left have given their own explanation of what took place there and their accounts are possibly more acceptable than mine. In fact, I do not attempt to discredit them.

But on the evidence as I know it, this is my reconstruction. A few minutes after Hitler had disappeared up the steps leading out of the Führerbunker I saw for myself a man who bore a startling resemblance to Hitler in stature and facial features being escorted by three uniformed SS officers into the Führer's private apartments. It was commonly accepted that there was on the Führer's staff, a man who was said to be his double.

EDITOR NOTE – It is generally accepted that this is not the real Hitler in this photo shot in the last days of the war. The nose, the ears and cheekbones are quite different than the real Hitler.

In conversations with Bormann, he was insistent that Hitler had been removed from the bunker under the influence of drugs on April 21st - the day I shook hands with him in the bunker corridor. Bormann would not give me any explanation as to how many apparently reliable witnesses had claimed to have seen and spoken to Hitler in the bunker right up until his reported suicide on April 30th, except to say that as creator of the Hitler suicide myth he had seen to it that all participants had been carefully briefed.

It is only left to me to believe that it was Hitler's double who, nine days after I left, was destined to play this most important role in the history of Nazism. It was this man who was shot through the mouth and whose body, dressed in Hitler's uniform, was burned alongside that of Eva Braun in the Chancellery garden that same afternoon.

I cannot swear to the truth of this story. I was not there. But seven years later I was to witness an incredible scene which was to reinforce my view that Adolf Hitler did not die in Berlin in April 1945.

Three hours after shaking hands with Adolf Hitler I left the Reich bunker and staggered up to ground level into a scene of the most appalling confusion and noise. Russian artillery was pounding Berlin to ruins. The capital seemed on fire. The sky itself was dark but the jagged outlines of the battered city showed starkly against a red backcloth of fire.

I lay close to a bomb shattered wall in the burnt out ruin of the Chancellery, waiting for a lull in the heavy shellfire from the Russian lines half a mile away. It didn't seem possible for one to live in this inferno; but in a momentary lull, a voice yelled in my ear:
	'Come on! Run!"

and I was jerked onto my feet. I recognized the voice of Colonel SS Wagner, Chief of Intelligence in Hitler's underground headquarters. With him was Commander SS Willi Oberbeil and together the three of us stumbled across the cratered ruins of the Chancellery garden. Wagner took the lead and we pounded after him. Staggering and occasionally sprawling, we scrambled over mounds of shattered masonry which littered the darkened streets outside. I might have been running for three minutes or three hours. I was so frightened that afterwards I found I could not reckon in terms of time - only of terror.

The streets of Berlin were full of dead and dying men and women, rubble and dirt and broken scaffolding. But around us the spattering of machine gun fire drove us on. I did not know how far I ran or where I was going. But suddenly the shadowy figure ahead of me stopped and seconds later, friendly hands were guiding me into the back seat of a large, black

Mercedes.   I fell into a deep leather seat, not knowing what was happening; only glad to be alive.

I felt rather than saw Oberbeil slump into the seat by my side, followed by Wagner and a fourth man unknown to me.   The steel-helmeted driver let in the clutch and the powerful car surged forward.   The great exodus from Berlin had begun.   Although the capital was lost, the brains of the Nazi party remained intact.

Three hours earlier, I had watched Hitler shuffle his way out of the bunker, attended by his Generals and personal staff.   My spirits could not have been lower.   For me, this seemed the end.   My Nazi masters were defeated and the cause which I had followed with so much enthusiasm seemed crushed beyond repair.

After Hitler's strange behavior, I found the bunker even more oppressive than usual and was relieved when Wagner announced we were leaving. He told Oberbeil and me that by the morning everyone of importance would be gone.   But at this time, there seemed to me little point in running away.   The messages I had seen the previous week spelled only one thing; Germany had suffered total defeat.

Yet here I was, being driven - apparently unhindered - out of Berlin. I had no idea where we were going, but the simple fact that there was still somewhere to go helped to repair my badly damaged faith.   But we were far from safe.   The Russians by this time had almost entirely surrounded   Berlin.   Only   the southwestern sector was still in the hands of the Germans.   Several platoons of our troops backed by Artur Axmann's *Hitler Youth* battalions, had succeeded in holding off the enemy long enough for us to make our escape

No one spoke as we twisted and turned through the city's back streets. Anxiously we watched for signs of enemy troops who might yet end our bid for freedom.   Many streets were partially blocked where blitzed buildings had collapsed.   Three times we were forced to stop and claw a way through the rubble with our bare hands. Once our driver careened straight over a three foot mound of bricks and broken concrete. Once clear of the deserted suburbs, our driver stopped the car. He told us it would be safer to wait for the others before going on to Munich. Within ten minutes, headlights flashed on the road behind, illuminating a convoy of about eighteen other cars coming in our direction.

EDITOR NOTE - When the top brass said they would fight to the last man; do you think they really meant they would fight to the last of everyone else while they and their families escaped? Keep reading - the defeat of Germany was anticipated more than a year before it finally ended and those at the top made sure that as many of them as possible could escape. Keep reading as this well-planned, well-executed escape operation becomes apparent.

The last I saw of Berlin was a smudgy glow on the skyline. The sound of gunfire had died to a distant rumble and with the immediate danger behind me, I took stock of my companions. At my side, little Oberbeil was complaining that he had lost his spectacles and could not see. Wagner was examining a deep gash in his right ankle - he had caught it on a half buried girder on our sprint from the bunker. And our other passenger, a round faced and pot bellied SS Colonel, his uniform crumpled and stained, was still sprawled in the seat where he had fallen. Fear and unaccustomed physical exertion had left him exhausted.

I found a half finished pack of cigarettes in my pocket and passed them 'round. Only when I came to light my own did I discover how badly I was shaking.

We continued south throughout the night, and dawn found us rushing through the German countryside, fresh and pleasant in contrast to the hell we had left behind us in the night. Only now in daylight, did I realize the extent of our getaway operation. We were the last car of a convoy of nearly two dozen vehicles. Practically all the key men who had staffed the bunker in those last desperate weeks were here. The nucleus of the Nazi High Command was moving en bloc to the last stronghold of the Thousand Year Reich. Many of them were destined to arrive.

Death swooped from the clear blue sky in the shape of a British fighter patrol. In seconds, the air was full of exploding cannon shells. Our driver braked and swerved into a hedgerow as the leading car of the convoy vanished in an eruption of flame.

I threw myself from the car and fought my way into the hedge. I was dimly conscious of the screams of the wounded above the roar of the aircraft engines, and saw a burst of fire from one of the planes above, cut a swath of death less than a yard in front of me. I didn't see what happened to the others - I hugged the ground with my belly, my head buried in my hands. In that kind of situation you don't worry about the others. The world ends with the person by your side; the rest cease to exist.

It was all over in a minute; yet in that minute twenty three people had died and at least a dozen others lay badly wounded along the roadside. Ten of the cars were destroyed completely. Some of the less badly wounded, we took in the remaining cars but the rest we left behind, wrapped in blankets and greatcoats, hoping that our own ambulance service or the Allied Red Cross would discover and take care of them.

For a time, we didn't feel like talking and once again I was thankful just to be alive. But soon my mind began to sort out the tremendous events I had witnessed in the past few days. Suddenly the SS Colonel, his name I believe was Lachner, broke into my thoughts and caught the attention of us all.

"The Führer wanted nothing more than to be left to die with his people." He shrilled. *"But Bormann wanted him out alive."*

I felt Wagner stiffen and Oberbeil peering intently at the Colonel. It was obvious he knew a lot more than we did about Hitler's fate.

"Bormann had left orders that the Führer was to be drugged, by force if necessary & taken out of Berlin. That's what happened."

Lachner, who had held a responsible position close to Bormann in the Party Chancellery, told us the full story of what had happened.

When Bormann appeared at the bunker the last time, Hitler was still determined to stay and if necessary, prepared to die defending the capital with the phantom legions which by then, existed only in his mind. But Bormann had already assumed command and gave orders that both Hitler and Eva Braun were to be evacuated from the bunker. They were both forcibly drugged with, it turned out, fatal results for Eva Braun.

EDITOR NOTE – DON ANGEL received faulty Intel of Eva's death as we interviewed people in Argentina who knew her. There is even a bit of evidence that she was still living into the 21st Century. This is not difficult, as she was born in 1912 so in 2002 she would be 90.

As Lachner spoke, I recalled Hitler's ashen grey face and his stutter which had been even more pronounced than usual. I had assumed his appearance had been due to the strong emotion he must have felt on leaving Berlin - but now it seemed more likely due to the side effects of the drugs he had been given.

The knowledge that Bormann had countermanded the Führer's last wish left us stunned. It seemed incredible that Martin Bormann, the man who had been Hitler's faithful lieutenant for twenty years could perform such a *'volte face'*. I had to wait almost a year to hear from Bormann himself, the true reason for this seeming piece of treachery.

Our flight across Germany lasted almost twenty hours. I still have a vague picture of the shattered towns and the blank faced people we passed on the long drive south. As the hours dragged past, Lachner grew more and more voluble, chattering endlessly on and on about the backstage intrigue at Hitler's court. Lachner was insistent that many of Hitler's worst blunders were due to the misguided advice he was given by a covey of astrologers whom he regularly consulted.

Some years after the war, I myself discovered how the British Secret Service had managed to bribe the so-called prophets and gave them certain information to pass on to the Führer in the form of predictions. An English Secret Service agent told me that without their advice, Hitler would never have attacked Russia. If this were true, and I had no reason then or now to doubt it, then this can be considered as probably the biggest single triumph in the long history of espionage.

At dusk on the evening of April 22nd, our depleted convoy arrived at its destination - Rottach am Egern; Germany's natural redoubt in the Bavarian mountains. It was here the Nazis planned to make their last stand against the advancing Allies. And as we approached the heavily guarded mountain fortress, I recalled the words of General SS Zimmermann, that here we might yet win an honorable peace.

2008 Sharkhunters Members in some of the bunkers still there in the "Southern Redoubt"

Long queues of vehicles waited to pass through the checkpoints along the road. At each point, we were thoroughly scrutinized by SS guards, and stage by stage, we penetrated deeper and higher into the redoubt; each car directed to its different section according to the number hastily painted on the sides. We were told to follow a narrow rutten track which wound us up the steep incline from the foot of one of the mountains. The driver finally pulled up outside the entrance to a tunnel, guarded by more SS men with sub-machine guns.

The tunnel at Rottach-am-Egern

Without a word, a young lieutenant led us through a steel doored entrance into a miniature bunker - smaller but similar in layout to the Führerbunker in Berlin.

For the first time in two days, our small intelligence unit was alone again; Lachner having left us at the main barrier of Rottach am Egern to rejoin his colleagues in another section. We had been allocated a tiny office near the bunker entrance, the new headquarters for Nazi Germany's espionage work.

Wagner exploded when he saw our miserable quarters. Apart from a heavy wooden table and four hard backed chairs, the room was completely bare. We were equipped neither with radio nor transmitter or files, code books and the necessary paraphernalia for our job yet we were expected to cope, we discovered, with the escape plans of some of Nazi Germany's leading figures.

PART IV

Escape from Germany

Fortunately, one of Wagner's angry outbursts brought quick results and twenty four hours after our arrival, a powerful radio transmitter and receiver was set up in a corner of our office.

In the week that followed we received and transmitted orders for the escape from Germany of dozens of top officials in the Nazi Party. Who most of them are, I shall never know. To me they were just code names on a piece of paper. But it was obvious that this mass escape had been planned a long time before.

Our two main escape routes out of Germany led through the Swiss border towns of Feldkirch and Kempten. Of these, the latter was far the safest route as our agent there was a member of the local Communist Party - a Nazi who had been planted there during the War among our bitterest enemies. It was one of the few pieces of foresight shown by the German Intelligence Service - probably one of the most inefficient organizations of its kind in the world.

I had been in Rottach am Eggern for just a week when Wagner called me into his private office. He had been almost without sleep for a week and he looked like a man about to acknowledge final defeat. But he forced a smile as he told me:
"My dear Gomez; I have good news for you. You have been ordered back to Madrid. There you are to contact members of your old organization & prepare to receive a very special visitor."

"Who is he?" I asked.

"That I cannot tell you. What I can tell you is that if the Nazi Party is to survive, then it is essential that this person gets safely out of the Reich and out of Europe. The job has been

*assigned to you.   You will receive instructions in due course.
They will be signed by the code name ZAPATO."*

I returned to my own quarters with mixed emotions. Glad to be getting
back to Spain but intensely curious as to who it was Wagner considered so
vital to the Nazi cause.

On the 29th of April, 1945 I left the redoubt - the last fragments of the
Nazi Empire which had spanned Europe only a year before.   That
morning, I said goodbye to Colonel Wagner and Willy Oberbeil. My last
vision of them was of two tired and dispirited men, their once arrogant
black uniforms now stained and creased. They answered my salute with a
weary mumbled *'HEIL!'*. I turned and left the bunker. Outside an SS
guard was waiting with an OKW car, topped up with fuel and a pass to
enable me to get out of the main gate.

I drove past the checkpoint, still heavily manned, and took the road to
München where I had been given the address of a garage to refuel.

I was still a long way from the advancing American Front but the evidence
of war was all around me.   The road to München was littered with
abandoned vehicles, a few intact but most of them partially or totally
destroyed.   Hastily arranged diversions set up by the Wehrmacht Police
enabled me to avoid the worst sections and I was able to make good speed
apart from a thirty minute holdup to allow a military convoy through. I
met few civilians on the roads and the little traffic I encountered was all
military.

SS Intelligence had supplied me with false papers, identifying me as a
Spanish chef in the Hotel Deutsche Kaiser in München. My papers were
barely glanced at by the guards at the checkpoints I passed. It was hard to
recognize in the blank faces of these guards, the proud army which had
once goose-stepped its triumphant way across Europe with such arrogant
ease.   And had it not been for the rigid discipline of their officers, I felt
sure that many of these men would have swollen the stream of deserters
who were daily giving themselves up to the advancing Americans.

But soon I had my own troubles. I had been assured that I would have no trouble getting fuel in München. None of the filling stations along the road had been open but it had not worried me. However, when I went to the address I had been given and the garage owner refused to serve me with gasoline, I became concerned. I told him no one at this time could run a car unless he were on government business. But he refused to be persuaded.

Just then, an SS detachment had turned into the street and was marching towards me. I waited until they drew abreast of me and I stepped out to speak with the sergeant in charge. I took the risk of confiding in him that I was on an extremely important secret mission which necessitated my traveling on forged papers. Had he not believed my story, I could have been thrown in prison and days might have passed with communications as they were, before Wagner could have arranged my release.

Fortunately, the man accepted my story and came with me into the garage owner's office. The sergeant, a huge crop-haired brute, threatened the cowering man with instant arrest unless he filled the tank of my car. The man did so; and I can't blame him.

The further towards Switzerland I traveled, the more obvious it became that the Third Reich was defeated. I began to meet groups of refugees; old men, women and children, trudging hopelessly away from the tide of battle. I questioned some of them, but they did not appear to know where they were going. They were just running away. The adults appeared thin and badly clothed, and I noticed that many of the children were without shoes. To one group, I tossed a few tins of meat and vegetables which had been stacked in the back of my car. They snatched them greedily without a word of thanks.

I stopped at a small roadside inn and asked inside for a cool lager, but the landlord shrugged and offered me the only thing he had in his cellar - a glass of water. I pressed them to look again and this time I produced a piece of butter, half the size of a matchbox. The landlord's wife accepted eagerly and moments later, a liter of foaming chilled beer was mine. Two miles further along the road, I discovered what price I really had to pay.

The car shuddered and stopped! My host had siphoned off my whole tank of petrol. In a fury, I considered having the man arrested, but common sense made me realize I would be wasting precious time. Instead, I filled a case with food and a blanket - and a spare pair of shoes, and walked.

In just over an hour, I arrived at a small railway station where I was amazed to find that trains were still running. But there was no question of buying a ticket.

"Are you mad?" Asked the porter. *"Nobody buys tickets any more. When the train stops, you just get on if you can."*

When it arrived, the train consisted of freight wagons and open coaches, but at least it took me to the outskirts Garmisch where, after a three hour delay, I was able to get a train through to Innsbruck.

The town was swarming with troops and the station itself was littered with stretcher cases and walking wounded. I decided to eat before continuing on the last stage of my journey to Feldkirch. I walked away from the station and threaded my way down a little side street until I came to a tiny coffee house away from the crush of field grey uniforms. I sat at a table near the cafe's entrance. It was dim in the blackout and at first, I did not notice the couple sitting adjacent to me.

I could scarcely believe my eyes when I turned to study them more closely and recognized the man. I had last seen him in the Führerbunker, exhorting us to the final defense of the Third Reich. It was General SS Zimmermann! He must have recognized me at the same instant and a flicker of disbelief crossed his face. He beckoned me over. I hardly sat down when he began to talk quietly and rapidly.

"This lady is my wife. I want you to take care of her. See that no harm comes to her, because I intend to kill myself."

I was speechless. This man was a comparative stranger, an influential SS officer who did not even know my name. He who a short time ago had been full of optimism now proposed to commit suicide, and thrust the responsibility of his wife's safety onto my shoulders.

I begged him to reconsider, but despite my pleadings, he explained that he could never leave Germany and since he had no intention of serving anyone but the Führer, the only course open to him was suicide. Seeing that it was pointless to go on arguing, I told him that I had been ordered back to Spain and would take his wife with me if he insisted.

Suddenly, as if fearing I might change my mind, Zimmermann stood up. He kissed his wife on the forehead, shook me firmly by the hand and without saying a word, walked out into the night. Frau Zimmermann, her name was Maria, half rose from her chair, then slumped back. She simply said: *"God help him, wherever he goes"*

Two years after the war I discovered that General Zimmermann had indeed carried out his promise and committed suicide.

Maria Zimmermann and I, the following night, made contact with our agent, a Catholic priest in Feldkirch named Father John. We decided it would be best if we traveled as man and wife, and Father John promptly forged an appropriate wedding certificate. We stayed with the priest for three days and it was in his house on May 1st that I heard the German radio announcement that Hitler
    "....had died at the head of his troops."

I was confused by this announcement, for I felt it could not be true. I knew of Bormann's instructions to transport the Führer to a safe place, away from the battle and the advancing Red Army. I had seen for myself the carefully planned escape of every other top Nazi, and I refused to believe that Hitler had been allowed to remain behind.

On the night of May 3rd, I crossed safely back into Switzerland, knowing that scores of high-ranking Nazis had preceded me through similar escape routes and countless others were to follow.

In Switzerland we presented ourselves to the authorities as Angel Donate Reca and Maria Pinto, man and wife, and asked for repatriation to Spain. Both of us were extensively questioned and passed from camp to camp until at last we were dumped in the refugee camp for Spanish nationals at lePlaine near the French border.

I was in this ghastly place on May 7 when I heard that the war was over. Germany had surrendered unconditionally. The misery of the filth at lePlaine almost defied description. We lived in unheated huts and slept on wooden bunks thinly covered with straw. The toilet was a hole in the ground at one end of the hut. The stench was indescribable.

On the second day there, I was lucky enough to find a pro-Nazi Swiss guard who agreed to pass on a message to a certain Father Ramon, whose name had been given to me by the Catholic priest who assisted us in Feldkirch. This monk took my case to the Spanish consul in Geneva, and shortly afterwards, I was visited by the Spanish Consul, one Senór Albazor. He pulled a great many strings and arranged with the Allied authorities on the Inter-Allied Commission for the Repatriation of Refugees to have Maria and I transferred to a hotel in Geneva under police supervision. From here it was a simple job to arrange a passage for the two of us to Barcelona.

I had cabled my wife when we were arriving, and she was waiting for us with a car when we docked late in July. After hearing our story, she insisted on Maria Pinto going back to live with us in Madrid. Maria stayed with us for three years before returning to Germany. Later I learned that she was working for the German Government in South America. Now Maria is once again settled in Germany, at Köln, and got engaged to an Englishman but now she lives under the name of Maria Danneworth.

By the time I reached home, the Allied nations were celebrating the crushing of Nazi Germany. But I knew that their victory had not been complete. Even as they rejoiced, scores of men, capable of keeping the spirit of Nazism alive, were being assisted to safety by those who still believe in their cause. I was one of those who assisted in these escapes. Two men came to me for help.....the first stands convicted for the murder of millions.

I met him the first time in 1946. In June of that year, a monk from a Swiss order, called at my home in Madrid asking me to give assistance to a

German refugee who had sought sanctuary with his brotherhood. The man's name he said, was Climents. He was described by the monk as:

"A good man who wishes to start a new life in the Argentine."

I said I might possibly be able to help, but first I would like to meet him. I accompanied the monk to the college of his order a few miles from Freiberg in Switzerland. I thought it possible that I might recognize Climents, but I did not. At that time he told me simply:

"I am an officer of the SS, and I am being hunted by the Allies. Will you help me?"

I agreed.

Climents returned with me to Madrid on a special passport issued to him by the Vatican. These passports were issued to many refugees after the war, but were valid for travel only inside Europe. I noticed that this passport was made out in the name of Didier. However, I asked no further questions and obtained an Argentine passport for him in the name of Climents. On the third day of July, 1947 I drove him to Madrid Airport to catch a plane for Buenos Aires.

As we waited together in the departure lounge, I asked if he could tell me his real name.

"My name in Eichmann." He replied. It meant nothing to me then. But now, all these years later, all the world knows what the name Eichmann means.

Who was the other man who came to me for help? It was Martin Bormann.

I stood with my companion on the conning tower of the U-Boat and stared out across the white-flecked Atlantic. The coast of Spain was a grey smudge in the thin light of early dawn. It was quiet except for the hollow slap of waves against the submarine's hull. Then my companion spoke:

"This is not running away. This is merely a pause. The war is not over as everyone believes. One day Germany - Hitler's Germany - will emerge victorious"

He gazed toward the distant coast. But I knew that it was not Spain that he saw. He was seeing Germany. A much diminished, war torn, scarred and defeated Germany.

"One day I shall return." he challenged. *"On that, I, Martin Bormann, give you my word."*

In silence we descended to the deck below. As Bormann dropped into sight, a 12 man Kriegsmarine guard of honor crashed to attention. Martin Bormann faced the U-Boat commander across the narrow deck and proudly drew himself to attention. Their arms came up as one and together they answered the salute. *"Heil Hitler."*

It was May 7, 1946 - exactly one year to the day after the signing by Germany of an unconditional surrender at Reims. A new chapter in the history of Nazism had begun.

After my escape from Germany, where I spent the last three months of the war in the Führerbunker, Hitler's headquarters beneath the Reich Chancellery, I thought for a time that I had finally finished with my Nazi masters.

On leaving the Reich, I had been instructed to alert the members of the Nazi espionage ring in Spain, of which I had been the wartime chief, to prepare for a *'special visitor'*. These were the instructions given to me by Colonel SS Wagner, Intelligence Chief at Rottach am Egern - scene of the Nazi's last stand against the invading Allies.

From time to time during the following months I recalled these orders, but was convinced they would never be put into operation. I little imagined I was soon to be plunged once more into the National Socialist cause, which I was certain had no further need for me. Until that day in December, 1945 when I received a visit from Felipe, a German who had worked with my organization in Spain. It had been several years since I had last seen him. Then, he had weighed a good 16 stones, but now he had lost considerable weight. He was tall, blond-haired & aged about 40.

He threw his arms around me and seemed very happy to see me again. We talked over old times together, before and during the war. I was not very surprised when Felipe told me he was still working for the Nazis. I knew that large sums of money had been deposited with different agents in various parts of the world - all men dedicated to the Nazi cause. These men, and Felipe was one of them, had been chosen to keep Nazism strong in the event of Germany losing the war. They were all fanatics. Some of them had even sold their homes and possessions to carry on their work. But Felipe was more fortunate and still had access to large sums of ready cash. His was a key position in the escape route that had been reserved for those top Nazis who survived the war.

Because of this, I felt sure that his surprise visit was not simply a social one. It was probably connected with the arrival of my long-awaited 'special visitor'. Felipe told me nothing of his mission, but before leaving he handed me a sealed envelope which he said contained important information.

I opened it in the usual way. My espionage training with the Germans had taught me how to handle this kind of message. I went to my bureau and selected a large plain envelope, a size larger than the one Felipe had left. I placed the one inside the other and sprayed the whole package with a liquid which I kept locked in my desk drawer. Quickly I plugged in an electric iron & pressed the twin package until it was dry. It became rigid.

Treatment with a second liquid spray caused the inside envelope to open. To have tried to open it in any other way would have resulted in the message it contained being destroyed. My instructions were in Spanish.

EXPECT SPECIAL VISITOR IN MADRID BETWEEN JANUARY 1ST AND 15TH. THIS PERSON, WHOM YOU

WILL RECOGNIZE, WILL BE BROUGHT TO YOU BY THE BEARER OF THIS LETTER.

ZAPATO

ZAPATO!   That was the code name which Wagner had made me memorize before leaving Rottach am Egern.

I spent the next four weeks in a frenzy of speculation. The peace of mind I had known over the past few months vanished, to be replaced by an undeniable compulsion to be once more back in the service of the cause. The message, though guarded in its phrasing, told me the one thing I wanted most to hear. At least one important Nazi had survived the war.

Felipe came to my house on January 3, 1946. But this time he was not alone. His companion I did not recognize at first. He was wearing a dark overcoat over a grey suit and wore a bottle-green trilby hat pulled down low over his eyes.

I knew I had seen this man before, but I could not see enough of his face to give him a name. Felipe introduced us.
   "Angel, I would like to present you to Herr Fleischmann,"

It was as I stepped forward to shake his hand that I recognized Martin Bormann. But a much changed Bormann. When I had last seen the Party Chancellor in the Bunker, he had been a good three stones heavier. His heavy jowled face had grown lean and his cheeks drawn. But there was about his eyes some unmistakable gleam, which reflected his insatiable appetite for power and limitless ambition.

He removed his hat and I noticed he was partly bald at the front, though I discovered that this had been artificially brought about. Plastic surgery had taken care of his prominent Greek nose.

Felipe was curious to learn the real identity of the man he had brought to my house and at the first opportunity, he took me aside and asked,

   "Who is this Herr Fleischmann?"

I told him:

"Who else should it be but Herr Fleischmann?"

But he pressed me to know what position the man held in Germany. I told him I had known Herr Fleischmann as one of Himmler's assistants. I could see that Felipe was not satisfied with that answer, but he shrugged and dropped the subject and left shortly afterwards.

As soon as we were alone, I took Bormann into the lounge, offered him a cigarette and a glass of Spanish brandy; both of which he accepted - and I waited.

He spoke first. *"Do you remember me from the bunker?"*

"Yes,' I replied. *'You are Martin Bormann."*

He smiled thinly and told me, *"That's right. But to everyone else, I am Herr Fleischmann. Do you understand?"*

"Of course." And then remembering to whom Felipe's message had been addressed, I added *"If you are Herr Fleischmann, then I am not myself, but Senór Gomez."*

Gomez was the name I had worked under in the Berlin Bunker. We talked in Spanish, though the Spanish of Bormann was a terrible thing.

"You will have to study hard if you want to improve your Spanish sufficiently to stay here undetected."
I told him.

"I shall not be staying in Spain permanently." He replied. *"But I shall take your advice and study the language."*

Then he handed me a white envelope, blank on the outside and unsealed. Inside were further instructions, signed **ZAPATO**.

I was told to take Bormann down to Condor, a Castle on the Mediterranean coast of Spain at Denia, 30 miles south of Valencia. I was further informed that Macario, a German who had been living in Spain for over thirty years and who had been working for the Nazis since before the war, was expecting us. He had a large house two miles from the castle, and the use of a small cottage built into the castle wall.

I assumed then that my part in the business would be over when I had delivered Bormann to Denia, but Bormann warned me,

"Get plenty of exercise. You must be fit to make a long journey very soon."

That night he slept in the guest bedroom of my home. He had arrived without luggage of any kind and I had to send out for pajamas and shaving gear.

PART V

Bormann the Prophet

During the next two days, my conversations with Bormann naturally revolved around the post-war situation in Germany. At this stage, he was not prepared to discuss the fate of Hitler but was only too willing to talk about the probable fate of other Nazi leaders, then awaiting trial at Nürnberg.

He happily prophesied, *"These people will soon be paid for the high treason they committed."*

He was particularly bitter against his former arch enemy at Hitler's court, Hermann Göring (photo right). *"That pot-bellied swine was the worst person Hitler could possibly have chosen to run the Luftwaffe."* he declared.

Ribbentrop too (photo left), he castigated, as the man responsible for Germany's premature declaration of war;
"He may have been a good ambassador; which I doubt - but he should never have been made Minister for Foreign Affairs."

These two men, Bormann claimed, pushed Hitler into a war for which Germany was neither economically nor militarily prepared. Göring, he said, had given Hitler a completely false impression regarding Germany's preparedness for total war in 1930 - 1939.

"No power in Europe can fight us in the air." Bormann claimed Göring had told Hitler. And Hitler believed him.

"For his part, Ribbentrop as Foreign Minister had done an unforgivable thing." Bormann went on, *"in failing to report truthfully and accurately to Hitler the character, morale, feelings and strength of Britain and her Empire when he returned from his last pre-war visit to London."*

"Hitler proved extremely wise in many of his decisions." Bormann explained to me. *"It was a pity he could not have been more wise in his choice of advisors."*

I never heard Bormann comment once on either Göring or Ribbentrop without he accompanied such comment with an insult.

EDITOR NOTE – The son of Joachim von Ribbentrop, tank commander **RUDOLF von RIBBENTROP (4189-1995)** was a Member of Sharkhunters.

Bormann stayed with me in Madrid until January 6th. On that morning, we left in my new Chrysler car for the eight-hour drive down to Condor Castle. It looked bleak and foreboding in the thin winter sunshine and the half-dozen white stone cottages nestling below its walls seemed deserted as we slowed to a stop outside the main entrance of the castle.

This place had been used during the war as an espionage center and the men living in the cottages had all worked for the Nazi regime at some stage of the war. The castle was built so as to command a perfect view of both the coastal plain and the sea, and was therefore an ideal hideout for a fugitive like Bormann. One room in the west tower had been roughly furnished and the glassless windows boarded up in preparation for Bormann's visit. Macario had been expecting us and approached in the doorway of his cottage as we left the car. He was then about 55 years old and dressed as he was in blue jersey, canvas trousers and sandals, he resembled the typical Spanish fisherman.

He greeted us briefly and without ceremony. We were just two more clients in the long list of faceless men who had passed this way. He led us through twelve foot high heavy oak doors of the castle and, holding a hurricane lamp above his head, ushered us towards Bormann's quarters less than a stone's throw from the main gate. We clambered up a short flight of very steep stone steps skirting the west tower and ducked through a narrow opening on our left. A heavy drape of sacking screened the doorway. Macario pulled it aside.

"It's probably not the best room you've ever had - but there are few safer."

Macario chirped, setting the hurricane lamp down on a flat-topped writing desk against the crudely hewn stone wall. An iron framed cot had been pushed into one corner and a pair of straight-backed wooden chairs and a small chest of drawers completed the furnishings. Instead of a carpet, a two-inch layer of fine white sand covered the stone floor.

Bormann seemed satisfied - at least he made no complaint about his Spartan hideaway. But he curtly rapped out an order in German. Macario scuttled away and reappeared a few minutes later with a basked of food and wine. I did not stay to join him in his meal, but bade him good night and set out on the return trip to Madrid.

I received no word of Bormann for three months and long before this I had accepted that my part in this drama was ended. Then, on May 1, Felipe turned up again at my house. Once again he brought a message and once again, it dealt with the escape of Martin Bormann. As usual, the message was brief and to the point. Herr Fleischmann would embark from Villagarcia - a fishing town on the north-west Gallegan coast of Spain, on May 7th. And that I would be accompanying him.

Bormann was to leave and I would accompany him - but to where?

But to where? There was no hint as to our final destination. I only knew that I would be getting further instructions from our agent in Villagarcia.

On the morning of May 3rd, 1946 I said good-bye to my wife, Conception. I told her I might be away from home for several weeks or perhaps months. I drove down to Condor in the Chrysler, urging the big car as fast as I could over the rough roads, for I was anxious to find out from Bormann where our journey would end.

He was waiting impatiently for me pacing up and down the cobbled courtyard below his room. He shook me warmly by the hand and greeted me in Spanish. He had not wasted his three months in Denia and had almost perfected the language, and looked a good deal fitter. I was unsure how to address him, but I decided to keep up the pretense of his pseudonym.

"Herr Fleischmann, it is good to see you again. I trust your stay at Condor has not been difficult."

Bormann grimaced. *"I would not say difficult, Señor Gomez. But nevertheless, I am not unhappy at the thought of leaving."*

Bormann had spoken to no one but Macario in those three months. He had not left the castle grounds, but at least his surroundings were beautiful. Acres and acres of rose gardens and lawns lay inside the castle walls. In this environment and under the warm Mediterranean sun, Martin Bormann had grown fitter, stronger and more confident. He was obviously excited at the prospect of action. The last twelve weeks had been spent in thinking and planning for the future and rebuilding of the Nazi Party. Now the time had come to translate those thoughts into deeds. He was in such good spirits that he sent Macario for a bottle of good Spanish wine and insisted that the faithful agent join us in a toast.

It was a bizarre scene. We stood, our shadows flickering in the candlelight against the bare stone walls. Bormann sloshed wine into three tumblers. He handed us our drinks and pulled himself rigidly to attention. He raised his glass.
"Gentlemen, we drink to the National Socialist Party and to its leader. Heil Hitler."

"Heil Hitler." We echoed and I felt a tingle of excitement rippling through my body. Could it be then that the Führer really was still alive? Bormann butted in on my thoughts.

"Come along, we must rest." He said. *"You and I, Gomez, have many miles to travel."*

Macario and I left Bormann standing alone in his cell-like chamber, and picked our way along the overgrown path to Macario's cottage. I dreamed that night a vivid picture of the Berlin bunker. And I heard again the voice of Adolf Hitler:

"Where goes this man without a motive?"

I was awoken at dawn to find Bormann dressed and waiting. After a hasty meal of bread, freshly landed langostino, washed down by mugs of hot, sweet, black coffee, Macario had prepared a satchel of food and a bottle of cognac to take with us. Bormann and I shook hands briefly with the man, and climbed into the Chrysler. We nosed out of the little town, the rising sun at our backs, on the first leg of our eight hundred mile journey across Spain. Bormann, dressed in a cheap blue suit and white cotton shirt, sat unspeaking at my side as we sped along the coast road towards Granada. Our only stopping points that day were Granada and Seville, and then only long enough to replenish our fuel tank. I deliberately chose small roadside filling stations where there was no risk of Bormann being recognized. We ate as I drove. Bormann handing me the cognac bottle from time to time. His bubbling good humor of the previous night had been replaced by his usual taciturn demeanor.

I had chosen a round-about route deliberately so as to avoid the bigger cities, and our first overnight stop was in the small market town of Merida, near the Portuguese border. We did not travel on passports and at the quiet hotel I had picked out I registered in my own name Angel de Velasco, showing my identity card and registering Bormann as Herr Fleischmann. I was paying the bill and the sleepy concierge did not bother Bormann for his papers. Our second night was spent in Ponferrada, barely a hundred and twenty five miles from our destination - Villagarcia.

But those hundred and twenty five miles - the last lap - took us the whole of the following day to cover. The road, an ill-made up potholed track, zig-zagged wildly across a chain of mountains and I arrived at Villagarcia exhausted. I drove directly to the house of one of my agents, a man named Martinez, who made us welcome. He was a genuine fisherman and greeted us wearing the traditional calf length canvas trousers, a blue seaman's jersey and wooden clogs. Inside the house was poor but clean, and Martinez had prepared a supper.

Bormann and I ate ravenously and while we were still eating, Martinez brought in his son, who he said would be going with us in their fishing boat the following morning. Martinez had another envelope for me, but he said:

"I have been given strict orders not to hand this envelope to you before you are embarked."

I protested. *"Why not now? I insist you hand it over."* Then I turned to Bormann. *"I am tired of this guessing game. I want to know where we are going."*

Bormann remained calm in the face of this outburst.
"My friend, even I do not know our exact destination. The organization which is arranging our transport is a highly efficient one - as you yourself must know. I need not remind you of the need for the strictest security. I have left the organization in the hands of trusted men. Let us not ask questions. Soon enough, you will know."

This gentle reprimand brought me back to my senses.
"Of course; I understand." I said to Bormann.

And to Martinez, *"Of course you must carry out your orders. I apologize for my rudeness."*

Bormann and I smoked a last cigarette before climbing the rickety stairs to a room where two single beds had been prepared for us. I was asleep even as my head hit the pillow.

It was still dark when Martinez shook my shoulder roughly. *"Señor, it is time to go."* He whispered, and I heard Bormann grunt sleepily.

We dressed by the light of a paraffin lamp and carrying a suitcase each, the former Nazi Party Chancellor and myself followed the old fisherman out of the house and down to the harbor.

In the darkness of a moonless night I could make out a dilapidated old fishing boat rocking unsteadily at its moorings. A stiff wind had risen and I could hear the crash of heavy breakers against the shore. Bormann was horrified.

"Mein Gott!" He exclaimed. *"Don't tell me we have to make our journey in this thing. It will sink before it leaves harbor."*

The old fisherman told him not to worry, and helped us aboard the aged craft, of which he was obviously but unjustifiably proud. I took a last look around before following Bormann aboard. I had made arrangements for my car to be driven back to Madrid and had given the driver a brief message for my wife, telling her that I might be away longer than I had at first believed.

Neither Bormann nor myself wore overcoats and we shivered, hurrying into the comparative warmth of the boat's main cabin. The craft had a crew of five and to an observer, it would seem that we were going on a normal nights fishing. Martinez's boat was a forty-five footer, propelled by a sluggish diesel engine. But despite Bormann's sarcastic comments and concern, she plowed a steady path through the white-topped waves toward the open sea.

We had come about two miles from the coast when Martinez slowed the engine and gave the order for the sea anchor to be dropped. He shouted to one of his seamen to keep a sharp lookout for any other shipping in the area, and we settled down to wait in silence. I noticed the lights of other boats in the distance and for the first time Bormann became agitated. But Martinez assured us that they were the lights of other fishing boats and were more than a mile away.

The sea was getting rougher, but the weather-beaten old fisherman was quite unconcerned by the nauseating roll of his battered tub. It was then that Martinez produced a bulky package from a pocket of his coat.
"This is the package for which you have been waiting, Señor."

He handed the packet to me. I wanted to open it then and there, but Bormann told me,
"No, wait until we get on board our next craft."

We had both known that there must be another boat waiting for us. Outside, a seaman shouted something and Martinez suddenly stood up and said, *"Alright. It is time you were going."*

On deck, I could see no sign of another ship, but two seamen were waiting to assist us over the side. I went to the rail and what I saw took my breath away. Bumping gently against the fishing boat's side was a rubber dinghy manned by two sailors wearing Kriegsmarine uniforms!

They gave a military salute as we lowered ourselves into the dinghy, and Bormann returned their salute. We shouted a farewell to Martinez, and the two sailors cast us loose and began paddling away from the boat. The yellow dinghy tossed violently on the waves and the sailors cursed their luck in German. Bormann and I still had our eyes fixed for some sign of an awaiting vessel. But there was nothing.

Then with incredible suddenness, the sea immediately in front of us began to boil, and from the foaming waves rose the unmistakable shape of a submarine lifting itself violently from the depths. The sea cascaded from its decks and had it not been for the seamanship of the two sailors, we should have capsized. Even so, we were forced to bail frantically.

Moments later we were scrambling over the wet curved steel deck and hauling ourselves up the slippery metal ladder that stretched to the lip of the conning tower. Bormann and I paused a moment on the narrow gangway circling the open hatch, from which came the pungent smell of diesel fuel. The U-Boat Commander, who had been waiting on the conning tower, had disappeared down below, leaving Bormann and I alone in the slowly gathering dawn. We caught a glimpse of the fishing boat heading back towards Spain.

Bormann gazed thoughtfully towards the coast and spoke softly as if voicing his thoughts to himself. *"Europe will see me again."* He murmured, *"leading a new and more powerful Germany."*

Then he turned abruptly and lowered himself into the bowels of the U-Boat. I followed him down the narrow ladder and the two seamen, having stowed the dinghy, came after me, snapping the clips of the watertight hatch behind them. Bormann faced the U-Boat Commander across the narrow deck and together they saluted.

Then the U-Boat Commander, in full naval uniform with an *IRON CROSS* glittering on his tunic breast, thrust out his arms and greeted Bormann in a firm embrace. He turned to me, extending a powerful hand and clicked his heels; *"Captain Karl Jui"* he announced formally and gave a slight bow. He was, I suppose, no older than thirty five and although still a handsome man, his hair was prematurely white. He was tall and arrogant, his height being emphasized in the cramped confines of the U-Boat's control room.
     EDITOR NOTE – Obviously not his real name.

While Captain Jui introduced his First Officer, ship's doctor and other officers to Bormann and myself, I noticed around me the crew alert at their diving stations, awaiting the order from Jui to submerge. They all wore white jerseys as did the steward who led Bormann and myself along a steel gangway towards the boat's bow.

As I stepped through a watertight door leading forward, I felt the boat surge and the deck ahead tilt downwards. We were going under, and I was embarking on the most fascinating voyage of my life. I glanced at my watch. It was 5:10am the morning of May 7th 1946. Exactly a year to the day after Germany surrendered unconditionally to the victorious Allies, I found myself in a German U-Boat diving beneath the waves of the Atlantic.

1222232..

.....

Apart from myself, there was only one other civilian on board this fully equipped and fully provisioned warship, the U-Boat under command of Captain Karl Jui. That other man was Martin Bormann, the most hunted fugitive of the Third Reich, the man around whom a storm of speculation had long raged. We were on our way to an unknown destination where Bormann planned the renaissance of the Nazi Party - a new Nazism which would conquer not Europe, but the indeed the world.

They had picked us up off the coast of Spain and now under full wartime conditions were thrusting its way on a three thousand mile journey beneath the Atlantic. One of the crew in the uniform of the Kriegsmarine led Martin Bormann and myself to a small cabin in the bows of the U-Boat. In this cramped steel box, Bormann and I were to share eighteen long days together. And here he laid before me his plans, plans he had prepared in the last months of the war, to ensure the continuance of the Nazi creed.

Captain Jui appeared at the door of our cabin as soon as the seaman had left. Bormann went to the door and they talked for a minute or two in German. I could not catch what they said but as Jui shut the door and left us alone, Bormann remarked:
"From now on Angel, we consider ourselves Argentine subjects."

Only then, three months after I had been instructed to help Bormann out of Europe, did I have revealed to me our final destination. Then Bormann referred to the bulky package of papers which had been handed to me by another agent as we left Spain.
"I think that now is the time to open the envelope." He said. *"If I am not mistaken, it will contain certain instructions for our Captain."*

I took the packet from my coat and laid it on the table. I examined it carefully. It was in a plain envelope - not the usual kind used by the Nazi Intelligence Service. I slit it open without further ado. Had it been the special type of envelope I had received so many times before, doing this would have rendered any message unreadable.

First I withdrew a single sheet of paper. On it were instructions typed in Spanish referring to Martin Fleischmann, the name Bormann used during his escape. I was to instruct him in the way of life, the political situations and the language of those South American countries known personally to me. I was to pay particular attention to life in the Argentine. From the envelope I also took out two Argentine passports. One was for Bormann in the name of Luis Oleaga; the other in the name of Adian Espana was for me

Although the passports seemed genuine enough - they were issued by the Argentine Consul in San Sebastian - there was another typewritten note attached to the inside page of mine saying that these passports were intended for use in emergency only and that the people who would meet us in Argentina would supply us with more authentic papers when we arrived. The message was signed *'ZAPATO'*. I knew then that it had come from Colonel SS Wagner, former Chief of SS Intelligence in the Berlin Führerbunker.

The last item in the packet was another sheet of white paper containing a lengthy message written in numbered code. I could not decipher it. I handed it to Bormann and he simply shrugged and said,
   "Give it to the Captain."

The message in fact was Jui's sailing orders. Bormann and I sat down to study our documents and take stock of our surroundings. There were two bunks in the cabin bracketed against the steel bulkhead to the right of the door, and placed one above the other. Over these there were shelves where we could put our only luggage; two small suitcases. Opposite the door was a table that folded back against the bulkhead when not in use. A single unshaded bulb glowed continuously from a bracket in the ceiling, and there was a small lamp screwed to a shelf above the table. The bunks themselves were firm but comfortable - each prepared with crisp, white sheets and pillow cases, and had a reading lamp above. The steel deck had a piece of threadbare carpet in the center of the floor. Our washing facilities comprised a small aluminum hand basin fixed to the gangway bulkhead outside our cabin. Two steel chairs completed the furnishings.

We had been in the cabin for something like two hours when I sensed the U-Boat tilting its nose upwards. Bormann and I glanced at each other wondering, but our unspoken query was answered almost immediately by Captain Jui who knocked on our door and entered briskly.

"Gentlemen, we have surfaced. We are just off the coast of Portugal. We shall be here for less than an hour to take on essential supplies."

Curious, I followed Captain Jui back to the U-Boat's operations deck and stood watching while two sailors opened the conning tower hatch and disappeared out of sight above us. A third seaman secured the hatch behind them and Jui rasped an order:

"Take her down three fathoms."

I heard the sound of ballast tanks filling, and then silence. By this time, Bormann had joined us on the bridge and we watched while Captain Jui made a 360° sweep with his periscope. Apparently satisfied, the captain came over to join us.

"Everything's all right - but we must wait."

He produced a chess board and pieces. He and Martin Bormann settled down to a game.

From time to time, Captain Jui excused himself to take a brief glance through the periscope. About an hour after the two seamen had left, Jui gave the order to surface. I felt a blast of fresh air as the conning tower hatch was opened and shortly afterwards the two men stumbled down the steps of the ladder, each carrying a small box about the size of a cigar box. I guessed they must have been extremely heavy for the men had difficulty carrying them down. The boxes were stacked on the deck and they returned for another load. All together, nineteen of these boxes were brought down. I suspected that they carried gold. But if Bormann knew, he was not saying and my suspicion was never confirmed. After these boxes, two larger wooden crates were lowered down and I was told they contained food.

Fifteen minutes later, we were submerged again and life on board the boat settled down for our eighteen day non-stop run across the Atlantic. For most of the time Bormann and I were closeted together in our cabin, occasionally speaking with a member of the crew, but generally conversing only between ourselves.

We were served excellent food in our cabin including crispbread, freshly baked on board twice a week. One of the marines (sailors) was detailed to wait on us. Occasionally, Captain Jui himself joined us for a meal, but he soon wearied of this, as it meant him standing to eat. There were only two places at our table.

Jui was a veteran U-Boat man with all the arrogance that life and death command gave these wartime heroes. Twice I was to cross swords with him. The first time was a trivial incident and occurred during my second day aboard. I had wandered on to the bridge, but was rudely ordered back to my quarters when Jui discovered me in conversation with one of his officers, and accused me of distracting the man from his duty. Upon my return to our cabin Bormann sensed my ruffled feelings and I told him what had happened.

He shrugged,
"Don't take it too seriously. You must remember that on this boat we are his guests. Jui is in command and we must accept what he says and try not to antagonize him."

I resolved to put the incident out of my mind.

The second time I quarreled with Captain Jui was a very much more serious affair, but it happened towards the end of our voyage and I shall tell you of it later.

PART VI

Bormann's Lessons

In accordance with my instructions, I started to coach Martin Bormann in the ways of fluent Spanish. Bormann applied himself studiously. Each night he studied a German Spanish phrase book and insisted I test his vocabulary, growing annoyed with himself if he forgot a word. My particular difficulty was in teaching him to speak Spanish the Argentine way, which had a different pronunciation to the Spanish used in Spain. I myself had been several times to the Argentine and knew the language and country well. I had passed several months there during the war, engaged on espionage work for the Nazis - arranging a spy network with Japanese Intelligence to relay information on the British-bound food convoys to our U-Boat packs in the North Atlantic.

In the first few days, Bormann did little except study Spanish and make notes in a leather-bound writing case. I gradually became aware that the man I was with was no longer the refugee Bormann I had greeted in Madrid three months earlier.

He had regained all his old authority and assumed again the air of a man who knows exactly where he is going. And as his confidence in himself grew, he began to talk more freely of the past and his plans for the future. During one conversation in which he had told me something of his plans for keeping Nazism alive.

I asked him,
"How is it possible for the National Socialist Party to continue after the battering it has suffered?"

He answered,
"Neither I nor many of the others understood until it was too late what were our possibilities for the future. But now I am fully

aware of those possibilities and will soon be in a position to take advantage of them."

At this stage he was unwilling to reveal his plans in more detail. But he expressed his belief that Hitler's Germany could win a second war of conquest; within the next six years.

"Hitler's Germany?" I asked, *"How can you talk of Hitler's Germany if the Führer is dead?"*

He regarded me seriously before answering.
"You yourself saw the Führer leave the bunker. And if you saw him leave, then he could not have died there."

"Yes, I saw him leave," I agreed,
"but I have no idea what happened to him after that. He could have returned, for all I know."

Bormann said nothing for a full minute.
"Do you want to know where Adolf Hitler is today?"

"I am more concerned to know if he is alive." I answered.
"As to where he is - it is not so important."

"You are right. It is as important for our followers to know that he is alive as for the Allies to believe him dead."

Then he told me the incredible story of Hitler's fate. He said
"Listen to me carefully and remember what I say. It is true. When Adolf Hitler left the Führerbunker, he was barely conscious of what was happening. After months of fighting the enemy on the battlefield and the treachery in his own camp, he was both mentally and physically exhausted.

"But time and again he expressed to me his resolution to die with German soldiers around him. This I could not allow to happen.

Hitler was the embodiment of the National Socialist cause. One could not survive without the other. At least not then.

"By the 21st of April (1945) it was obvious that the war was lost. It became necessary to countermand the Führer's wishes and remove him physically from the bunker. I arranged to have him driven secretly from Berlin to Rottach am Egern, escorted by officers from my personal staff. Only a handful of people besides myself knew that the Führer was there, and these were people whom I knew could be trusted to keep the secret of his escape for as long as it was necessary.

"From Rottach he was driven across Germany and smuggled by ship to Norway. Two of my agents kept him in a place many miles from the nearest village until arrangements were completed for him to leave Europe."

I asked, *"What of Eva Braun and the suicide?"*

"Eva Braun never arrived in Norway. Unfortunately she was given an overdose of drugs from which she later died. As for the suicide, I was the author of the story that Hitler and Eva Braun committed suicide and their bodies burned with petrol. Those witnesses who afterwards testified to this end had been carefully briefed on my instructions."

EDITOR NOTE – As previously stated, there is very strong proof that Eva Braun (Hitler) did not die and was indeed in Argentina.

Bormann leaned intently across the table;
"That Hitler did not die I know. I also know that he is still alive but more than that I am not prepared at the moment to tell you."
with that I had to be content.

Yet later in a fantastic and on reflection nightmarish mission, I was to be shown near conclusive evidence that what he had said was true. But even now I gradually began to accept the incredible fact; Hitler was still alive.

Bormann told me he believed the news of Hitler's death was a source of satisfaction and pleasure to the Allies. He believed that with Hitler dead, the Allies would accept that Nazism could not be rebuilt. Bormann also wanted to perpetuate the myth of his own death for the same reason. On a number of occasions throughout our U-Boat journey, he asked me what I would ever do if his name cropped up in conversation. During one such conversation, I assured him:

"Martin, from me everyone will believe you are dead."

This pleased Bormann. *"That is what I wanted to hear."*

But he added,

"Not that I died here. Tell them I died on the battlefield fighting the Bolsheviks."

Then I suggested to Bormann that he had given me so much information, and since I was the only person in the world who could tell the world that he was still alive, he might never allow me to return from this journey.

"I am more or less your prisoner." I told him.

Bormann chuckled and rose from his bunk on which he had been lying. He reached out and clasped my hand in his.

"There is no question of your remaining my prisoner. You have proved yourself a good friend and a loyal member of the Party. There are of course, certain things I cannot tell you. It is simply not convenient that you know everything, but that does not mean that I do not trust you. I am more than confident that you will not reveal the secret of my escape when you return to Spain."

It was the closest that Martin Bormann and I came to intimate friendship.

Life in a submarine is so claustrophobic that it is impossible for two men to be confined almost entirely to one cabin without their nerves stretching to the breaking point. There were times when I positively loathed Bormann. I remember clearly one incident - we had been at sea for a week when one of the crew fell seriously ill and the U-Boat doctor reported that the man's condition was extremely grave. For want of something to do, I remarked to Bormann,

"I think I will go and talk with this poor fellow. Perhaps I might be able to cheer him up."

Bormann's reply shocked and surprised me. Testily he snapped in a harsh voice, quite out of character,

"Why waste your time. This is of no importance to you. Do not bother yourself with it. What happens to this man can in no way affect our future."

This sort of insensitive attitude shook me. It might have been acceptable coming from the warped brain of a man like Himmler. But from Bormann, who loathed Himmler in any case, it seemed unnecessarily brutal. In due course, the sailor died. Bormann was quite unaffected by the man's death and when I asked what they did with a man who died on a submarine, he leered and replied

"Yes, we eat them."

In fact, shortly afterwards, we had surfaced and the crew were ordered onto the upper deck where I presume the poor wretch was given a naval funeral.

But in the main, I must say Bormann proved an interesting and pleasant companion. Our talks together ranged over every conceivable subject. When you are shut in a steel tomb under the sea, it becomes necessary to find an outlet in talking about everything, and also nothing.

Within a week I had developed a kind of U-Boat craziness and experienced bouts of depression and physical sickness. Bormann comforted me by telling me that this was not unusual even in hardened U-Boat crews, and advised me to think of the future.

"At the moment, everyone is talking about the destruction of our cause." He told me.

"For them, the battle has been fought but for us, this is not the case. While they content themselves with editing their diaries, we prepare a new chapter in the history of the Nazi Party. Time will soon come when their nerves will be as shattered as

ours are down here. You must cheer up. We will soon be off this damned submarine and back on dry land - and it has not really been very long since we left Spain."

But to me it seemed that we had been at sea and trapped in our metal box for half a lifetime and I refused to be comforted. I envied Captain Jui his patience and acceptance of this unnatural life. However, I knew that he had spent the whole war in U-Boats. He had been in the early years a First Leutnant in a submarine similar to this, operating in the North Atlantic. Most of his war had been spent patrolling the Western Approaches to Europe, and he had been in at the sinking of seven Allied ships. For his part in these actions he had been awarded the *IRON CROSS* and in late 1944, had been given command of his own U-Boat. He had been at sea at the end of the war and had received special orders to take his boat to a secret island base off the South American coast and await further orders.

EDITOR NOTE – Brazil removed her personnel from their island Trindade (not to be confused with Trinidad) before the war and German personnel took possession there. In the early days, they provided radio support while in the closing months of the war and until middle 1947, they maintained herds of pigs and goats as well as providing fresh water to the '**Black Boats**' and many

other vessels taking thousands of high ranking members of the Reich to Argentina. Photo left was the landing place, a plain strip of sandy beach with some huts seen in the photo below right. Both photos were taken by the German contingent in 1939. They also erected a radio shack with tall antenna, photo next page.

Throughout our journey, the U-Boat remained in radio contact with its base, and daily during the last part of our trip Bormann received messages from the agents awaiting him in South America. To kill time, I repeatedly offered my services to Bormann to help him with his constant writing, but apart from asking one or two questions concerning intelligence work, he refused my offers of assistance.

The radio station on Trindade built in 1939
Translations of the writing at the top of the photo:
Secret Reich Affairs   Secret Commander's Affairs   Chief's Affairs

Other translations:
Trindade Island   Radio station, second Plateau, March 1939

Consequently I faced long stretches of boredom and took to wandering about the submarine. However, most of the crew to whom I spoke with, were guarded in their answers even in response to innocent questions about their duties. I found that my only escape was sleep, and in order to sleep, I asked the ship's doctor to provide me with tablets. This officer, whose name he told me was Willy, proved more approachable than most. Oddly enough, he was also the ship's radio officer, but in neither capacity was he needed for more than a few hours each day.

We became good friends and spent a lot of time talking about our families. Willy's home was Hamburg, where he had a wife and son whom he had seen only four times since he joined the U-Boat Service in 1939. He was aged about forty and in contrast to most of the crew, had jet black hair. However, in common with them all, he was on the small side. It was a curiosity of the U-Boat service that the men who manned them were almost invariably short.

Willy was a very enthusiastic sailor and liked the life of a submariner, but for myself I had quickly lost any enthusiasm I may have had for underwater vessels. This boat was fitted with the then newly invented *'snorkel'* apparatus which was supposed to maintain a good supply of fresh air when the boat was submerged. I had been full of praise for it in the first two or three days, but after a week I found the poor circulation of air, the stench of diesel and almost unbearable heat made me feel sick. And I damned the *'snorkel'* along with every other piece of machinery on the boat.

EDITOR NOTE – This is the early version snorkel which was retrofitted on many boats (Type VII and Type IX) at the end of the war. Unlike the newer version which was built onto the type XXI and Type XXIII which were hydraulically operated, these were hinged and had to be raised manually from the deck. They had a watertight connection at the deck level but they had their share of problems.

The diesel exhaust port was in the same small head that contained the fresh air inlet and so, as **DON ANGEL** points out, the incoming air smelled badly of diesel exhaust. If a wave rolled over the intake, the diesels continued to run, sucking huge amounts of air out of the boat causing the crew to bleed from nose and ears. In some rare instances, crewmembers were overcome by carbon monoxide.

For Bormann, it did not seem so bad. He rarely left our cabin and spent hours at a time writing in his book. Even this was a torment for me, for at such times he answered me with grunts; for long stretches refused to acknowledge my presence at all. During his long silences, Bormann whose shaved head had grown and who had by now, a thick stubble of beard, developed a maddening habit of tugging endlessly at his left jowl. It was just one of those little things that can drive you crazy on a long submarine voyage.

After politics, Bormann's favorite topic of conversation was his family. I was surprised to learn that he was married and had a daughter, then aged fifteen. He said he hoped to arrange her passage to the Argentine as soon as he himself had settled. Years later I learned that the girl had managed to join him and she now lives in Buenos Aires, and is married with children of her own.

However, if I was feeling in a state of nervous collapse, I became aware that my condition was shared by large numbers of the crew. Halfway through the second monotonous week at sea, one of the crew caught his foot in the engine room machinery and was quite badly injured. As a result, he had to spend his time in the seamen's mess area quite near our cabin. Since the poor fellow couldn't escape, I fastened on to him as some to talk to and soon deducted that he was as anxious as I was to see this voyage over. However, he said that this was not as bad as some of the trips he had made, but added his hope that the injury to his foot would be good enough cause for Captain Jui to put him ashore with Bormann and myself when we reached South America and although it caused him some pain, he seemed almost pleased to have been injured.

From the remarks of other crew members, I began to suspect that he had arranged the accident himself and many of the crew openly congratulated him on his prospects of quitting the boat. It seemed to me that the attitude of some of the more outspoken seamen bordered on the mutinous and my impression of them changed from that of a smart, well drilled and enthusiastic crew to that of a group of dispirited men who only hoped to end their wanderings under the waves. And I thought that Captain Jui might have trouble with them before our voyage was over.

One day I caught Bormann in a philosophical mood. For hours I listened to his explanation of the past, and his hopes for the future. He began by comparing National Socialism with some of man's most ancient religions, pointing out that as in all beliefs, Nazism looked for a super-human leader to free its people and lead them to world superiority.

Bormann believed that there were only two possible theories in man's living; Communism and National Socialism. Bitterly he condemned Communism.
"Who wants all men to be equal like animals?" He snorted.

"Nazism is the only way. We believe there should be rulers; supermen for the masses to follow. We want to breed a race of men with the brains and physique to lead the world.

We started this with the SS because none of the people selected for the SS had any physical or mental defects. We want to procreate our race, and in a thousand years, the Reich will produce a race of splendid men and women."

Pacing up and down the cabin, he went on,
"I am convinced that National Socialism will rise again in Germany. It may take a few years; even a generation; but it will come back."

I protested that this was an impossible dream, since Germany would be occupied for many years to come and the Allies would certainly crush any reawakening of Nazi feelings. I added that the world is not full of heroes, and men would soon forget the war and this period of German history. They had lost the war; that was enough for most.

Bormann turned on me in a fury.
"You bloody fool! Have you lost your faith?"

He shouted,
"Can't you see that just by occupying Germany, the Allies will always give the Germans cause to turn against them?"

Bormann ended this tirade by predicting,

"The fools will think they have won the final victory, but if they are so stupid as to go on hating the German people and showing that hatred, then the Nazi cause will never die. They will look to us again for freedom."

He talked optimistically for finding in South America, a people who would lend themselves to the Nazi teaching of a super-race.

"They must be a very clever people." he remarked.

But on this, I had to disillusion him.
"If you expect to find a super-race there, you will be disappointed, Martin." I told him.

"But is it not true that we have followers there?"

I replied,
"Yes, but you do not yet know the South Americans. Today they will call you HERO. Tomorrow they could just as easily shoot you in the back."

At this point, our discussion was ended by the urgent blaring of klaxon horns and a fierce hammering on the door of our cabin. I realized that the U-Boat's motors had stopped.

A rating entered the cabin and told us that Captain Jui wanted to see us urgently, and he led us at a rapid walk to the hatchway leading down to the engine room. In front of a huge bank of accumulators, Captain Jui was talking excitedly to a group of engineers. When we joined them, Jui broke off and told us seriously,
"We shall have to stop to make emergency repairs to one of the accumulators."

EDITOR NOTE – Accumulators means batteries

He pointed to one of the huge accumulators and indicated a crack running the full length of it from ceiling to deck. He explained that in its damaged condition, it would seriously affect the supply of electricity to the motors and unless repaired immediately, would make it necessary to continue our journey on the surface using the diesel engines.

"I have no need to tell you how dangerous this would be for all of us." He added.

But already the engine room crew had begun to seal the crack, which meant that the immediate danger would soon be passed. Escorting us back to our cabins, Captain Jui again apologized for the defect in his ship, but remembering my conversations with the crew, told him,
"I am not surprised to find things going wrong. I do not think your crew is a happy one, Captain."

Jui laughed,
"Don't worry about the crew. We have been in worse situations than this together. I believe the cause is simply that my ship has been heavily depth charged several times and this has weakened the accumulator casings."

The next day our spirits were given a boost when we neared the River Platte estuary. It meant that we were only a day or two from landfall. Bormann became excited and pulled out a large scale map of South

America. He drew a large cross over our point of disembarkation, the tiny port of Puerto Coig in the Argentine district of Patagonia. That same afternoon my belief that the crew were determined not to sail again on this boat was further strengthened when another mysterious crack was found in another bank of accumulators. In my nervous state I even imagined disaster overtaking us within a few miles of safety. I was quite certain of sabotage, and I told Captain Jui so.

"It is incredible that between your officers and yourself there is no one who can see how this trouble was caused. It was sabotage, you fool. Can't you see that?"

Captain Jui exploded with anger. In language that would shock a Hamburg dock worker, he raved at me for fully two minutes. At this moment, Bormann stepped between us.

"Captain Jui," he roared.

"You will come to attention and keep quiet!"

Jui was shocked into obedience. Red faced with fury, Bormann viciously abused the stunned Captain. Pale and trembling, Jui suffered an outburst which only Hitler himself could have matched.

In a screaming temper, the Führer's Deputy tongue-lashed the young captain and ended by telling him,

"You do not deserve to be in command of a German ship. This gentleman,"

and he indicated myself,

"I consider to be a hero. It is thanks to him that I am here at all. And if you insult him, you can consider yourself as having insulted the leader of the Nazi Party!"

He thrust his face close to that of the shivering Jui and snarled,

"Need I remind you Captain, of the consequences of such a serious blunder?"

With that, Bormann turned and walked away.

After Bormann had left, the officers and crew on the bridge took moments to recover. But by this time, my temper had evaporated and to ease the tension, I stepped forward and held out my hand.

"As far as I am concerned Captain, this matter is closed. Believe me, I regret it having taken place at all."

Jui seemed glad to accept my friendship, and together we went to his cabin and split a bottle of French wine.

While we were in the Captain's cabin, Bormann joined us, seeming also to have forgotten the incident. Almost immediately, a rating appeared with a message. It read:

"Everything is prepared and we await you."

It was signed *'Rodriguez'.* This message, our first direct contact with our agents ashore, brought a whoop of relief from us all.

Bormann asked me if I knew Rodriguez personally, and I told him I did not.

"This is strange," he said,
"I have been told that he is a priest, and that you will know him."

"I have only known one priest who worked for us in the Argentine," I replied,
"and his name certainly was not Rodriguez."

Bormann smiled,
"Your name is not Adian, is it Angel? And mine is not Luis. So why should this priest's name not be Rodriguez?"

The message was not in code, I noticed. And a second signal a few hours later made us certain at last that we had finally reached safety.

It said;
"You may proceed in perfect safety. We are in complete command. Heil Hitler!"

We had less than twenty-four hours to go before disembarking and the tension was tremendous. But Bormann and I spent the night restlessly tossing in our bunks and were unable to sleep. Willy, the doctor, gave us both a sedative and even suggested that I might like an injection to put me out for those last agonizing hours of suspense, but I would not agree. Even now I could not forget my espionage training and my cardinal rule; never trust anyone. I was the only witness to Martin Bormann's escape. I was taking no last minute chances.

On the morning of May 25th, Captain Jui gave the order to surface and I felt the rhythmic *'THUMP THUMP THUMP'* of our diesel engines take over from the electric motors; the U-Boat thrust onwards on the surface.

Bormann and I raced for the bridge in time to see Jui returning from a brief reconnaissance. Around his neck were a pair of powerful Zeiss binoculars,

"You have a reception committee waiting for you." He told Bormann.

"How many?" asked Bormann

"I have counted eight men and two cars." Jui replied

But I could wait no longer. I brushed past Jui and scrambled up the steel ladder to the observation platform on the conning tower. It was my first sight of land in eighteen nerve-racking days. Through the mist I could see the beach quite close, and a number of figures waving at us.

Once ashore, I watched Martin Bormann walk up the beach near the tiny town of Puerto Coig with a feeling of intense satisfaction. My most important job as an espionage agent of the Nazi cause had been accomplished. Bormann, the most wanted war criminal in the world, had been safely smuggled out of Europe and was now safe on the friendly shores of the Argentine.

I stood on the stony beach that morning in May 1946 and took a last look at the vessel which had brought us out of Spain. In the mist I could vaguely make out the glistening steel plates and her crew standing stiffly to attention on her upper deck, their arms outstretched in the Nazi salute.

Bormann turned, a thick-set, wind-blown figure at the crest of the steeply rising beach, and stretched his arm toward the distant U-Boat. Three minutes later, the rubber dinghy which had brought us ashore had returned to the boat and eager hands hauled it aboard. I gazed seaward and caught sight of Captain Jui alone now on the conning tower. Moments later he too, disappeared and the U-Boat vanished in the mist. Its last mission completed, the boat was heading for Buenos Aires - surrender and asylum.

EDITOR NOTE – The boat did not reach Buenos Aires. We believe it was scuttled by her crew in an area revealed to us in letters from Don Angel after this file was sent to us. This photo, we believe, shows the boat that **DON ANGEL** rode along with another German U-Boat, scuttled in the Caleta de los Loros.

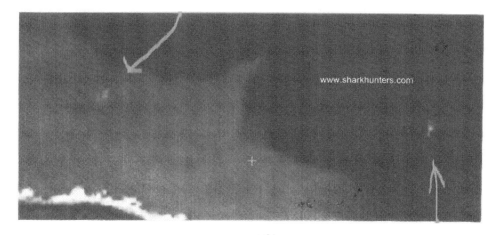

We had been met on the beach by the Nazi agent Rodriguez, a priest whom I had recognized as a man who had worked with me some years before in that country under the name of Father Vogamiz. Rodriguez, wearing Roman Catholic garb, greeted Bormann enthusiastically. I doubt whether the good priest or anyone else there, realized that they were the Welcome Committee for the new Nazi Führer.

PART VII

Half Buried Hatreds

Ever after these years, the face - the name and the recorded voice of Adolf Hitler are still sufficient to stir half-buried hatreds and unforgettable fear in the hearts of millions who suffered and fought in the last war. Yet to those who shared his beliefs - and I was one of them - he was considered a genius. The memory of the madness of those last weeks I spent with him in the Berlin bunker are still vivid in my mind, and I still remember as if it were yesterday the words of the Führer's deputy, Martin Bormann as we fled the shores of Europe in the Spring of 1946.

"Only under Hitler can Germany ever hope for real spiritual and geographic unification."

But the image that springs to my mind at the mention of Hitler's name is not that of the dynamic, dominating dictator. It is of a grotesque cripple, a man feebly clinging to life in the deathly wastes of the South Polar ice cap.

The most macabre adventure of my career as a professional espionage agent began one July day in 1952. I had left Spain to live with my wife and family in Mexico three years before and settled in Cuidad Juarez, a small town close to the U.S. border.

Ostensibly, I was working for the *CARCIA VALSECA* newspaper group as Literary Editor of a weekly supplement. But as always, my real work was with the Nazis - helping establish, for the expanding Party in Central and South America, a communications system for their intelligence service. It was a routine job with little travel and no risk. I began to think that my usefulness to the Nazi cause had passed its peak.

That is, until the day in July 1952 when I received a routine message ordering me to report to an isolated region on the southern tip of South America where I would be taken to see a *'most important person'*. I naturally assumed that this most important person referred to in my orders would be my old friend, Martin Bormann. But I was wrong. Even now, after years of self-interrogation, I am forced to the conclusion that the man I met was no less a person than the Führer himself - Adolf Hitler.

I felt the old excitement as I drove to the airport. Once again, I was called to serve my Nazi masters. I wondered what mission they had in line for me. I was still wondering when, after several changes of aircraft and many hours of frustrating delay, I finally arrived at the airfield named in my instructions. The airstrip was in wild, forbidding country in the southernmost part of the Argentine. I had been expected and when I entered the only building, a rough wooden shack in one corner of the field, I was greeted by a blond Aryan type who turned out to be a former Luftwaffe pilot.

Our transport, a twin-engined freight plane, was parked, already fueled, at the far end of the runway. Without further delay, the pilot told me to follow him and we boarded the aircraft. To me sitting in the co-pilot's seat, it seemed impossible that the big plane could take off from the tiny strip. But my pilot coaxed her into the air and within an hour, we were crossing the coast five thousand feet below.

I had asked him where we were bound, but was not surprised when he refused to discuss our destination. He simply explained that there was no difficulty involved in our flight, since there had been none of the usual formalities at the airstrip we had used. The only clue to our ultimate destination was that the aircraft was fitted with skis as well as wheels and now as we flew, I noticed that our compass was bearing steadily southeast. Incredibly, we were flying towards the South Pole!

For several hours we flew over endless wastes of ice with never a sign of life or vegetation. My pilot seemed to know our route well, for he made few references to maps or navigational aids. Finally, after the briefest check on the, to me, meaningless and patternless terrain below, he eased back the twin throttles and dipped towards the ground.

We came to land on a smoothed tract of snow, and it was not until the aircraft was almost stationery that I picked out the angular outlines of a snow covered hangar and a cluster of buildings grouped a hundred yards further on. We taxied towards the main hangar and, with a final burst of power from the engines, slid to a halt. After the continual roar of the motors alongside me, the silence of that Arctic waste was unearthly. I hardly expected to find other human beings in what seemed a ghost town in the snow, but as soon as our aircraft stopped, a party of well-muffled men left the shelter of the hangar and walked towards us. They greeted my pilot as an old friend and welcomed me in polite German. One of them provided me with a heavy, fur-lined topcoat and urged me to hurry to the nearest house, one hundred paces away.

EDITOR NOTE – We believe that either Don Angel made an incorrect assumption that he flew to Antarctica or that he is deliberately giving mis-information, not an uncommon thing for *'spooks'* to do. We are quite certain that he landed far to the southwestern part of Patagonia and we have been at the complex where Hitler lived for some years after the war.

This is the main house of the complex which consisted of several small guest cottages, a small building for power generating, another small house for cooking and a boat house where boats and float planes were kept. This area is totally blanketed in white over the hard Patagonian winters and this complex could only be reached by boat or float plane. More photos available at **www.sharkhunters.com**. There were also several guest houses. The complex was built in the closing moments of the War with German money, allegedly for the chief executive of a well-known German auto maker but in reality, it was for Adolf Hitler.

Once in the house, a wooden single-story affair, I was handed a steaming hot drink and shown to my quarters. My room was hardly bigger than a normal sized bathroom, but there was a comfortable bed and a chest of drawers, which was quite sufficient for my needs. I found there were similar rooms in the building, plus a larger room where all the occupants ate their meals together. At that time, there appeared to be only myself and the three men who met me, and a white-jacketed servant who cooked and served our food.

Dinner that night found me no nearer the solution to the mystery of this desolate settlement. No one had volunteered why I, or anyone else for that matter, was here. My few attempts at questioning my companions had brought me stares as blank as our surroundings and an infuriating stone wall response.

EDITOR NOTE– The abandoned boat house. When we returned in 2009 and were walking across the expansive lawn, our Argentine boat captain began goose-stepping with his right arm extended in the air. We asked what he was doing, he said,
"I know who lived here. I lived here in my childhood. My father was the caretaker – I know who lived here!"

During the meal, I was excluded almost entirely from the other's conversation and was thankful to excuse myself on the grounds of tiredness, and retreat to my room. I lay on the cot that night with a thousand questions buzzing around my brain. Why was I here? Where was I going? And - most important of all - who was I to meet? And what were the connections between this God-forsaken outpost and the photo of two teen-age children I had been instructed to bring with me?

I took the photos from my briefcase and studied them again. I knew these children well. In the past six months, I had received repeated instructions to check on their well-being. Several times I had visited their hometown of Las Cruces, New Mexico. I understood they had been brought over from Lisbon, Portugal in 1951. Often I had watched them from a discreet distance and taken photographs of them on their way to and from school. In what way were they linked with this mystery man I had flown three thousand miles to meet?

It was nearly mid-day August 10th when one of the men who I had met, came to my room and announced,
   "Señor Gomez, today you are going to meet the Führer."

He mentioned the title so matter-of-factly that at first I did not grasp what he meant.
   "The Führer?" I asked.

"Who do you mean when you say the Führer?"

The man stared at me as if I was mad.

   "There is only one," he replied. *"Adolf Hitler."*

Abruptly, he motioned me to follow him and turned on his heel. Dumbfounded, I let him lead me out of the house and across the snow to another, larger building. Just inside, he stopped and knocked on the door of a room leading off from the hallway. A muffled voice answered his knock. He threw open the door and ushered me in. There were four men in the room. Three of them were standing. But these I scarcely noticed. My attention was riveted on the fourth man, who was seated behind a large wooden desk facing the door. I knew instantly that this must be the man I had heard referred to as the Führer.

But if this was Hitler, then he was barely recognizable as the man whom I had seen leaving the Berlin bunker in April, 1945. To recognize in this person the Hitler who had dominated Germany for twelve years, it was necessary to have a willing imagination.

Compare for yourself. Left 1940; right in the 1960's

This man had no mustache. He was completely bald and the skin of his cheeks and temples had been stretched out of shape and left taut across the cheekbones. Yet his forehead and chin were heavily wrinkled and lined, and an inch-long scar showed white on his left temple. This sinister face was framed against a huge scarlet and black Nazi banner which hung on the wall at his back.

One of the three men standing to my left led me forward and introduced me to the figure behind the desk. I came to attention and gave the Nazi salute. The man behind the desk smiled fleetingly and acknowledged me with a slight wave of the right hand.

Hitler, if Hitler it was, received me sitting down and later I learned that he had difficulty in standing. I could see that his left arm was semi-paralyzed and useless. His face was grey and every few moments, he had to wipe a trickle of saliva from his sagging chin. When he did this, I noticed that his thin, wrinkled hand trembled violently. He looked like a man from whom most of the life had been wrung and his eyes were dull and almost devoid of spark. He wore a dark blue double breasted suit with a Nazi Party emblem in the lapel. The suit fit badly and hung limply from his narrow shoulders.

The man who ushered me to the desk now bade me sit down and produced a file of papers which he set in front of the old man before me. After a brief glance at the papers, he began to ask me questions in a thin, hesitant voice; questions about South America, and the political and economic states of various countries of that continent. But he spoke as if not really interested, and I had to lean forward in order to catch his words properly. I was gripped with such a strong feeling of dream-like unreality that I had to concentrate hard to answer intelligently.

He continued to ask questions, now about the strength of the Nazi movement in South America and about my work for the cause of National Socialism. Yet only once did he show any signs of life and real interest, when with a sudden clench-fisted movement of his right arm, he asked me
"Have you the pictures of the two children?"

It was as *'the children'* or *'that boy'* that he referred to them throughout, never giving a hint of his relationship to them, if any. I only knew the boy's name was Adolfo and he was then about sixteen. The girl's name was Stern; German for Star.

When he asked, I produced a pack of some fifty or sixty photographs of the children. I told the Führer that they seemed well and happy. As I spoke, he pored eagerly over the pictures and when I had finished, the questioning ceased. Without further sign from the old man behind the desk, the interview was over. One of the others in the room stepped up and tapped me on the shoulder, motioning me silently to leave. I rose, bowed slightly to the man at the desk, and left the room. The following day, I was flown back to Argentina.

I never again saw the man they called the Führer.

Throughout the flight, I cast my mind continually back to the macabre meeting with the hunched, shriveled man sitting in a Swastika decorated room in that little hut on the South Polar ice cap; the man his companions referred to as '*the Führer*'. Could this shrunken old man have been the one-time ranting, dominating dictator whom I had last seen in the Berlin Führerbunker during the collapse of Nazi Germany?

Was this poor creature, now presiding over a million square miles of nothing, the same as he who had conquered a continent? Was this Hitler? I remembered the long conversations I had had with Hitler's deputy Martin Bormann, during our long flight together out of Europe six years before. Then, Bormann told me how he had planned the escape of the Führer from the flaming hell of Berlin and how he planned to keep him hidden away until Nazism was again strong enough to lead Germany to freedom.

Now, as our aircraft droned on towards South America, I was filled with excitement. It seemed likely that all Bormann had told me was perfectly accurate, and that the Nazi Party would indeed prove strong and resilient enough to re-emerge.

Upon my return to my home in Cuidad Juarez, a little Mexican town close to the U.S. border, I settled down to await orders from the Nazi underground movement which I still served. My task - under the guise of working for a newspaper group - was to organize and seek contact with Nazi sympathizers in Central America, and to this end I received orders on a radio receiver-transmitter which I kept in the bedroom of my house.

It was just strong enough - it had a range of some 100 miles - to keep me in touch with the next link in the chain of Party workers strung the length of South America. But the days of waiting for the big news stretched into weeks; the weeks into months; and the months into years. The messages I did get were trivial. There was no sign of a call to arms from Bormann or any of the other high-ranking Nazi Party chiefs who had escaped to the sub-continent.

In early 1957, I decided to quit working for my Nazi masters. I yearned to return to my native Spain and settle there once more with my wife and children, and spend the rest of my life making up to them the time I had spent on the Nazis. But my plans were delayed.

On June 6th, 1957 my radio receiver brought me news which was to send me chasing through South America for yet another meeting with Martin Bormann. At first I balked at the uninformative order to proceed to Panama City and await further contact with another Nazi agent. Instead of following my orders as I had done for so long, I decided to take the bold step of flying direct to Germany to make contact with the men at the heart of the Nazi cause.

Here I hoped to get more definite instructions. If I did not, I resolved to quit the organization altogether and move back to a quiet life in Madrid.

To cover my trip, I proposed to my newspaper boss that I fly to Europe for a series of interviews. I managed to arrange one with General Franco, and this was sufficient to justify my journey, and I duly left. But immediately after my audience with Franco, I set out across Europe to the German town of Köln. Köln had replaced München as the new shrine of Nazism and it was here, I knew, that men such as Bormann came from all over the world for top-level talks on the Nazi situation at least once a year.

The way I made contact with the Nazi underground movement was to insert a specially worded advertisement in a Köln newspaper, giving my whereabouts. The day the ad appeared, I took a telephone call at my hotel and was instructed to attend a rendezvous at a certain cafe in the city.

There I was met by a man I had known during the war - a former SS officer, who is now among the group of highly important men who control the new Nazi party in Germany. This man took me to his home on Wagner Straße where I stayed for two days. I explained my feelings to him and asked him to be more explicit about the trip I was supposed to make from Panama City, but he refused to be drawn. He simply said that the High Command had requested me to attend one of their meetings somewhere in South America. He only added that when I got there, I would appreciate the reason why I had been sent for.

This news reversed my pervious decision not to go. I resolved that I would make one more journey into South America, for I guessed that a request from the High Command could only lead to a meeting with Martin Bormann - the Nazi fugitive I had not seen since the day we stepped from a *'pirate'* U-Boat off the coast of Argentina ten years before.

I returned immediately to Mexico and laid plans for my last journey at the bidding of Nazi Intelligence. First, I packed my wife back to Spain and told her I would rejoin her quite soon. Then, with my eldest son Angel, I moved to Chihuahua.

The next step was to shake off the American counter-espionage agent of the C.I.A. who had me under observation. This was not difficult since I had passed on considerable information about the activities of a Communist cell in Mexico to the U.S. military attaché in Mexico City. The CIA agents who kept tabs on me did not seem unduly interested when I let it be known that I was to embark on a tour of Latin American countries with a bullfighting circus. I had great fun setting up my traveling bullring. I'd been a pretty good bullfighter myself in the arenas of Spain in the early 1930's and I looked forward to the trip as a pleasant holiday.

As I say, I took my son with me and also recruited a young woman who was trying to make a name for herself in the somewhat crude bullfights of Latin America. It would be useful to have her along, I thought. Having her in the show gave it an attraction and made my travels appear to be a serious business venture. I bought all the equipment we needed in Mexico City. We set out for Panama, traveling via El Salvador, Nicaragua and Costa Rica. All the way down, my little show and the woman bullfighter, whom I had christened *'Lola Montez'* proved a big attraction.

EDITOR NOTE – Is it possible Conchita Cintron was the lady bullfighter **DON ANGEL** meant? She was the only well-known female bullfighter in the western hemisphere at the time.

Just outside Panama City, in a little town called Davis, I met my contact agent. He was a German named Karl who had taken up cattle breeding. He had apparently been in the business since about 1947. I guessed his story. Anyway, he informed me that I was to travel to Ecuador, and he gave me the location of a farm in the state of Cuenta in that country where, he said, the High Command meeting was due to take place.

I plodded on with my traveling bullring. It was hard work, since I found myself having to go into the ring myself to rouse the bulls sufficiently to make a show of it for the now deadly efficient Lola. It was usual when we arrived in any town, for me to travel around searching for reasonably impressive bulls, which were hard to come by. Consequently, when we finally got to Cuenta, I hired a truck and gave the driver the address of the farm, as told to me by Karl.

Unfortunately, the truck was unable to go the whole way and I had to resort to hiring a mule, which picked its way towards the farm, nestled in the foothills of the Andes. The journey on the back of a mule proved as hair-raising as any I had ever made. Some of the ravines we were forced to cross here were spanned by planks of wood, no more than 18 inches wide, and I found myself hanging on terrified to the neck of the mule.

Worn out but thankful that I had not come to any great harm, I reached the farm. It was a large, splintery wooden house with several smaller cabins dotted around, and as I walked across the dusty ground towards the house, I was approached by the apparent owner, an Ecuadorian, and a posse of about fifty Indians. Quickly, I explained that I had come for the meeting.

"Meeting?" he said without emotion.
"There is no meeting here."

Mystified and more than a little annoyed, I turned to go. But the man called me back and said that since I had obviously come a long way, he would be pleased if I would join him in a drink. He led me into the house and poured me a glass of the local spirit, a rather fierce drink rather like brandy to taste but with twice the kick. We talked in Spanish about nothing very much for a minute or two at the end of which, I drank up and made my farewell. I was just about to leave the house when a sunburned but obviously European man appeared in the doorway.

"Are you Don Angel Alcazar de Velasco?"

He asked in German.

"Yes." I replied.

"Then come this way." he said, and led me through a door and up a flight of narrow wooden stairs. At the top of the stairs, he hesitated a moment, then threw open the door and bade me enter.

I walked into a very large room where seven men were seated around a long, cloth-covered table. And there, smiling a welcome from the top of the table was Martin Bormann. I recognized him instantly, but ten years had left their mark on his features. He was now almost completely bald and had deep pouches on his cheeks, but in his eyes and smiles there was no mistaking the man I had brought out of Europe.

I made the Nazi salute as I entered the room and the group responded immediately by rising and answering, *"Heil Hitler!"*

Martin was first to speak, *"Man, you've grown old, Angel."*

"And the years have made a difference to you, too Martin."

I countered with a chuckle. Bormann invited me to sit down at the table and join himself and the others for coffee. He made no attempt to introduce me to these men, mostly Germans, and I recognized none of them.

He ladled my coffee out from a large bowl on the table and as he did so, he remarked,

"I have been keeping track of you ever since we parted, Angel. I have seen plenty of reports about your good work for us, plus a few reports which you have made out yourself I wanted to tell you personally how pleased I am with the work you have done for the Party."

I sipped my coffee, thanked him, and went on,
"I myself have thought often about you and of the trip we made together."

Bormann insisted then that I should go downstairs and wash the dust from my body and rest before joining him at dinner. As I left the room, I nodded curtly to the other men at the table, each of whom had a pile of papers in front of him, as if each had been given an agenda for an important board meeting.

I went downstairs and was shown to a room where I lay down on a single bed and slept for about an hour. I was woken and invited upstairs again, where Bormann and his friends were preparing to dine. A place for me had been laid on the rough wooden table on Bormann's right-hand side. During dinner, thick soup eaten from heavy earthenware bowls, Bormann talked earnestly to me, questioning with great enthusiasm. He wanted to know everything I had learned about Central and South America in the years I had lived there since last we met.

Further, he wanted to know who I knew in South American politics and what the situation was, as I saw it, with the organization of underground Nazi agents in the continent. He listened intently while I outlined the social, political and economic affairs of those agents I knew personally. Then he pressed me for my views about certain Latin states and their ripeness for revolutionary take-over. On this subject, the other men began interjecting with their own questions; about armaments, finance and the structure of various governments until at the end of an hour, I felt like a well-squeezed lemon.

I did not mention that I had recently been to Europe and they did not mention that part of the world.

Bormann did not tell me too much about himself and his life in South America, but I gathered that he had been well employed and dug his fingers into many different political pies, but he did mention that he had been successful in setting up a number of youth movements along the same lines as the old Hitler Youth; those children who had proved their worth in the battle-scared streets of Berlin in 1945.

EDITOR NOTE - The Reich certainly was deeply entrenched in South America. This is one grave marker in a remote cemetery in Brazil. Many grave markers are the same, with swastika and a German name. They are dated 1936.

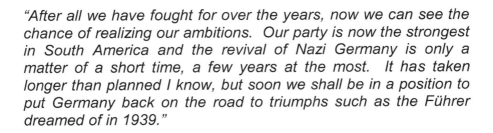

But there was one thing above all that I wanted to tell Bormann; and one question above all, that I wanted to ask.

First, I informed Bormann that I had decided to end my work for the Nazi cause and return to Madrid and my family. He did not seem surprised, but asked me to think again.

"This is not the time to think about leaving us," he said fiercely.

"After all we have fought for over the years, now we can see the chance of realizing our ambitions. Our party is now the strongest in South America and the revival of Nazi Germany is only a matter of a short time, a few years at the most. It has taken longer than planned I know, but soon we shall be in a position to put Germany back on the road to triumphs such as the Führer dreamed of in 1939."

He paused after this speech.
"It seems silly for you to leave us," he concluded,
"when everything you have been working for is about to take on some meaning."

But I would not be persuaded.
"I am glad that things are turning your way, Martin" I answered.
"but I have lost much of my energies. I do not feel up to taking on further work. In a word, I am tired."

Bormann accepted my decision without further comment and changed the subject. I waited for my opportunity during the meal before asking my million-dollar question.
"What of the Führer?"

The question brought dead silence from all around the table. Bormann answered slowly.

"I don't follow. What about him?"

"Is he still waiting?" I asked.

"I planned to bring the Führer back into Germany at the correct psychological moment," said Bormann.

"That plan has now been abandoned."

"Does that mean Adolf Hitler is now dead?" I asked.

Bormann shrugged. He refused to answer me, but turned the subject quickly and pointedly. Bormann's last question during that strange meal was to ask me an out of character inquiry for this once publicity-hating man. He wished to know if people in Europe still talked about him.

"The people, yes. They are still talking about you. But you are rarely named in the press these days." I told him.

"That is good; that is good." came his reply.

I left Bormann the next morning. We parted solemnly, both expressing the wish and hope that we would meet again some time, some place and in more happy circumstances. The last words he ever spoke to me were these.

"I promised you once that I would return to Germany and that is still my promise. The destiny of the Fatherland lies with the National Socialist Party and its Führer. Heil Hitler!"

I clambered onto my mule and without looking back on the group of men standing near the farmhouse at the foot of the Andes, I returned to Cuenta. As soon as I could arrange a booking, I returned at the first opportunity to my home in Madrid. I had finished serving my Nazi masters. I had given them two decades of my life; two decades in which I had risked my life and made myself prematurely old with worry.

I do not work for them now, but thousands of others are helping to keep the Nazi cause alive and I am sure of that. However hard the democratic powers try to delay it, the re-emergence of the Nazi creed in Europe is bound to occur.

I know. I have seen the men who are working for that end. They have power. They have influence. They have the financial determination to put Germany back on top of the heap. They also have Martin Bormann. While men like him live, Nazism will never die.

This is the end of the file sent to Sharkhunters International by the Spanish spy, **DON ANGEL ALCAZAR de VELASCO** who worked for the Reich. It was typewritten, single space and 114 pages in length.

Now we read authoritative comments on Hitler, his escape and the hierarchy of the Reich who also escaped the crumbled Europe and for the most part, lived out their lives in relative safety thanks to their benefactor, Perón.

PART VIII
Details and Proof

Now that we have read the thoughts & memories of Don Angel Alcazar de Velasco, let's see who else knew Adolf Hitler escaped the Führerbunker.

Soviet Field Marshall Georgi Zhukov led the Red Army in the attack and overrunning of Berlin. It was his troops who were in complete and total control of the city – of its entrances and exits. After a long and thorough investigation, Field Marshall Georgi Zhukov told Josef Stalin;
   "We have found no corpse that could be Hitler's"

The Commanding General of the U.S. Sector of Berlin, Major General Floyd Parks, stated for publication that he was present when Marshall Zhukov stated that Hitler might have escaped.

Marshall Zhukov   Major General Parks   General Bedell Smith

12 October 1945, Eisenhower's Chief of Staff General Bedell Smith said;
   "No human being can say conclusively that Hitler is dead."

Thomas J. Dodd, U.S. Chief Trial Counsel at the Nürnberg Trials said,
   "No one can say Hitler is dead."

In his book '*Ten Days to Die*', Nürnberg Judge Michael Mussmanno wrote;

> *"Russia must accept much of the blame that Hitler did not die in May 1945."*

In his book '*Frankly Speaking*', Secretary of State Jimmy Byrnes wrote;

> *"While in Potsdam at the conference of the Big Four, Stalin left his chair, came over and clicked his liquor glass with mine in a very friendly manner. I asked what was his theory about the death of Adolf Hitler and he replied;* **Hitler is not dead. He escaped either to Spain or Argentina.***"*

Thomas J. Dodd   **Jimmy Byrnes**

In 1952, General Eisenhower said;

> *"We have been unable to unearth one bit of tangible evidence of Hitler's death.'*

Colonel W. J. Heimlich was Chief of U.S. Intelligence in Berlin and was in charge of determining what happened to Hitler. After thorough research, Colonel Heimlich stated;

> *"There is no evidence beyond that of hearsay to support the theory of Hitler's suicide. On the basis of present evidence, no insurance company in America would pay a claim on Adolf Hitler."*

During the Potsdam Conference, President Harry Truman directly asked Soviet leader Josef Stalin if Hitler was dead. Stalin simply said,
"No!"

The magazine ***DIARIO ILLUSTRADE*** of Santiago, Chile published an article on 18 January 1948 in which it reported on an incident at Templehof Airfield on 30 April 1945. The writer was friends with a gunner in a JU 52 that had young SS troops for the defense of Berlin. He reported this;

"During this refueling operation, he was suddenly elbowed in the ribs by his radio operator with a nod to look in a certain direction. At about 100 – 120 meters, he saw a sleek Arado AR 234. He and the radio operator saw, without any doubt whatsoever, standing in front of the jet, their Commander in Chief, Adolf Hitler dressed in field grey uniform and gesticulating animatedly with some Party functionaries who were obviously seeing him off. For about ten minutes whilst their plane was being refueled the two men observed this scene and around 4:30pm they took to the air again. They were extremely astonished to hear during the midnight military news bulletin some seven and a half hours later that Hitler had committed suicide."

An article published in August 1952 entitled '*Hitler did not die*' said;
"Adolph (sic) Hitler's fake suicide in the Berlin bunker is now exposed as History's greatest hoax."

Otto Günsche was Hitler's Aide de Camp in the Führerbunker and it was he who poured gasoline on the bodies – but whose bodies? After release from Soviet captivity, he would not talk about that day. In the early part of the 21st Century, his wife passed away and friends speculate that Günsche was about to end his decades long self-imposed silence.

He celebrated his 88th birthday with friends who said that Günsche was still a large and strong man, in perfect health. Perhaps someone feared that he might decide to open up – who knows, but just a short time after his 88th birthday, his housekeeper found him in the sauna at 9am.....where he had been since 3pm the previous day – with the temperature set at 85° Celsius (about 185° Fahrenheit). Beef isn't cooked at that temperature and certainly not for that long.

Or maybe the death of Otto Günsche really was just a heart attack.........

Captain **ROBERT THEW (333-1987)** was in U.S. Navy until he retired, then went into the NSA which as we all know, means No Such Agency. Captain **THEW** flatly stated to us;
   "We (the Intel community) knew Hitler did not commit suicide."

We cannot forget the *'official DNA evidence'* of the government but we also remember that it was the government that stated unequivocally that President John F. Kennedy was assassinated by a lone gunman, Lee Harvey Oswald, using a rifle whose reputation for inaccuracy was exceeded only by its reputation for its lamentable quality. Anyone who believes any government on history of such monumental importance would buy a tower in Paris or a bridge in Brooklyn.

The DNA proved that the skull held by the Soviets in the basement vault of the Red Army Museum was that of a young woman! It obviously was not that of Adolf Hitler, so that entire argument falls apart especially since Field Marshall Georgi Zhukov and Josef Stalin had earlier stated flatly that they did not find the corpse of Adolf Hitler in Berlin.

In The Beginning.....

Cruiser *DRESDEN*, sole survivor of the 1915 battle.

During the Battle of the Falkland Islands in 1915, the cruiser squadron of Admiral Graf von Spee was destroyed except for the light cruiser *DRESDEN*. Badly damaged, she made her painful way through the Straits of Magellan toward escape and freedom. Aboard the cruiser was a young Oberleutnant zur See, Wilhelm Canaris. With dreams and plans for the future, Canaris was carefully plotting all the hidden coves and harbors they passed in the Straits for future use. He was destined to become Admiral Canaris and head of the Abwehr, Germany's Intelligence unit in the Second World War.

He plotted a great many hidden harbors known as "*U-Plätze*" where a boat or ship could lie at anchor hidden from the outside. In true German fashion, he made detailed notes. *DRESDEN* then made it to Chile and Canaris was interned with the crew but he either escaped or bribed his way out then on horseback, he traversed the Andes and arriving in the little village of San Carlos de Bariloche just over the border into Argentina. Canaris was astonished! The little village looked very much like any little Bavarian village back in his homeland of Germany. This too, was burned into the brain of the man to be spymaster of the Reich.

www.sharkhunters.com   Photo by Nahuel Coca

San Carlos de Bariloche in 2008

In 1938 the old German line ship ***SCHLESWIG-HOLSTEIN*** retraced this route and updated the notes to perfection.

All this data, charts and more have been published in the monthly magazine of Sharkhunters. Here are just a few of those secret charts on the next pages.

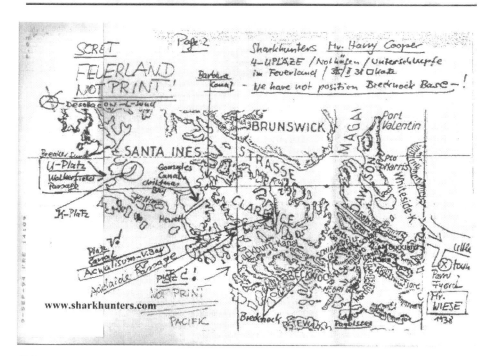

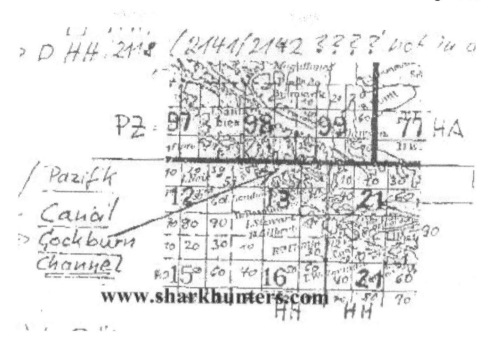

There were more and detailed instructions to find and enter these hidden harbors. They contained sailing directions, how to spot the entrance, what the bottom was like, the prevailing winds, distance from steamer routes and towns, how many ships of what size could hide there and much more.

The island Trindade (not to be confused with Trinidad) is a rock in the middle of the southern Atlantic and has been a possession of Brazil for centuries. They keep a small naval contingent on the island to raise and lower the Flag daily so they can claim ownership and thereby control the fishing rights for 200 miles around. It literally is in the middle of nowhere, but it has great strategic importance.

Shortly before the war, Brazil removed her personnel and within a week, a group of German ships arrived. German personnel occupied the old huts that were built by fishermen in the early 20th Century and they built the radio station seen in the preceding chapter '*Bormann's Lessons*'.

(above left) Northern plateau where the second radio station was built.

(above right) Southern plateau where the first radio station was built.

(below) Remains of the hut foundations – these photos shot in 2009

In 1944 as the Reich was already crumbling, Großadmiral Karl Dönitz told one of his aides that Germany had found an impregnable Shangri-La for the Führer. We believe that he meant San Carlos de Bariloche. The majority living in Bariloche by this time were Germans and thanks to a relatively unknown German named Otto Mehling who arrived in the early 1930's on a '*spook*' mission, there was surveillance all around the huge deep fresh water Lake Nahuel Huapi and there was an armed German security force both on land and on the water.

From the house he built by hand (above left), which he named the Berghof, Mehling could oversee a large part of Lake Nahuel Huapi and he built a watch force that left no corner of the lake or the nearby town unseen. The view from Mehling's Berghof over the lake is seen in the photo above right and the prominent island there is Heumel Island on which German scientists built a nuclear research laboratory – in 1947.

Item #1 on this map is Golfo San Mathias where our files indicate that many U-Boats and specially equipped sailing ships came and went with all the works of the German Abwehr: spies, personnel, money, radio sets and a tremendous amount of items needed for the South American spy service. The little town at the NW corner of the Gulf was the terminus of one rail line running to Buenos Aires and the other to the west, ending at the Estancia San Ramon outside Bariloche.

An unknown German Skipper made this run many times with his secret sailing vessel code name "*MARY*". Kapitänleutnant Heinrich Garbers was decorated with the **Knights Cross** for his work here.

In 1944 when it was obvious that the Reich was going to lose the war, Garbers was quizzed about his voyages. He assured the leaders of the Reich that a wooden boat would not be detected by radar, and that he could bring anyone to Patagonia. We know that he made at least one post war voyage here – we think he made more.

In the war years and for decades later, it was not possible to go by train all the way to the town of Bariloche. The rail line ended at the Estancia San Ramon and from there, it was necessary to arrange transportation the last 20 or so kilometers to the town.

In the winter, this was impossible because of the heavy snowfalls in Patagonia. Our findings indicate that Adolf Hitler and Eva Braun (Hitler) arrived in late June or early July 1945, right in the dead of the Argentine winter and were guests at the Estancia until the snow melted – and their quarters readied for them outside Bariloche.

The Estate Inaco at Lake Nahuel Huapi

As the war was rapidly coming to a close with disastrous results for Germany, work began rapidly on the estate called Inalco far up a finger of Lake Nahuel Huapi. This estate was built in 1942 for a German '*entrepreneur*' then to Jorge Antonio, Perón's frontman for German companies but in reality it was to be the home of Adolf Hitler. The only access to Inalco was by water, usually by boat but occasionally by float plane. To reach the estate from one direction, it was necessary to pass immediately off this watchtower as we see in this photo shot in 2008 from our boat passing under the tower. There were sleeping quarters and cooking facilities for a dozen or so men. Any boat that passed this tower was sure to be spotted and quickly reported to the security forces and definitely to Inalco.

If a boat would approach from the other direction, a bunker on a cliff overlooking that part of the lake would spot it and again, would report the presence to the security forces and to Inalco. The bunker is nothing but rubble now, being dynamited as '*an Army exercise*' in the early 1960's. Author Harry Cooper explores this bunker that housed a dozen or so men with bunk and cooking facilities and furnished security from that end of the lake.

The Remote and Hidden Estate Inalco Hitler's Home for Many Years?

You have seen photos of the main house and the boat house in the preceding chapter '*Half buried Hatreds*' but there were guest houses as well as support and servant's quarters on the grounds. There are many more photos to be seen on our website at **www.sharkhunters.com.**

Sharkhunters 2009 Explorers in front of....
www.sharkhunters.com

When our small group came in 2009, we used two small cabin cruisers to get to the now deserted estate. As we walked across the grass, one of the boat captains began goose-stepping with his right arm high in the air. When asked what he was doing, he said he knew who had lived here.

When asked how he knew, he said that his father was the caretaker here in the 1950's and the captain grew up here. He smiled again and set off again with his right arm in the air, goose stepping across the grass.

Why This Little Town - and Who Else?

Kurt Tank, the brilliant aeronautical engineer who designed the Fw-190 fighter plane, escaped Germany via Norway to Argentina where he designed fighter planes for Argentina. He lived out his years in Bariloche.

SS Hauptsturmführer **ERICH PRIEBKE (7598-2011)** made it to Bariloche shortly after the war where he became Headmaster of the German School in that town. Even today, there is a large German

School and a large German Cultural Center. **PRIEBKE** was brought back to Europe where he stood trial and was convicted. He served a life sentence under house arrest in Rome.

These men and others came to this tiny town, seemingly like a transplanted Bavarian village, at the foot of the Andes. They came because there was a large community of similar people from the Reich, because there was good security for them by their own forces, because it was so remote and hidden that no one would find them much less even look for them. And above all, this was like their beautiful Bavaria except for the reversal of the seasons.

Hundreds of former SS Officers lived in and around this little village of San Carlos di Bariloche and even some just over the border into Chile and all a short distance from Hitler's estate and other places of importance.

A very short distance out of Bariloche stands this magnificent resort named Llao-Llao, built in 1938 with German money and reportedly the site of many celebrations by people of the former 3rd Reich, especially on 20 April, the birthday of Adolf Hitler.

And they had a guardian angel – Juan Domingo Perón!

Ike to Llao-Llao

The above photo shows U.S. President Dwight Eisenhower on a visit to Llao-Llao in 1960. The original of this photograph hangs in the lobby of Llao-Llao and we shot it from that.

One can only wonder what was the real reason an American President was at a resort so far from……..from anything shortly after the end of the war.

The German Nuclear Research Laboratory

The population of scientists, weapons makers, SS officers, high ranking men of the Party etc. quickly swelled the population of Bariloche in the months immediately following the end of the war – about the same time that Perón came to power. They came along what the Allies called *'the Ratline'* out of Europe either by air to Brazil at the *'bulge of Brazil'* at the area of Natal or more commonly by submarine, sailing ship, tramp steamer to the Golfo San Mathias while some came directly into Buenos Aires on board Italian cruise ships.

Perón was eager to help these men escape; principally for two reasons. First of course was the vast sums of money they brought with them but the second reason was more important – nuclear power! Nuclear scientist Dr. Ronald Richter (photo right with some of his scientific team) was one of Germany's top

nuclear scientists, now all but forgotten to history, and he came with his team to Bariloche to build their nuclear research laboratory complex on Heumel Island in the lake. The remains of the laboratory buildings and the reactor itself are there today as seen in these photos taken in 2008.

It was reported that Dr. Richter's scientists achieved a cold fusion reaction that lasted a short few moments but it was supposed to remain a secret operation. Juan Perón however, wanted to make a spectacle and announced that Argentina was the first Latin American nation to be an atomic power. According to the book *"Nazi International"* by Dr. **JOSEPH FARRELL (7353-2008)**, the shadowy figures behind the Reich in Argentina caused Richter to sabotage the tests conducted by an Argentine scientist who studied the laboratory and concluded there was no cold fusion – thanks to the sabotaged tests.

The Nuclear Research Laboratory Complex

Above left – the only building that has been dynamited is the reactor.
Above right – one of the laboratory buildings.

Above left – these spherical objects are outside the reactor building.
Above right – inside another abandoned laboratory building.

A great many more photos of the ruins of the atomic research laboratory complex are to be found on our website **www.sharkhunters.com.**

Was Perón the benevolent angel when he built his army's mountain troop training school directly opposite this laboratory complex on the mainland less than 400 yards distant? Or was he keeping a close eye on it?

So Many Interesting Hotels in Faraway Places

www.sharkhunters.com   Photo by Nahuel Coca

In 1938, a year before the outbreak of World War Two, German interests built the magnificent luxury hotel Llao-Llao outside Bariloche, about 700 miles SW of Buenos Aires in the middle of nowhere. It was badly damaged in a fire but rebuilt and reopened in 1939. What is even more mysterious about this hotel is the photograph hanging in the entrance hall, that of Dwight Eisenhower standing in front of this hotel a few years after the end of the war.

Traveling several hours west out of Bariloche, crossing the border into Chile we find another very fine luxury hotel where, local sources tell us, many SS officers would meet for a celebration every year on 20 April. To refresh your memory, that's Hitler's birthday.

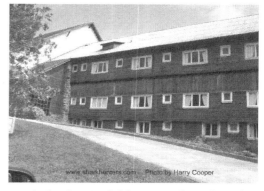

www.sharkhunters.com   Photo by Harry Cooper

We are told that these celebrations ended after Priebke was found and arrested.

One might wonder why these beautiful upscale hotels built by Germans were so far away from civilization. We must remember that at the time these hotels were built, 700 miles SW of Buenos Aires was accessible only by rail and could conceivably be likened to the American frontier of the 1860's. Let us not forget to mention that at least one plastic surgery clinic was built in Bariloche in the closing years of the war.

During our first visit to Bariloche, January 2008, we stopped for dinner in a nice restaurant where the owner greeted us at the door. He was a man of about 80 years, tall with blond hair and blue eyes. He could not speak any English and I cannot speak Spanish. His explanation of the special dinners was not working through my two Argentine friends so, in German, I asked him for an English menu. Without blinking an eye, he replied in German. We spoke for about two minutes in German and I do not think he realized that he had changed into German. I asked how he spoke such good German. He looked shocked for a moment then he said;
   "I am Swiss."

Later in the evening when our host and a friend were entertaining us with gaucho songs on the clavier and guitar, I asked him to sing the Matrosenlied. That is the song the U-Boaters would sing as they departed on their war patrols. No, sorry he said – he did not know that song. I went back to a superb cut of Argentine beef when suddenly, after a few minutes, he did indeed begin to sing the Matrosenlied.

He smiled back and then went through the entire Panzerlied, the song of the armored divisions. When he finished, I applauded then gave him a *'thumbs up'*. He smiled, stood up, clicked his heels and lifted his right arm in the air.

While the two aforementioned hotels were built a very long distance from Buenos Aires to the southwest of Buenos Aires, there were two other hotels of great interest some 500 miles to the northwest of Buenos Aires in the province of Cordoba. Both are now in various stages of ruin, but the history of their participation in WW Two – and afterward – is critical.

The Eden Hotel in the little town of La Falda was built by a German hotel magnate in the late 19th Century but bought by a German family (the Eichhorn family) in the early 20th Century. This family and especially Frau Isa Eichhorn, adored Adolf Hitler and sent him great sums of money to help his political career in the early days.

This hotel had every possible amenity for the day – elevators, outstanding cuisine (they had their own farm and cattle ranch), there was a fleet of Ford Model T cars for the guests and one staff for every two guests. There is a letter at the hotel from Hitler written in his own hand, thanking Frau Eichhorn for her financial support and there are photos of the two of them together. There are also F.B.I. documents on file there in which the F.B.I. states that they believe Hitler was living in that area after the war. One of these documents is found at the beginning of this book.

It was said that the only radio reception and transmission in all of South America was through the Eden Hotel. This may or may not be true, but it is fact that radio broadcasts of Hitler's speeches and news of the war was broadcast here on a regular basis. The hotel boasted a high powered radio transmitter, tall antenna – and a German eagle on the hotel near it.

www.sharkhunters.com

Listening to Hitler's speeches

Was Hitler really here?   The F.B.I. thought so; a waitress (Catalina Gamero) that our S.E.I.G. Agent **SECOND SON** interviewed said that she served Hitler and Eva several times in the private home of the Eichhorns in 1949. The short interview was taped and a copy is here.

Our research indicates that the couple was forced to leave Bariloche about 1955 because the area was found to be great for tourism with the vast, deep lake enticing the fishermen in the summer then skiers flocked to the area in the winter. There are even photos of Hitler's top special ops guy, Otto Skorzeny, skiing in the Andes at Bariloche. Again one might wonder why a man like Skorzeny would go to ski in the Andes by Bariloche when the Alps were so much closer to him in Europe.

After the war, the Eichhorn family was declared *"Nazi sympathizers"*. They lost possession of the hotel and it fell into ruin. The local government is currently trying to resurrect the hotel but it appears that time and the elements are winning the war. The cost to rebuild this once magnificent palatial hotel to its former grandeur is staggering and with no possibility of ever getting that money back, the hotel is crumbling. There are many more photos of these two hotels on our website.

While the Eden Hotel was built approximately five decades before the war began, the Hotel Viena was built in the closing moments of the war and apparently for a very secretive purpose

In the secluded village of Miramare we find the ruins of the Hotel Viena. This was one of the most beautiful, most magnificent hotels at the time in all of South America and it was built late in the war as the war was already turning against Germany.

This hotel not only boasted elevators but air conditioning as well – in 1944! Naturally, there was also a plastic surgery clinic in the hotel complex. The resort complex was built on the shores of a huge inland salt lake, which rose over the years, flooding the first floor to a depth of a several feet. The hotel complex was abandoned; today it sits in ruin even though the waters have receded and the hotel property is high and dry.

Nahuel Coca photo

We see in these photos taken in Jan. 2010, there is no hope for this hotel.

Beauty and the Beast?

The beauty in the photos to the left was Austrian born Hedwig Eva Maria Kiesler. American movie goers of the 1940's and 1950's knew her better as Hedy Lamar. The man in the right photo is her first husband, Austrian Fritz Mandl. He was a very successful arms dealer and once he gave Hedy to Hitler for

a night, presumably to make sure he got arms contracts from the Reich. She quickly emigrated to the USA prior to the war and helped the American war effort with some very important inventions.

When the war ended and the greater Reich was in ruins, Mandl went to the Argentine and, like the other well placed Germans, met with Perón and got the contracts to provide weapons to the Argentine military. He accumulated such an incredible fortune that he palatial homes all over South America but probably none so magnificent as '*El Castillo*' in La Falda. Today this operates as a very expensive hotel.

www.sharkhunters.com
Jim Preston photo

Another of his mansions, now a hotel seen above, is equally as nice, but smaller and less expensive............although not by much.

This was a time and an era of great opulence.

FILES, LETTERS & History

The Third Reich had a huge presence in Latin America, primarily in Argentina, from the middle 1930's and onward. While we are aware of the huge rallies in Madison Square Garden in New York City and other cities in the USA, but they were just as big and open in Latin America too.

On this page and next – rallies in Luna Park in Buenos Aires in the 1930's

Many of the Reich came to Argentina..........including:

Werner Baumbach (left), top bomber pilot and Squadron Commander of the ultra-secret KG 200. He was killed in a plane crash in Buenos Aires while training two Argentine pilots aboard an Avro Lancaster heavy bomber when it crashed into the River Plate. Baumbach could not get out of the plane and drowned.

ADOLF GALLAND (2854-1993) (center), super ACE with more than 100 aerial victories and commander of JV 44, the jet fighter squadron.

Hans-Ulrich Rudel, the most highly decorated of all German warriors in any branch and probably the best pilot ever.

These three Luftwaffe greats reorganized the Argentine Air Force. Here we see Rudel with his beautiful wife at the home of Juan Perón; in the middle of this photo. A great many Germans were friends of Juan and Evita Perón.

The Peróns had many other friends from the Third Reich as well.

Doctor Ronald Richter

Very shortly after the end of the war, Dr. Richter moved to Argentina where he initially went to Cordoba Province, Cordoba City where, thanks to his contact with Kurt Tank, he was employed at the headquarters of the Argentina Air Force. Tank was intrigued with Richter's ideas of nuclear propulsion of aircraft. He worked in Cordoba until Juan Perón sent him to Patagonia, to the little town of San Carlos di Bariloche and the nuclear research laboratory on Heumel Island where he went by the name Dr. Pedro Matthies. The project cost some $300,000,000.

Richter at Heumel

In 1951 Richter reported that he had achieved a controlled cold fusion but Argentine scientists, jealous of his connection with Perón, insisted on an investigation. Upon testing, it was confirmed that the reaction never happened. However, there were two schools of thought on this.

The Argentine scientists claimed that Richter was a fraud and that he never achieved this cold fusion reaction. On the other hand, Dr. **JOSEPH FARRELL (7353-2008)** states in his book "*Nazi International*" that Richter did achieve this success but that contrary to wishes of Martin Bormann to remain quiet about it, Perón widely proclaimed that Argentina was the first Latin American nuclear nation. In this book it is claimed that Richter deliberately disconnected some of his equipment to make sure that the test failed, thereby giving Bormann and his movement cover.

Either way, the Argentine scientists convinced Perón that Richter was wasting all these huge sums of money and in 1952, Perón shut down the Heumel Island nuclear research laboratory. Richter went back overseas where his whereabouts and activities remain clouded. It seems that he did spend some time in Libya but he eventually returned to Argentina where died in 1991. His daughter still lives in Bariloche.

Doctor Richter's Laboratory System on Heumel Island

Sharkhunters groups have been on this island and all through these ruins on two separate occasions. We will return and if you would like more information about our *"Patrols"*, go to the website at the web address at the bottom of each page and check for information about our tours.

Hauptsturmführer ERICH PRIEBKE (7598-2011)

Hauptsturmführer (SS Captain) **PRIEBKE** lived in Bariloche from shortly after the war until his arrest in the middle 1990's for alleged war crimes.

He was Headmaster at the German school as well as head of the German Heritage group in Bariloche. He was brought before a military tribunal in Rome in the mid-1990's and found not guilty. He was not back in Bariloche long before a certain group protested and he was brought back to Rome to stand trial again, only this time before a civilian court.

The civilian court found him guilty and sentenced him to life in prison, but rather than prison he was under house arrest for the rest of his life.

He was allowed daily walks in the park near his apartment and he could shop in the nearby markets. He passed away 11 October 2013 just past his 100th birthday. **PRIEBKE** was just another of the Third Reich who lived out much of his later years in Argentina.

Doctor Friederich Bergius

In the early 20th century, Dr. Bergius earned his PhD in chemistry from the University of Leipzig and his thesis was on sulfuric acid as a solvent. He later worked a short time at the University of Karlsruhe in the development of the Haber-Bosch Process then at the University of

Hamburg where he worked with Professor Max Bodenstein with the process of chemical kinetics.

During the war he worked with the I. G. Farben Company which put a cloud of suspicion over him and his citizenship was questioned. He had to depart quickly and after spending time in Turkey, Switzerland and Spain, he made his way to Argentina where he worked as an advisor on processes to make fuel from coal as well as making sugar from wood.

War Criminals

We will not waste space here attempting to describe what a war criminal is. That definition can change with the wars and the times in which they are fought. Despite the claims of the Allies in World War Two that all the Germans were terrible people, no nation can claim clean hands. However, let us remember that all the war heroes were on the winning side and all the war criminals were on the side that lost. Amazing, isn't it?

The winning side therefore, is able to create the definitions of a war criminal and because they are able to create such definitions, they are able to tailor these definitions to fit certain individuals and specific types of people. The winners have the time, money and other resources to relentlessly pursue those determined to be war criminals indefinitely while the alleged war criminals do not usually have the money to keep running or the specific talents to be protected.

Adolf Eichmann

One such escapee who had no fortune when he arrived Argentina nor great talent was SS Standartenführer (Colonel) Adolf Eichmann, Commandant of Auschwitz concentration camp.

When he escaped the crumbled Reich and made his way to Argentina, he did not have great wealth as most of the others, and he had no talent that was in great demand by the Perón Government like most of the others. He was a poor factory worker who lived in a tiny house at 6067 Garibaldi Street.

He and his sons built this tiny house, about 20 feet by 20 feet in a poor neighborhood, now a very dangerous neighborhood, on Garibaldi Street. He first worked in the factory at FV Manufacturing, a company that made fixture for toilets. Later he worked in the factory at Orbis making water heaters and water softeners. The last place he worked was

in the factory at Mercedes Benz which required a three hour bus ride each way. One night as he returned from work at about 9pm, half a dozen men of the Mossad lay in wait for him as he got off the bus near the railroad embankment and kidnapped him. Here is the little house with the Reich Flag raised by Eichmann's oldest son protesting the kidnapping of his father. As we see in the photo of his oldest son, the young man carried the protest even further by putting on the Swastika armband.

To protect their father's identity in the early days, the two sons referred to Eichmann as their uncle stating that their father had been killed in the war. When Adolf Eichmann first arrived in Argentina, he was welcomed by many of the elite including the Eichhorn family who owned the Hotel Eden in La Falda in Cordoba Province.

This exclusive Sharkhunters photo was taken in the late 1940's at a picnic grove called El Chorito located some distance behind the Eden Hotel. During the Asado, the cooking of the meat over an open fire, he was using his Hitler Youth dagger to cut the meat – it is in his belt in this photo. He is at the left in the photo and his hat is at its usual rakish tilt.

We spoke at length with Francisco, the tailor who made Eichmann's suits when he lived on Garibaldi Street. Francisco said that his kids and the two sons of Eichmann were friends and played together when they were young. He said that the younger Eichmann son told Francisco's kids that they lived for some time in the Vatican before coming to Argentina and that they had met the Pope on several occasions.

To make ends meet, Eichmann also sold fruit juices at the beach on weekends. Both his sons still live in Buenos Aires, but they have changed their names for obvious reasons.

Doctor Carl Värnet

A Dane, Värnet received his Doctorate at the University of Copenhagen and practiced medicine in that city. He studied further in Germany, France and the Netherlands and he became interested in hormonal treatments to modify certain types of behavior.

During the war he held the rank of SS Sturmbannführer (Major) and was a doctor at the Buchenwald concentration camp. He was introduced to various important men of the SS and eventually to Heinrich Himmler himself. He performed glandular experiments on seventeen homosexuals in Buchenwald in an effort to show that their homosexuality can be changed but after some time with no solid results to show, he was more or less defunded.

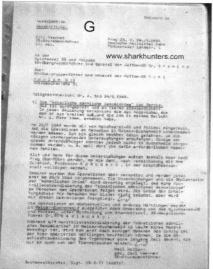

After the war he was arrested in Copenhagen and Danish authorities were going to bring him to trial, he pretended to have heart trouble. When his chance presented itself, he escaped first to Brazil then to Argentina. He died there in 1965.

This is a memo of Värnet's describing his treatment to change homosexual behavior. During my expedition to Argentina in in January 2014, I visited what was once his clinic. It is now a residence hotel.

Ludwig Freude

Ludwig Freude (his name is German for Joy or Delight) was a high level German businessman and in the 1940's was the Director of the Banco Aleman Transatlantico, a subsidiary of the massive Deutsche Bank. At that time he was one the ten wealthiest businessmen in Latin America, was president of the German Clubs in Buenos Aires and one of the most influential men of the Third Reich. He was also a friend of Juan Perón as we see in this photo. The arrow points to Freude and we see Perón putting his hankie into his pocket.

Even before the war ended, Freude worked to help preserve the vast fortunes of individuals on the Reich as well as the treasures of the Reich itself. When things were closing in on Freude, he fled to Argentina.

Because of his friendship with Perón and his financial power, he was instrumental in helping organize "*die Spinne*" better known as "*Odessa*"! And when the Allies requested Freude's extradition, Perón more or less said that Freude was his personal friend and that he was not going to be extradited. His grave is in the beautiful German Cemetery in Buenos Aires, not far from that of Kapitän zur See Langsdorff.

ABC Restaurant

This restaurant, right in the center of Buenos Aires only a few steps off the ultra high-buck Calle Florida, is where many men of the Third Reich met for lunch in the years after the fall of Germany. Two of these were Doctor Josef Mengele and Adolf Eichmann.

Since this restaurant is only a few blocks from the Navy Hotel where I always stay, my guide and I went there for lunch.

The food was great and while the service was adequate at best, the decor and ambiance put us right back into the post war years. One could almost feel the presence of former warriors all about in the place.

It was a bit out of place when two beautiful Irish lasses finished their lunch and brought their half-finished bottle of wine to our table and said it was for us. That was the good memory. Then we watched the waiter go to a table that had just been vacated where he took the guest's water glass, splashed a bit of water on the used bread plate and wipe it with the napkin then put the plate on another table. Memories, eh?

Doctor Josef Mengele

We all know this name so there is no need to go into his history but we traced his movements through Argentina. An important man, Gerhard Malbranc, picked up Mengele at his hotel a few days after he arrived in Buenos Aires and brought him to the Malbranc home where he lived for some time. In the photo left we see Mengele on the porch at 2460 Aeronales with the cat.

Malbranc was a close friend of Juan and Evita Perón.

The Malbranc house at 2460 Aeronales.

Soon afterwards, Mengele bought a nice house at 968 Juan Jose Vertez, just around the corner from 1065 Gaspar Campo, the Presidential Palace of Juan Perón. Mengele ultimately owned three houses in Buenos Aires.

Fridolin Guth

Fridolin Guth was born in the Tyrol and was involved in the 1934 attempt to place the NSDAP in Innsbruck. He fled to Bavaria then in 1938, back to Innsbruck. He held the rank of SS Hauptsturmführer (Captain) in the SS Police Regiment 19 and was sent into Slovenia in March 1944. The 2nd Company was headed by Guth stationed in Annemasse.

After he made his way to Argentina, he ended up in Cordoba Province in the town of Agua de Oro. It means *"Golden Water"* because there was a brewery in the area.

Guth however, was an excellent baker and it is said that his Black Forest Cake was excellent. He opened a restaurant called the Nueve Tyrol. Guth died some years ago but the restaurant is still open and we ate there in January 2014. No Black Forest Cake at the time, I am sorry to report.

This photo shot by the author in January 2014. There really isn't anything in this remote area. Fridolin Guth apparently was afraid that he would be grabbed and taken out of Argentina as he almost never left this house/restaurant except when the German Ambassador came by. They would go for a drive together. Other than that, Guth never went out.

Kurt Christmann

He was a Member of the Hitler Youth and participated in the "*Beer Hall Putsch*" on 9 November 1923. He then joined the SS and received his Doctorate in Law. Quite athletic, Christmann won the German championship in canoeing and he worked as a sports instructor of the SS.

He was transferred to the SS Police at Gestapo Headquarters in Vienna in 1938 then to Innsbruck in 1939. He was there until July of 1942 where he was a Task Force Leader with an Einsatzgruppe in Krasnodar. Lateron he was Gestapo Chief in Klagenfurt, Austria when he was promoted to SS Obersturmbannführer (Lieutenant Colonel).

He worked for the British Army occupation under the name Doctor Ronda until 1948 when he flew through Rome to Argentina. He was helped by "*die Spinne*" (*Odessa*) then he participated with this organization to help others escape Europe.

In 1956 Christmann tried to return to the Federal Republic of Germany as a lawyer but was denied admission. Returning to Argentina, he quickly rose in the real estate business and soon owned a company.

On 19 December 1980 the München Regional Court convicted Kurt Christmann of war crimes involving the activities in Krasnador and sentenced him to ten years in prison. He appealed but on 11 November 1982 the German Federal Court of Justice confirmed the sentence.

Kurt Christmann (alias Doctor Ronda) died on 4 April 1987.

Martin Bormann and the Plaza Hotel

Martin Bormann was the second most powerful man in the Third Reich and apparently, at some point, he assumed control of the Party and Adolf Hitler was not much more than a figurehead. As you have already read, Bormann assumed control of the Party and everything else pertaining to the Third Reich. We know that he came to Argentina aboard a U-Boat thanks to **DON ANGEL ALCAZAR de VELASCO (158-1985)** and that he quickly took quarters in the Plaza Hotel, the most elegant hotel in Buenos Aires.

This hotel is only four blocks from my hotel, so I walked there and entered the lobby. Senora Rodriguez at the front desk was cordial; I introduced myself and told her I was doing research for this book. I also told her that we had reason to believe that Martin Bormann lived here for some time after the end of the war. Without any expression, she said:

" Oh yes, room 470: the Presidential Suite. "

Naturally I was a bit taken aback and asked how she knew this. She told me that everyone there knew that Bormann stayed in the Plaza for quite some time and, she added, this was about the same time that Adolf Hitler came to Argentina. I grabbed a thick book about the history of the Plaza Hotel, thumbed through it and asked Senora Rodriguez why there was nothing about Bormann in the book.

She said this was not really the kind of advertising the Plaza thought was positive. Guess she has a point there.

Professor Kurt Tank

Kurt tank was one of the most brilliant aircraft designers of the war years and his most famous aircraft was the Focke-Wulf FW 190 fighter, called the Würger (Shrike) by the Luftwaffe but more accurately called "*the Butcher Bird*" by Hermann Göring. The various versions of this single seat fighter were Tank's brainchild throughout the war.

When the war was over, naturally the US tried to bring him to America in Operation "*Paperclip*" and other countries wanted him and his talents as well. The US did not snare him nor did the Soviets. Tank had been talking with the British as well as the Nationalist Government of China but to no avail.

He did not reach agreement with China, and the British felt he was too important and could not be incorporated into an already smoothly working group. The US and the Soviet Union could not tempt him so he went north then south.

He went north into Denmark then over the Denmark Straits to Norway where he obtained transport to Argentina. He brought with him about fifty of his engineering team and worked in Argentina until Perón was ousted from power. Many of his team went to the USA but Tank went to India and designed aircraft there for a while.

Dr. Ronald Richter was one of his team and as we have already learned, he went to Heumel Island by San Carlos di Bariloche, Patagonia Province which incidentally, is the area where Adolf Hitler and his wife Eva lived until 1955 when they had to move to Cordoba Province.

Kurt Tank's two children still live in Argentina.

Ante Pavelic

His pre-war activities are well known including his involvement in the planned overthrow and assassination of King Alexander and his wartime activities as leader of the Croatian Nationalist Movement and their ties to Adolf Hitler and Germany. Here we focus on his post war history.

He moved through Europe on a Peruvian passport identifying himself as a Catholic priest named Don Pedro Gonner. He went through Venice and Florence and into Rome where he was given shelter by the Vatican and he lived there for some time. While living in the Vatican, he organized the Croatian State Committee but communist dictator Tito confronted the Vatican about Pavelic, now living in the Papal summer residence at Castel Gandolfo, claiming that Pavelic, with the help of the Vatican, was trying to revive Nazism.

He hid in a Jesuit house near Naples and in the fall of 1948 he met Father Krunoslav Draganovic and the priest helped him obtain a Red Cross passport identifying him as Pale Aranios, a Hungarian. Draganovic had other ideas and was going to deliver Pavelic to the Italian police, but Pavelic smelled the plot and escaped. He rode the Italian ship *SESTRIERE* and disembarked in Buenos Aires on 6 November 1948. He lived with the writer Vinko Nikolic in Buenos Aires where he worked as a bricklayer. His wife Maria and oldest daughter Visnja soon joined him.

Thanks to a friend who was close to Juan and Evita Perón, Pavelic took a job as security advisor to Perón. In 1950 he was given amnesty and allowed to remain permanently in Buenos Aires and further, some 34,000 other Croats also emigrated into Buenos Aires, naturally including a great many who were wanted by the Allies but they were safe here.

Branko Benzon, who had been the Croatian Ambassador to Germany in the war and knew Hitler personally, was close to the Peróns. Thanks to him, Pavelic was also close to Perón. Thanks to such influence, he soon owned a construction business in Buenos Aires and built some of the huge buildings that stand today. We visited some of them.

At the end of the 1940's, there was a rift in the Croatian movement in Argentina and many drifted away from Pavelic. Many sought the revival of the Independent State of Croatia and one of the leaders was Vjekoslav Luburic, former head of the concentration camp network in his country. Luburic lived in Spain but in Argentina, Pavelic used the "*Croatian Home Guard*" immigrants to expand his power. He founded the Croatian Statehood Party which evaporated as quickly as it began.

Then on 10 April 1951, the 10th anniversary of the Independent State of Croatia, Pavelic announced the new Croatian State Government in exile. Many more Croatian emigrees poured into Argentina and most joined with Pavelic who was actively engaged in attacking the Communist government in his home country.
LEFT – Pavelic as a bricklayer
BELOW – With his family

On 10 April 1957 on the 16th anniversary of the founding of the Independent State of Croatia, Ante Pavelic was ambushed and shot in the back by Blagoje Jovovic, an agent of the Yugoslav Federal Secret Police. Pavelic had just gotten off the bus on the corner of his street in the Palomar District of Buenos Aires when the ambush occurred.

While he was in hospital, Perón fell out of power and the Yugoslavian extradition request was granted but Pavelic flew to Chile and then to Spain, arriving Madrid 29 November 1957 still with a bullet in his back that he refused to have removed.

Although he attempted to remain politically active, the Spanish Government refused to allow him to appear in public. Pavelic died in the German Hospital in Madrid on 28 December 1959.

I spoke with the lady who, with her attorney husband, now own Pavelic's house and told her I was gathering evidence that Adolf Hitler lived out his live in Argentina. She was surprised. **She said she thought everyone knew that; they did in Argentina.** She pointed out the little monument on the corner where Pavelic was shot as seen here in the photo by the author in January 2014.

The Maid Knew!

Catalina Gamaro worked for Walter and Ida Eichhorn at their Hotel Eden. She was a young woman and was more like a daughter to the family and she was with them for years. She knew that Hitler was there.

In the year 2004, Abel Basti contacted her and made arrangements to come to La Falda to interview her and look at any documents and photos Catalina had. He told this author that Catalina was ready and willing to speak with him openly and to show him what she had. This was going to go into the book that Abel was writing about Nazis in Argentina.

Her cooperation abruptly vanished and she informed Abel that he should not come and she said that.......... *they* told her that she could not speak with anyone or show photos "while the lady was alive".

"*They*?" "*The Lady*?" We are quite certain that "*They*" refers to "*die Spinne*" otherwise known as "*Odessa*". They do exist today. No, not the original men of the SS as they are either very old or passed away. Their grandchildren however, are very active. This author met one such young man in Villa General Belgrano in 2010. He was a handsome young man of thirty years of age with blue eyes, blond hair and straight white teeth. His grandfather had been a Generalleutnant with Kurt "*Panzer*" Mayer.

We also think that "*the lady*" refers to Eva Braun-Hitler. She was born in 1912 and so in 2002 she would be 90 years of age, not impossible at all.

A few years ago Catalina made an interview which has been provided by our friend Martin Gomez. Here it is, translated from her Spanish.

CG: I never worked in the Eden Hotel; I worked in the annex.

Q: Did Hitler have holidays in the annex?

CG: No. He stayed just a few days.

Q: How did you know that was Hitler?

CG: We, the employees, are one – very united. We talked about this.

Q: He presented himself as Hitler?

CG: No, no, no. We don't see him. He stayed in a private place. Nobody can see him.

Q: And why do you think that he was Hitler?

CG: Because of the attitude of the Eichhorns. He stayed in 1936 and then after the war.

Q: Is there a picture of Hitler in La Falda?

CG: Yes. The Eichhorns had one, but they burned it.

Q: Is there someone else who saw Hitler here?

CG: No. They are all dead.

Q: What happened to Hitler?

CG: He stayed here in 1949 and he died in San Juan, Mendoza.

Q: When you stayed in the annex, did you receive some calls from Hitler asking about Ida Eichhorn's health?

CG: No. There were calls from Mendoza but someone else talked.

CG: He did not die in Germany! No! No! No!

Q: We thank you.

CG: At this time, all was very quiet not like today. La Falda was very small, very private.

Q: Did you receive pressure from anyone to shut up?

CG: No. No. I talk about what I want.

The Secret Hidden Compound

You can't see it………..you do not even know it is there unless you know where to look and what to look for. As we fly down a new, modern four lane highway, we must know precisely where to look for the little slash in

the treeline where just as hint of a gap appears for a fleeting moment. It is the beginning of a narrow, one lane dirt road that goes back through the trees. As we enter this hidden dirt road we pass the abandoned building that had once served as a guardhouse.

We bounce along for perhaps half a mile when we come to a tunnel. If you came here in the late 1930's and managed to pass the guardhouse, you would be stopped here as you see in the photo left.

There were no guards when we arrived (photo above right) and we drove right in. It is so narrow that only one vehicle can make it – only a car, it is too small for trucks or anything bigger than a car. After a short way, maybe a quarter mile or so, the tunnel opens up and we drive at least a mile, it seemed like more, through the wilderness and on the way we passed several signs that said "*Sharkhunters Welcome*"……actually they said "*No Pasar*" but we know this means the same as "*Eingang Verboten*" in Germany which we know means there is something in here that we must see – and so we press onward over the horribly rough dirt road towards the remains of the compound.

Finally we arrive at the compound - and we walk back in history so many decades. It is just the way it was when the German personnel walked out in, we believe, the 1950's except that time and nature have taken their toll.

On the left we see an abandoned building through the trees and on the right, one of those signs that say *"No Pasar"*. We get out of our *limousine* (a two door Renault with a one liter engine) and explore the compound on foot.

We learned much that was going on in this compound. Not sure yet what its function was prior to the war and during the war, but post war many of the men of the Third Reich had to come through here to receive their new identities, their new assignments etc. We were told that even for some years after the end of the war German troops were billeted here and trained here. The white building in the photo top appeared to be a staff or clerical function while the yellow building behind our *limousine*

appeared to be a cookhouse or similar. Meals were taken here in this outdoor area where there were approximately forty stone tables that sat six men each. The *"grinder"* to the right of this photo is where the men drilled and they had weapons and infantry training in the woods beyond. We are not sure when this compound was deserted – but some of it still works.

Here is the "baño Caldera" which I am told means "hot baths". The water is still flowing in the pipes as we see in the lower right photo although it is not known if the showers are hot.

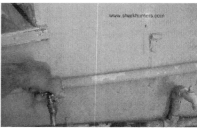

There was a huge swimming pool and a grotto with a shrine (above).

(below) The HQ building and a barracks where there were two sets of bunks stacked three high in each room. The bathrooms were strategically placed along the corridors for easy use of the personnel.

There are a great many more photos posted on our website. The web address is at the bottom of each page and when you get to the site, click on "*Previous Tours*" then let your fingers do the walking.

Here we bring you just some of the files and letters we have in file that, along with our personal visits, leave absolutely no doubt that Adolf Hitler, his wife Eva Braun-Hitler, Martin Bormann and countless others of the Third Reich did indeed, reach safety in South America, primarily Argentina, and with but a handful of exceptions, lived out their lives in safety and depending on each situation, from comfortable to quite plush.

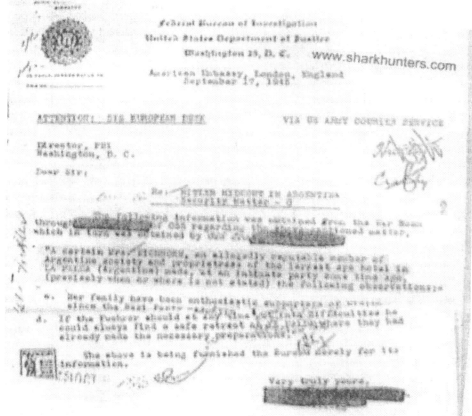

This FBI file dated 17 September 1945 is kept in the Eden Hotel in laFalda, Argentina.

DIRECTOR

Federal Bureau of Investigation
United States Department of Justice
Washington, D. C.

September 4, 1944

CAG:FCS

www.sharkhunters.com

MEMORANDUM FOR THE DIRECTOR

Re: Possible Flight of Adolph Hitler to Argentina

Mr. E. A. Tamm
Mr. Clegg
Mr. Glavin
Mr. Ladd
Mr. Nichols
Mr. Rosen
Mr. Tracy
Mr. Carson
Mr. Coffey
Mr. Harbo
Mr. Mendes
Mr. Kramer
Mr. McGuire
Mr. Piper
Mr. Quinn Tamm
Tele. Room
Mr. Nease
Miss Beahm
Miss Gandy

Many political observers have expressed the opinion that Adolph Hitler may seek refuge in Argentina after the collapse of Germany.

Political ramifications lend credence to this possibility when it is recalled that the duly appointed Argentine Consul Hellmuth, ostensibly assigned to a Consular post in Spain, had plans which included clandestine meetings with Hitler and Himmler for the arranging of importing arms and technicians into Argentina. Hellmuth, intercepted by the British at Trinidad, never completed his mission.

Argentina remains a mysterious maze of questionable characters. ████ who will be recalled for her notorious affair with the German diplomatic representative in New York, is presently residing in Buenos Aires. ████, former Austrian munitions king and ex-husband of ████ recently converted his bicycle factories into an Argentine plant for the manufacturing of munitions. Arnulfo Arias, pro-Axis ousted President of ████ conducts a long range political campaign from Buenos Aires. ████ well known as the sweetheart of the American industrialist Vivien Spillers, still claims to be in Argentina as the postwar planner for the German cartel Metallgesellschaft.

A large wealthy German colony in Argentina affords tremendous possibilities for the providing of a refuge for Hitler and his henchmen. One of the members, Count Luxburg, has been mentioned as operating a ranch which would serve in providing a haven.

By the very nature of any plans formulated for the abandoning of Germany in its collapse, it is virtually impossible to substantiate any allegations with regard to Argentina's serving the Nazis after defeat; however some significance may be attached to the fact that Argentina remains silent despite all the accusations that she will serve as a terminus for Hitler after a non-stop flight of 7,376 miles from Berlin to Buenos Aires in an especially constructed plane or as a passenger in a long range submarine.

This matter continues to be the subject of a coordinated investigation by the Bureau representatives throughout the world. Information developed to date has, of course, been furnished to other interested governmental agencies.

Respectfully,

D. M. Ladd

58SEP

456

Above file was uncovered by S.E.I.G. Agent **TAUCHER**

This four-page file was uncovered by S.E.IG. Agent **TAUCHER**

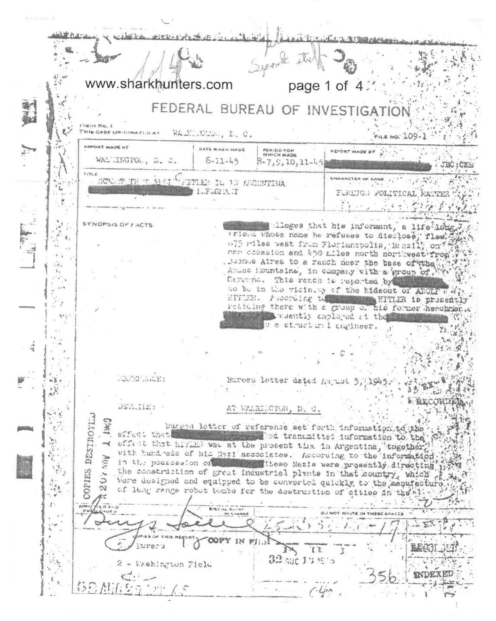

www.sharkhunters.com   page 1 of 4

FEDERAL BUREAU OF INVESTIGATION

........page two of that file from S.E.I.G. Agent **TAUCHER**

WFO 109-1

United States and Brazil.

This hideout was purported to be beneath a German owned hacienda located about 675 miles west from the Brazilian port of Florianopolis and 450 miles northwest of Buenos Aires.

██████ ███████ presently resides at ████████ ... W., and was interviewed at the Washington Field Office by the writer. Mr. ██████ stated that he had transmitted the information in his possession concerning the whereabouts of HITLER to Senator PIERCE and also to ██████

██████ stated that he obtained ██████ address from a ██████ last name unknown, the Washington representative of the "Chicago Times".

When ██████ was interrogated concerning the source of his information, he stated that a life long friend of his had told him in the strictest confidence that HITLER was presently residing in Argentina, near the base of the Andes Mountains, and instructed him explicitly never to reveal his name as the source of this information. According to ██████ this life long friend speaks many languages fluently, including German, Spanish, Portugese and French. ██████ stated that he did not know his occupation, but did know that for the last twenty years he had traveled all over the world, particularly in South America. He stated that he apparently represents various countries and various corporations in many different localities. On one particular occasion ██████ informant was selling manufacturing equipment in South America.

According to ██████ his informant had told him that on one occasion he posed as a German national and flew 675 miles west from the Brazilian port of Florianopolis with a group of German nationals. ██████ stated that they landed at a ranch near the base of the Andes ██████ and during the course of their trip he had ascertained that this ranch was to be the hideout of ADOLF HITLER, and a group of his cohorts.

On another occasion, according to ██████ this informant again posed as a German citizen and flew from the port of Buenos Aires, Argentina, 450 miles north northwest from Buenos Aires to this same ranch. ██████ stated that his informant could not recall any town near this ranch and, therefore, could not identify the particular spot in which the purported hideout of HITLER is located. He stated that he had informed Senator HITNER that the ranch was located 450 miles northwest of Buenos Aires, whereas, it was more nearly 450 miles north northwest of Buenos Aires.

- 2 -

…..page three of that file from S.E.I.G. Agent **TAUCHER**

www.sharkhunters.com   page 3 of 4

[REDACTED] ....en that his informant had been in South America
in May or June of this year and had contacted him in Washington, D. C.
upon his return from South America. It was at this time that [REDACTED]
was informed that HITLER was presently hiding out in Argentina.

[REDACTED] refused under any circumstances to reveal the source
of his information, in view of the fact that he had given his word of
honor that he would not reveal the name of his informant. However, he
did state that his informant apparently was in constant travel status,
but that when he was in the United States he spent most of his time in
New York City. He also stated that his informant was about his
[REDACTED] age, Jewish and a very brilliant man, speaking many languages.
[REDACTED] stated that he never did ascertain his informant's connection
with any business concern or any Government, but believed that he
associated himself with anybody who needed his services.

[REDACTED] stated that his informant added, just prior to his
departure, that HITLER has shaved off his mustach and dyed his hair
blond. Other than the above changes, his appearance has not been
altered to any great extent.

[REDACTED] advised that upon the next occasion that his
informant comes in, he would try to prevail upon the informant to
any additional information, in strictest confidence, and also to give
stated that he knew of nothing further concerning the information about
the whereabouts of ADLF HITLER, other than that reflected above.

In order to ascertain the reliability of [REDACTED]
a background check was made of this individual. [REDACTED]

Special Agent, [REDACTED] checked The Credit Bureau
and Stone's Mercantile Agency at Washington, D. C. for a record on
[REDACTED] with negative results. A check of the indices of
the Washington, D. C. Police Department failed to reflect any record
on this individual.

[REDACTED] is not listed in the Washington, D. C.
Telephone Directory or the City Directory.

It was ascertained that [REDACTED]
the [REDACTED] Washington Field Office, [REDACTED] employed at
F. W., Washington, D. C. A check of his personnel file at [REDACTED]

- 3 -

358

.....page four of that file from S.E.I.G. Agent **TAUCHER**

reflected that [REDACTED] is born [REDACTED] and has been
employed as a structural engineer at the [REDACTED]
[REDACTED] at a salary of $3600.00 a year since February 1, 1945.
Prior to this time he was employed in the [REDACTED] and
the [REDACTED] an engineer at a salary of
$4200.00, from [REDACTED]

[REDACTED] file at the [REDACTED] reflected
that he was employed for five and one-half years as a bridge designer
for the [REDACTED]
He was also employed for a period of ten years as a structural engineer
consultant for the [REDACTED] and
for thirteen and one half years by the [REDACTED]
as editor of the magazine [REDACTED]. His personnel file reflects
that his permanent residence is [REDACTED]
and that his sole dependent is [REDACTED]

[REDACTED] prior to his transfer he received
an efficiency rating of "very good", dated February 17, 1944.

No further investigation is being conducted by the Washington
Field Division unless advised to the contrary by the Bureau, and this
case is being considered closed.

- CLOSED -

SECRET   Madrid, July 3, 1943.

www.sharkhunters.com

MEMORANDUM

Subject: HITLER

HITLER is hiding at the finca of the Conde de
MAYALDE in the aldea of Mazarambroz, Province of
Toledo, near Sonseca and near Pulgar, in the jurisdiction of the town of Orgaz. MAYALDE was former
Spanish Ambassador in Berlin up to about 1943, and
is said to have been friendly with HITLER. The
bearer of these good tidings is one Augustine
MARTINEZ, native of the town of Sonseca and between
1928 and 1937 chief of the Spanish telephone service
in that town. He now is in Madrid, proprietor of the
Pension Roldan, Calle Cruz 53, segundo derecho,
telephone 26215. MARTINEZ seems to have pronounced
democratic ideas and has been in jail on political
grounds. I have an idea that the Pension Roldan
is a very interesting place. Some of MARTINEZ's
relations live in Sonseca, and he believes he
could obtain confirmation of this bulo by going
back to Sonseca and talking to his friends in the
service of the MAYALDES. He wants no money but his
expenses, and offers to do odd jobs without pay except expenses.

MARTINEZ is unknown to me but he looks like a
shrewd old rascal who hates the present regime and
is sincerely attached to the Allied cause.

EOT/jra

This file uncovered and sent by S.E.I.G. Agent **PIZZARRO**

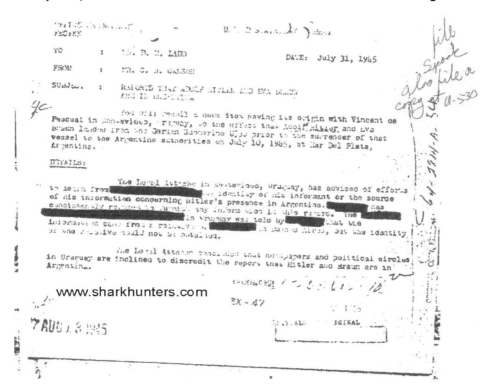

This file uncovered and sent by S.E.I.G. Agent **PIZZARRO**

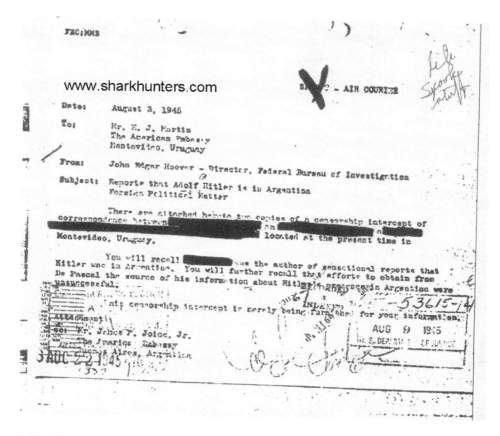

This file uncovered and sent by S.E.I.G. Agent **TAUCHER**

Office Memorandum • UNITED STATES GOVERNMENT

TO   :   Director, FBI   DATE: August 14, 1945

FROM : SAC, Los Angeles

SUBJECT: ████████████ AND REPORT ON
          ████ ██ ███████ HIDEOUT
          INTERNAL SECURITY - G

The following information was brought to the attention of the Los
Angeles Field Office by ████████████████████████████████
who advised that the information was originally received by an individual on
the ████████████████████████

████████████████████████ Hollywood, who it has been
ascertained is a radio actor and "bit" parts movie player, reported that
certain sources placed Adolf Hitler in hiding in Argentina. According to
████████████ he met a man named ████████ who is of Spanish-Argentinian descent, at
a club in Hollywood, and after several hours of general conversation ████████
told ████████ about a tremendous problem that was bothering him and wanted to
know if ████████ could help him. It followed that ████████ who speaks fluent
Spanish, was one of four men who met Hitler and his party when they landed
from submarines in Argentina two and a half weeks after the fall of Berlin.

"The first submarine reportedly docked at approximately 11:00 at
night, and the second submarine about two hours later. Hitler was reported
to have been aboard the second submarine and with two women, a doctor, and
several other men numbering in or about fifty persons came ashore. Pack
horses were waiting for the group, and at daylight an all-day trip inland
toward the foothills of the Southern Andes was started, and at dusk the party
arrived at the ranch where Hitler and his party are now in hiding. According
to ████████ this affair was arranged by six top Argentine officials as far
back as 1944, and ████████ further reports that if Hitler is apprehended the
names of these six top officials will be revealed. ████████ is ready also to
reveal the names of the three other men who, with ████████ helped HITLER
inland to his hiding place.

████████ advised that he was given $15,000 for helping in the deal,
and wishes to state at this time that he does not want to become any further
involved, and realizing that it is only a matter of time before Hitler is
apprehended, he is desirous of clearing himself at this time.

████████ informed that two interesting things were mentioned on the
inland trip. One was that the reason the French channel ports held out against
the Allies after the fall of Berlin was to allow Hitler to leave from one of

COPIES DESTROYED
R 207 NOV 1 1900

80 SEP 7- 1945

www.sharkhunters.com

Director, FBI

August 14, 1945

them by submarine, and secondly that shortly after leaving France the submarines were fired on by the British gunboat. According t▓▓▓▓▓▓ Hitler is suffering from asthma and ulcers. He has shaved off his mustache and has a long butt on his upper lip. ▓▓▓▓▓▓nsists that if arrangements can be made he will have a man available to conduct a party to Hitler's hiding place. This man, followin▓▓▓▓▓ instructions, will meet the interested party at a hotel in San Antonic, Argentina."

Efforts are being made by the Los Angeles Field Office through ▓▓▓▓▓▓to recontact▓▓▓▓▓▓hose whereabouts are unknown at present, for the purpose of conducting a full detailed interview regarding this matter. The Bureau will be advised of the results of this interview at the earliest possible date.

Page 2 of 4

EAF:rg
105-410

This two-page file uncovered and sent by S.E.I.G. Agent **TAUCHER**

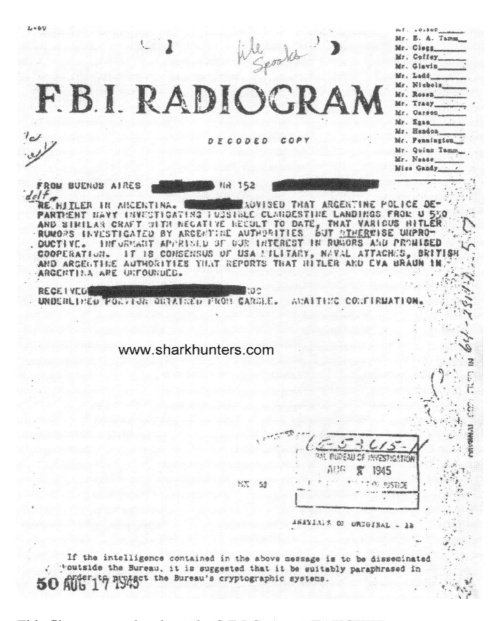

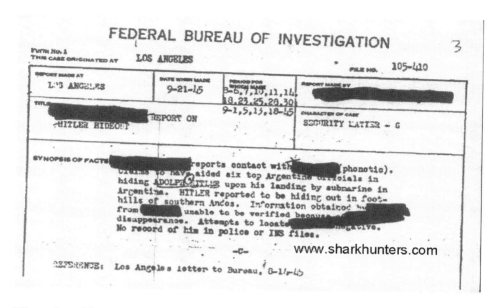

FEDERAL BUREAU OF INVESTIGATION

3

THIS CASE ORIGINATED AT   LOS ANGELES

FILE NO.   105-410

REPORT MADE AT	DATE WHEN MADE	PERIOD FOR WHICH MADE	REPORT MADE BY
LOS ANGELES	9-21-45	8-5,7,10,11,14, 18,23,25,28,30 9-1,5,13,18-45	▓▓▓▓▓▓▓

TITLE ▓▓▓▓▓▓▓▓▓▓▓▓▓ REPORT ON
HITLER HIDEOUT

CHARACTER OF CASE
SECURITY MATTER - G

SYNOPSIS OF FACTS: ▓▓▓▓▓▓▓ reports contact with ▓▓▓▓▓▓ (phonetic).
Claims to have aided six top Argentine officials in
hiding ADOLPH HITLER upon his landing by submarine in
Argentina. HITLER reported to be hiding out in foothills of southern Andes. Information obtained ▓▓▓
from ▓▓▓▓▓▓ unable to be verified because ▓▓▓▓
disappearance. Attempts to locate ▓▓▓▓▓▓▓ negative.
No record of him in police or INS files.

www.sharkhunters.com

REFERENCE: Los Angeles letter to Bureau, 8-14-45

Note that this FBI Radiogram suspects that Adolf Hitler was hiding out in the foothills of the southern Andes – precisely where San Carlos di Bariloche is situated. The various "Spook" agencies knew where he was.

This file uncovered and sent by S.E.I.G. Agent **TAUCHER**

DECLASSIFIED AND RELEASED BY
CENTRAL INTELLIGENCE AGENCY
SOURCES METHODS EXEMPTION 3B2B
NAZI WAR CRIMES DISCLOSURE ACT
DATE 2001 2007

NO. ⊏   ⊐

www.sharkhunters.com

INFORMATION REPORT
⊏ ⊐

COUNTRY: Spain/Germany/Argentina

SUBJECT: Nazi Aid Organization in Argentina

DATE:

INFO:

DIST: 20 February 1948

ORIGIN: ⊏   ⊐

PAGES: 2

Evaluation of source: see below   Evaluation of Content:

SOURCE: ⊏ ⊐ & ⊏ ⊐

1. Reference: DB-6882.

2. ⊏ ⊐ comments as follows on information reported under reference:

"We regret we have no traces of any of the people mentioned in your letter.

"We have, however, information on two escape organizations in Spain, one of which might be the organisation referred to in your letter, even though the first one is reported to handle collaborators:

A. A Franco-Spanish religious order, the CONGREGATION DU CHRIST-ROI, is reported to be at the bottom of a powerful escape organization for collaborators, militiamen and prisoners of war. The congregation takes escapees into its various monasteries in France and disguises them, often as priests. They are taken by various lines into Spain. Two of those concerned with the running of these lines are two doctors named MOUNIC and VIDAL. It is said that, when escapees are arrested on the frontier by customs officials, they are set free on use of a password.

In Spain Pere VALETTE of the 'CONGREGATION' is in charge of getting the escapees set free more or less rapidly and helping them if possible to get to the Argentine. He is assisted by the following persons from the French Embassy in Madrid:

FRANCOIS PIETRI (ex-ambassador to Vichy, now private Monsignor BOYER-MAS, and
Monsignor PETIT   individual).

christian

SECRET

www.sharkhunters.com

- 2 -

page 2 of 2   NO. ⊏   ⊐

2.   An entirely German escape organisation involving the following names and addresses in Barcelona:

   a. SEITHER, a German bookshop at 72, Rambla de Catalunya.
   b. A German photographer at Calle Balmes 90.
   c. Another German bookshop, LIBRERIA HERDER, Calle Balmes 22.
   d. Padre BOOS, Calle Mallorca 211 2ª 1º.

"Apart from the fact that the LIBRERIA HERDER provides clothing chits for Germans which are accepted at the department store 'EL AGUILA', Plaza Universidad, Barcelona, we know nothing of the workings of this organisation.

"We are making enquiries in Spain and Argentina about this organisation and the personalities concerned in it, and we will let you know the results."

⊏   ⊐ comments as follows on the general subject of Nazi escape routes:

"We have at the moment a great many undigested reports coming in from Belgium, Holland, France and Spain of rumoured escape organisations for Nazis, but it seems early days to comment on their strength and ramifications. We will, however, remember your interest in this subject and will pass to you such information as comes to us that bears on this matter."

This two page file uncovered and sent by S.E.I.G. Agent **TAUCHER**

DECLASSIFIED
authority N ND 897127
NARA Date 5-2-07

Since the Allies let him go I don't think there is much to be done. Is it worth while advising B. A.? SWW.
G-C It

file
Spirit

SECRET

www.sharkhunters.com

DECLASSIFIED
Authority NND 897127
AT   Date 3-5-04

MEMORANDUM   SECRET

TO: PCO
           J. Millar- Miss Howell
           M. Gabriel
           Chancery

FROM: Hudson Smith

       I have had in my Department today a visit from
a German ex-POW who escaped from France to Spain last
year. This man was most indignant over the fact that
he was in the same prison as the famous SS leader(in
San Sebastian) otto SKORZENY.

       The POW was indignant because he declares that
whereas he was in the prison several months, SKORZENY
was liberated before he had been there two months and
issued with all the necessary documentation to proceed
to the Argentine where he now is.

       You will know doubt recall that SKORZENY achieved
notoriety by rescuing Mussolini from his mountain
prison in Italy on Hitlers direct order, and is a person
who after the war was taken prisoner by the Allies and
considered as of some considerable importance. Several
war books have it that this man was detailed to assas-
sinate General Eisenhower when the laters Headquarters
were in Paris.

       The POW who reported this matter was questioned
closely as to whether he was certain that the man who
was in jail with him was indeed SKORZENY, but could not
be shaken in his asseveration,saying that he had known
SKORZENY personally from war time days and could not be
mistaken.

                                          HS.

January 4th, 1948.

HS/mh

This file uncovered and sent by S.E.I.G. Agent **TAUCHER**

Wonder which scientists went where? This six-page report will help.

~~TOP SECRET~~

C9

'235

Copy no. 3

13 April 1949

www.sharkhunters.com

page 1 of 6

MEMORANDUM FOR: Director,
                Joint Intelligence Objectives Agency
                Joint Chiefs of Staff

SUBJECT   : Nominations of Austrian Scientists to Critical List

REFERENCE   : JIDA 1034

1. In response to the request of the Director, JIDA, there is
attached hereto a list of Austrian scientists.

2. Since the requirement is flexible as to number, the list has
been divided into four groups:

A. Scientists whose prominence makes their denial to the
Soviets highly desirable.

B. Scientists of second-rate importance who may be considered
for List A if denial capabilities on the part of the U.S. increase.

C. Scientists of Austrian derivation not now in Austria
but whose return should be forestalled at all costs.

· D. Scientists under Soviet control whom it would be advantageous to have under Western control.

3. The information given as to location and present occupation is
the best now available. It is, however, subject to change and it is
therefore suggested that immediately prior to action the addresses be
checked again for accuracy.

[   ]
Assistant Director, OSI

Attachment:
List of Austrian Scientists

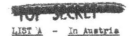

~~TOP SECRET~~

$C)\emptyset$

LIST 'A - In Austria

(Scientists whose prominence makes their
denial to the Soviets highly desirable)

www.sharkhunters.com

page 2 of 6

BRODA, Engelbert B., (Dr), Birthdate unknown. Address: Vienna, XIX Formanekgasse 40,
(a/o Jan 1948; Akademie fuer Wissenschaft und Kunst, Vienna, Austria. (a/o Feb. 1949).
Employment: Chief, Research (planning) Section, Ministry of Energy; also conducts
theoretical nuclear research in chemistry faculty, Univ. of Vienna; teaches at Soviet
sponsored Akademie fuer Wissenschaft und Kunst and at Communist Party School at
Villa Recht, Vienna. (a/o Feb. 49).

HECHT, Friedrich, (Prof), Birthdate: 3 Aug 1903. Address: Mosern 52, Grundelsee,
Upper Austria (a/o Dec. 47); Geological Inst., "Palais Guttmann" Vienna II, Rustenschacherallee, Austria. (a/o Feb 1949). Employment: Geochemist, Geological Inst.
Vienna (a/o Feb. 49). Has investigated micromethods of analysis of uranium, thorium,
radioactive minerals and determination of atomic weights; microanalysis and separation
of single elements of silicate minerals.

ORTNER, Gustav, (Dr), Birthdate: 31 July 1900. Address: Vienna XIII (Br. Zone)
Maxingstrasse 42 (a/o Jan. 49); Geological Inst., Palais Guttmann, Vienna II,
Rustenschacherallee, Vienna, Austria. (a/o June 48). Employment: Head, X-ray
Laboratory.(research on cathode rays), Geological Inst. Vienna (a/o June 48).
Completed a new book recently on atomic physics sponsored by the Soviets.

PRIZBRAM, Karl, (Prof. Dr.), Birthdate: 1878. Address: Vienna IX, Strudelhofgasse 4,
Austria (a/o Feb 49). Employment: Professor of physics and radiology and Director of
the Second Physical Inst. of Univ. of Vienna. Took trip to Moscow in 1947 and on his
return began research in infra-red field. Alleged to be working for Soviets and to be
visited frequently by Russians, but lacks Eastern inclinations. Told visiting
American physicists he is now engaged in studies of luminescence. (a/o Feb 49)

STETTER, George, (Prof.Dr), Birthdate: 23 Dec. 1895. Address: Thumersbach, Zell-am-See,
Austria (a/o Dec. 47). Employment: Has gathered data for meteorological experiments
and is developing device to extract coal dust from air in mines. (a/o Feb. 49).

THIRRING, Hans, (Dr.), Birthdate: c.1898. Address: Inst. for Theoretical Physics,
Univ. of Vienna. Has negotiated with Austrian Ministry of Electrification and Power
Conservation for a subsidised research program aimed at derivation of plutonium from
natural sources. Although considered an outstanding physicist, devotes all present
efforts to pacifism and general philosophical questions. (a/o Feb 49).

(Scientists of second-rate importance who may be considered for
List A if denial capabilities on the part of the U.S. increase)

EBERT, Ludwig, (Prof.Dr.), Birthdate: 19 June 1894. Address: Vienna IX,
Waehringerstrasse 42. Austria (a/o Feb 49). Employment: Director, 1st Chemical
Inst. Univ. of Vienna. Unconfirmed reports indicate that he is working on Soviet
orders on analytical problems of fluorine. (a/o Feb 49.)

HERNEGGER, Friedrich, Birthdate: 23 May 1908. Address: Vienna IX, Boltzmanngasse 3,
Austria (a/o Dec. 47). Employment: Professor, Radium Inst., Univ. of Vienna, (a/o
Dec. 47).

HERZOG, Richard, (Dr.), Birthdate: 11 Mar. 1911. Address: First Physical Inst. of
Univ. of Vienna. Strudelhofgasse 4, Vienna IX, Austria. (a/o Feb. 49).
Employment: Assistant to Dr. Ehrenhaft at First Physical Inst. of the Univ. of Vienna.
Physicist, specializing in mass spectography. (a/o Feb 49).

KAINDL, Karl, (Dr.), Birthdate: 1890. Address: Spittelwiese, Linz/Donau Austria
(a/o 28 Jan. 49). Employment: Nuclear Physicist, formerly assistant to Prof. Stetter.
Wrote recently from address listed to Willibald Jentschke, Austrian scientist in the
US stating, "You inquire why none of the Austrian physicists contributes articles to
the magazine "Nucleonics". Who should do it? Lintner works on other problems.
Apart from the fact that you and Schintlmeister were the best men in this field, and
both of you have left Austria. Incidentally, I heard in a roundabout way that
Schintlmeister can be seen in Vienna once in a while. You will also be interested
to learn that Kober (Gemma) is in Vienna. He is working with Wieninger, who with
his cathode evaporation device develops quartz protection layers over mirrors."

KARL-KROUPS, Edith, (Dr.), Birthdate: 11 Sep. 1910. Address: Vienna, Austria
(a/o May 47). Employment: Now employed in a chemical factory in Vienna engaged in
the preparation of simple medicines, kitchen scouring materials etc. for Austrian
industry. Until the end of the war was Prof. Hecht's assistant at the Chemical Inst.
(a/o May 47).

KARLIK, Berta, (Prof.Dr.), Birthdate: Unknown. Address: Institut fuer Radiumforschung Boltzmanngasse 3, Vienna IX, Austria, (a/o Feb. 49). Employment: Nuclear
physicist, Director of Radium Inst., Vienna, Austria. Had orders from Soviets for
construction of radioactive measuring instrument. Current experiments at Radium
Inst. include study of nuclear reactions using new Ilford plates. Collaborates with
scientists of all occupying powers in Vienna. (a/o Feb. 49).

LINTNER, Karl, Birthdate: 28 April 1917. Address: Vienna, Austria (a/o Feb 49).
Employment: Dr. Karl Kaindl wrote recently in a letter to Willibald Jentschke,
Austrian scientist in US stating, "You inquire why none of the Austrian physicists
contributes articles to the magazine "Nucleonics". Who should do it? Lintner works
on other problems. Apart from the fact that you and Schintlmeister were the best men in
this field, and both of you have left Austria. Incidentally, I heard in a roundabout
way that Schintlmeister can be seen in Vienna once in a while. You will also be
interested to learn that Kober (Gemma) is in Vienna. He is working with Wieninger,
who with his cathode evaporation device develops quartz protection layers over mirrors."
(Feb. 49).

C/2

NOWOTNY, Hans, Birthdate: Unknown, Address: Vienna, Austria (a/o Jan 48).
Employment: Professor Extraordinary for Systemology Univ. of Vienna. His
specialty is structural analysis, corrosion and particularly supersonic cavitation.
He is politically unbiased. Also Director of the Institut de Recherches Scientifiques
at Schloss Tettnang (Fr.Zone), Germany where he is located during Univ. vacations.
(a/o Jan. 48).

SEIL, Theodor, Birthdate: Unknown. Address: Institut fuer Radiumforschung,
Boltzmanngasse 3, Vienna IX, Austria. (a/o Feb 49). Employment: Experimental
physicist and lecturer at the Radium Inst. of the Univ. of Vienna (a/o Feb. 49).

UNDESSER, Karl, Birthdate: c.1919. Address: Nuclear Physicist and former
assistant to Professor Stetter reportedly engaged in private research. (a/o Sept. 47).

Keep reading………..pages 4 and 6, for some reason, are only a half page.

LIST C - Outside Austria
(Scientists of Austrian derivation not now in Austria
but whose return should be forestalled at all costs)

EWALD, Heinz, Birthdate: 16 June 1914. Address: Tailfingen/Wuertemburg,
Germany (a/o Oct. 47). Employment: Last reported in Oct. 1947 at address
noted working for the French.

FLAMMERSFELD, Arnold. Birthdate: 10 Feb. 1913. Address: Tailfingen,
Kreis Balinger, Germany (a/o Oct. 48). Employment: Nuclear physicist at the
Kaiser Wilhelm Inst. for Chemistry at Tailfingen (Fr.Zone), which was to be
moved to Mains. (a/o Oct 48).

GHOFFER, Stephen E., Birthdate: Unknown. Address: Argentina (a/o May 47).
Employment: Physico-Chemist, Austrian-Jewish refugee formerly with the Curie
Inst., Paris, France and reported in May 1947 to be in Argentina.

GUNDLACH, Franz, (Dr.), Birthdate: 16 June 1905. Address: Spangenburg, near
Kassel Germany. (a/o 46). Employment: Physicist. Research on radio tubes,
Member of the Inst. II for Physics of the Vienna Univ. Formerly assistant to
Professor Stetter, Thumarsbach. (a/o 46).

JENTSCHKE, Willibad, (At Wright Field).

MATTAUCH, Joseph, Birthdate: 21 Nov 1895. Address: Mains, Germany (a/o Oct 48)
Employment: Kaiser Wilhelm Inst. fur Chemie, Tailfingen, Kreis Balinger until
recently when he transferred to Mains. Reportedly the world's best authority on
mass spectrometers he travels twice a week to Berne, Switzerland to lecture at the
Univ. there. It is further reported he is seriously considering emigrating to
Berne to set up a new nuclear physics Inst. at the Univ. to continue his work on
mass spectroscopy. (a/o Oct 48).

MEITNER, Lise, (in Stockholm)

PANETH, Frederich Adolph, Birthdate: 31 Aug 1887, Address: SouthRoad, Durham,
England. (a/o 1948). Employment: Professor and Head of Dept. of Chemistry,
Univ. of Durham since 1939. (a/o 1948).

PAULI, Wolfgang, Birthdate: 25 April 1900. Address: Inst. of Experimental
Physics, Univ. of Zurich, Switzerland. (a/o Feb. 48). Employment: Theoretical
physicist and Nobel Prize winner working at address listed as of Feb 1948.

SCHROEDINGER, Erwin, Birthdate: 12 Aug 1887. Address: 67 Merrion Square,
Dublin, Ireland. (a/o 1948). Employment: Professor of Theoretical Physics, Royal
Irish Academy since 1940. Also Senior Professor, Dublin Inst. for Advanced
Studies. (a/o 1948).

www.sharkhunters.com
page 6 of 6

LIST D - In USSR

(Scientists under Soviet control whom it would be
advantageous to have under Western control)

RIEHL, N., Birthdate; Unknown. Address: Electrostal, Moscow Oblast.
Employment: Formerly Chief Chemist, Auergesellschaft, Berlin.

√ SCHINTLMEISTER, Joseph, Birthdate: 16 June 1908. Address: Vienna, Austria
(a/o Feb. 49). Employment: Was removed to the USSR in 1946 where he reportedly
was located at a Nuclear Physics Inst. near Moscow. A more recent report (jan 48)
states it is rumored he has been transferred to Prague and in a recent letter from
Dr. Karl Kaindl in Austria to Willibald Jentschke, Austrian scientist in the US,
Kaindl states, "You inquire why none of the Austrian physicists contributes
articles to the magasine "Nucleonics". Who should do it? Lintner works on other
problems. Apart from the fact that you and Schintlmeister were the best men in
this field, and both of you have left Austria. Incidentally, I heard in a round-
about way that Schintlmeister can be seen in Vienna once in a while. You will
also be interested to learn that Kober (Gemma) is in Vienna. He is working with
Wieninger, who with his cathode evaporation device develops quartz protection
layers over mirrors. (a/o Feb 49).

The previous six-page long file was uncovered and sent by S.E.I.G. Agent
TAUCHER.

Keep reading............there are more files to see and they all prove that
Adolf Hitler and others did not perish in the Führerbunker or any other
place in Germany. They made it to South America.

Keep reading.

SECURITY INFORMATION

www.sharkhunters.com

MEMORANDUM FOR RECORD   **page 1 of 4**   2 January 1952

SUBJECT: Project 63 Personnel Now in the U. S.

REFERENCE: Conversation between [＿＿＿＿] and Col. B. W. Heckemeyer,
Chief, JIOA on 29 December 1951

1. Purpose of reference conversation was primarily with regard
to the interest of Professor [＿＿＿＿] of Purdue University
in Professor [＿＿＿＿] (see attached copy of teletype from
Chicago Field Office of OS/C.) Col. Heckemeyer cleared the visit
of Professor Ruska to Purdue University. He stated furthermore that
the Services did not have a spot at present for the employment of
Professor Ruska and he would be grateful if we could make arrangements through Professor [＿＿＿＿] for [＿＿] employment at Purdue.

2. Col. William H. Speidel, Hotel Alamac, Broadway at 76th Street,
New York City is the Director of Project 63, and Project 63 personnel
come under his jurisdiction. There are, at present, 12 German scientists in the U. S. under this project and 30 more in Germany who are
under contract. These scientists come into the U. S. under military
jurisdiction and under the general jurisdiction of JIOA. They do
not have diplomatic passports. They are brought here primarily for
employment by the military Services. If, however, these Services
have no spot for them, JIOA attempts to place them in private
institutions, universities, or industry. Col. Heckemeyer stated
that Project 63 personnel are supposed to be top-flight German
scientists. The reasons for bringing them to the U. S. are: 1) To
prevent the Russians from inducing them to go to the East Zone of
Germany, or to Russia. Theoretically these scientists are not use-
fully occupied in Germany, have no funds to subsist on, and might
be subject to such inducement. 2) Their previous work has qualified
them for useful occupation by the Services. They are only placed
privately if they can not be so utilized.

3. They remain under military jurisdiction after they are
hired and until it is clearly shown that they are working out
satisfactorily, after which JIOA takes the necessary steps to legalize
their stay in the U. S. either through the required passport procedure
or through naturalization. When they travel around the U. S., they
must travel with military escort. If they are placed outside of
New York, the military jurisdiction will be transferred to the local
area such as a ROTC setup at a university. This military jurisdiction
does not limit their movement and is not generally evident. It
amounts to the military keeping an eye on them and their activities
to see that they do not enter into anything subversive or detrimental
to the U. S. and to see how they are adjusting to life in America.

SECURITY INFORMATION

C16

4. The procedure to be followed with regard t [   ] and which
will apply generally to other similar cases is as follows:
Col. Heckemeyer telephoned, 29 December 1951, to a Lt. Cooper in G-2
to authorize Col. Speidel to arrange the trip of [   ] to Purdue,
for which trip JIOA will pay. Col. Speidel will ....nish the military
escort. [   ] of OO/C will request the Chicago Office to contact
Professor [   ] as to the date which is convenient to him. When
this information is received, [   ] will have the New York Office
contact Col. Speidel to make the necessary arrangements and will
inform the Chicago Office of these arrangements so that Professor [   ]
may be notified. He will also tell the Chicago Office of JIOA's desire
to have Ruska employed by Purdue University, if possible.

5. Biographic Register, OCD [   ] has the background
data on all Project 63 personnel in this country. Col. Heckemeyer
said that there is no reason why we can not interrogate these people
if we wish but he suggests that we make arrangements through him
because of the military jurisdiction aspect and also because most of
these people are employed by the Services who might impose some
objection to CIA interrogation if such application were made direct.
This has been our experience with some of the Paperclip people.
Col. Heckemeyer is very cooperative and I feel sure will work with
us in every possible way, particularly on a quid pro quo basis if
we place some of his strays.

[   ]

OSI:AHA/fd
Orig.: Repatriate Program File
cc: Chrono
    Daily Reading File
    OO/C - [   ]
    Vital Documents File

EMPLOYMENT STATUS - - - - "PROJECT 63" SPECIALISTS

C 17

page 3 of 4

20 Feb 1952

Aust. BRUEDA, Botho
Negotiating with CIBA Co., Summit, New Jersey. Fields of drugs,
pharmaceuticals, anti-biotics, hormones, etc.
Salary - To be determined.

Aust. DUSSIK, Karl
Negotiating with Boston State Hospital, Boston, Mass. (Mental Instituti
Salary - To be determined.
NOTE: Now on duty with this hospital which is deeply interested in
subject's abilities.

Aust. GANTSCHNIGG, Gottfried
Employed at Glenn L. Martin Co., Baltimore, Md. (Aircraft Industry)
Salary $505. per mo.

Aust. GREIL, Karl
Employed at Glenn L. Martin Co., Baltimore, Md.   "   "
Salary $505. per mo.

Aust. GUERTH, Fritz
Employed at Naval Air Missile Test Center, Point Mugu, Calif.
Salary $23.08 per day.

Ger. GUNDLACH, Franz
Employed at Wright Air Development Center, Wright-Patterson AF Base
Salary $450. per mo.

Ger. HARGIES, Wolfgang
Negotiating with Bell Aircraft Industries; (also commitment from
Distillation Products, Rochester, New York)
Salary $7500. per annum (approx)
NOTE: Position assured at either company.

Ger. HELMBOLD, Heinrich
Employed at University of Wichita, Kansas (Navy contract)
Salary $6,000. per annum.

Aust. HINTEREGGER, Hans
Employed at Cambridge AF Research Center, Cambridge, Mass.
Salary $600. per mo. (approx)

Ger. MUELLER, Erwin
Negotiating with University of California (Berkeley) (Aircraft). Very
good offer in which he is interested.
Salary - To be determined.
NOTE: Air Force now requesting sub-allotment of funds for the universit
for this contract.

Ger. RUSKA, Helmut
Negotiating contract with N.Y. State Public Health Service
Salary $6,000. per annum (approx)
NOTE: Civil Defense program-directors of State Health Services are
anxious to obtain personnel with this type of experience.

Ger.   TUEBBECKE, Julian
         Contract awaiting approval by Under Secretary of Army for
         Ordnance employment.
         Salary $7200. (approx)

Aust.   UNDESSER, Karl
         Employed at Glenn L. Martin Co., Baltimore, Md. (Aircraft Industry)
         Salary $550. per mo. (approx)

Aust.   WENDL, Ernst
         Has offer from Chicago Luxi/Air as Asst. to Director (Technical Advisor
         Salary $7200. per annum

The previous four-page long file was uncovered and sent by S.E.I.G. Agent **TAUCHER** and continues listing German//Austrian scientists who came to (or were brought to) the United States after the war.

NAL ARCHIVES

Security Information
www.sharkhunters.com

C/9

OFFICIAL - INFORMAL

page 1 of 3

18 March 1952

MEMORANDUM TO: Mr. [⎯⎯⎯]
2430 E Street, N. W.
Washington 25, D. C.

FROM   : [⎯⎯⎯]

SUBJECT   : Project 63

REFERENCE   : [⎯⎯⎯ ⎯⎯] dated 6 March 1952

1. The flurry of cables preceding the arrival of the twenty-man mission from JIOA apparently achieved the desired result; namely, a little coordination before the conquest of German science was begun. Although Colonel Crabbe had indicated in a cable that he would get in touch with me on 24 February, he did not do so until 6 March when we held a meeting jointly with [⎯⎯] and others. In the meantime the JIOA group was well on its way to the repetition of previous blunders in the form of several invitations to top German scientists to come to Heidelberg for discussion of contracts.

2. Principal members of the twenty-man group are Lt. Col. G. W. Crabbe (JIOA), Col. Arthur S. Randak (USAF), and Col. E. S. Berry (G-2). With them are an assortment of lesser military personnel, four U. S. service civilians, and six German Paperclip specialists. The group is armed with a list of Germans to be contacted. The group, or members thereof, will be present in the theater until some time in April.

3. On 6 March the military members of the mission met with [⎯⎯ ⎯⎯], other members of local organizations and myself for a frank discussion of Project 63, its good points and bad points and how to implement it. [⎯⎯] concern was for the preservation of good relations with the German scientific community as a practical matter for those of us who must work here as well as the U.S. foreign relations involved in recruitment. My concern was for the prejudicial effect of inept recruitment on relations between Germans and Americans which would affect adversely our intelligence operations. All of us however agreed that an exchange program of some sort is desirable and in this respect we are all in sympathy with the aims of the project.

4. After an initial period of shooting barbs at each other, perhaps containing too sharply pointed criticisms, the meeting

 Security Information

~~Secret~~ Security Information

www.sharkhunters.com

straightened out and became a useful exchange of ideas which I feel
was entirely satisfactory. The local people brought out the need
for careful consideration on a case-by-case basis of each individual
before making an approach. We pointed out for example that the recruitment list contains names of people too old, too rich, too busy
and too thoroughly disgruntled with past experience with Americans to
justify a renewed approach. We also pointed out the impropriety of
making an open-ended contract with a man who in this community occupies
a position comparable to that of the leaders of science in the U. S.
Negotiations for a specific job at a specific place with adequate description of conditions and salary are the only proper approach when
dealing with scientists of high caliber. This point appeared to be
accepted by the mission.

5. I raised the question of propriety in connection with the
use of ex-Germans as recruiters having in mind resurgent German
nationalism and the possible attitude among present-day Germans that
the Paperclippers are in effect traitors. The mission did not seem
to be impressed with this consideration which is understandable since
they are primarily salesmen who are not sensitive to more subtle
dangers. The mission apparently feels that the good done by ex-Germans
in explaining to prospective candidates on the basis of first-hand
experience outweighs the harm which may result from the traitor concept.
I did not press the point at length.

6. The important point which evolved from the discussion is that
in the future the recruiters promise to consult [   ] and myself
on all cases so that foreign relations and intelligence interest can
be provided for adequately. [   ] is furthermore making [   ]
services available to the group in furnishing background on individuals,
making interviews and introductions, and laying out the schedule of
contacts. Local advice and consultation were something we were most
anxious to have incorporated into the implementation of the project.
[   ] agreed to write letters to the leaders of German science as
well as to his British and French counterparts which will in effect
take them in a limited way into confidence on the scope of the project.

7. If performance lives up to promises, I feel that much has been
done to remove the friction built up between military and civilian
groups responsible for, or at least concerned with, this project. The
storm we kicked up by our cables seems to have had the desired result
of forcing the military into consulting with us before proceeding on
a project the effects of which were so poorly understood by them.
Time will tell how well we succeeded but there is at least some cause
for hope.

8. Incidentally after the meeting Barry who seems rather alert
and Crabbe who is largely salesman told [   ] and me that we had
been regarded as saboteurs and obstructionists prior to the meeting.
Afterward they said they felt we had been helpful and well-intentioned,
even though our motives had been misunderstood for a long time. The

-3-

sad part is that such a meeting could have been held a year ago when we also set up a clamor. The slow awakening seems to be characteristic of the breed.

The previous three-page long file was uncovered and sent by S.E.I.G. Agent **TAUCHER.**

We now cover the findings of our *"DELTA Team"*, a group of excellent researchers who have been through many archives.

CONFIDENTIAL INFORMATION
HUSH MOST SECRET

Strictly Confidential Document

"Routes to South America"

Secret Reich Matter!
Minister's Matter

Secret Reich Matter!

Secret Command Matter!

---for the Boss---

Secret Command Matter!

By
The Delta Team
1995

Serial number 2509951

www.sharkhunters.com
page 1 of 12

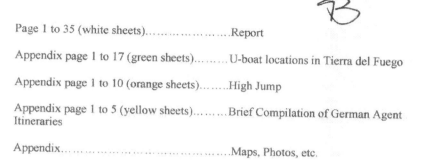

The twelve-page long file was sent by S.E.I.G. Agent **PIZZARRO.**

He is a superb S.E.I.G Agent and he headed up this group.

There will be several questions raised in this text. Look to page 181 and we will do our best to explain and questions that might arise.

These secret and confidential reports have 35 pages and 40 pages of appendix.

Prologue:

If Knight's Cross recipient Navy Lieutenant (S) **Heinrich GARBERS**---who ran agents for the German Abwehr in 1943 in Operation "Mercator 2" to Brazil/Cape Frio, and in 1944 with "Passim 1" [a 16-meter long sailing yacht in] Operation "WOLIN" to Punta Mogades, south [to] La Plata/Argentina for return transfer by freighter of agents---had not left the mystery of a secret German Abwehr rendezvous point behind,

And

if it had not been for the report of

Don Angel Alcasar de Velasco (Report: Conceil de securite Paris)

Case in Point: Don Angel de Velasco allegedly published a lengthy escape report in the U.S. (1995)

And

Had the Hotel "Maison Rouge" in Strassbourg secret meeting on 10 August 1944 not happened, then this secret report would never have been written.

TO REPEAT:

This secret and confidential report has 35 pages and 40 pages [of] appendix.

The content of this report is the result of years of laborious and conscientious research by the DELTA TEAM (tel. # ************). It is hereby expressly prohibited to commercially publish this report, its contents, or parts of its contents. This report offers many surprises and will promote further inquiries. We have deliberately addressed many hitherto unknown details of German history. This report will clear up hitherto surmised facts only by virtue of the reader's [subject] knowledge.**

[www.]www.sharkhunters.com

Now according to the clues and evidence:

--The existence of a German Abwehr ocean-surface base in 1944
--The existence of a German Abwehr ocean-surface base until at least 1952

So we're talking about a base of the former Third Reich after 1945!!!
Which apparently was supposed to have existed from 1944 (first mentioning) until
1952 (last mentioning). This report follows the trail. (Rep[ort] OSS/CIC/DA/PH/DC
and South American sources.)

**FROM WHAT WE KNOW TODAY, THE GERMAN ABWEHR BASE COULD
HAVE EXISTED IN TIERRA DEL FUEGO--ON CHILEAN TERRITORY--
SOUTH OF THE ADMIRALTY FJORD, SOUTH-EASTERLY OF THE PARRY
FJORD, AND NEAR A NARROW, SMALL BUT LONG SECONDARY FJORD,
WHICH IS STILL TODAY AN EXTREMELY ISOLATED AND HARD-TO-
ACCESS NATURE PRESERVE.**

From what we know today, the base could have been activated on orders of Abwehr boss
CANARIS as early as 1935 or 1936. Vm (BE) PARLOW officially began working for
Ausland Abwehr IV of the OKW (Armed Forces High Command) in September 1939.
A German Navy {Vm (BE)} was designated by Abwehr IV in the secret files of
operations orders/commando missions for May 1940 in relation to the V-Ship for Tierra
del Fuego for the **U-boat locations** in the environs of **Tierra del Fuego**.
The inference was that one could depart from a secret base, in which a pilot from the V-
Ship (a Vm) waits, in order to bring the V-Ship to a safe holding point, noted on all
extant maps as land. The U-boat locations in Tierra del Fuego, especially CLAERENCE,
only makes sense if they had logistics, supplies, pilotage, etc.

The following 5 pages pick up the mystery that HEINRICH GARBERS left behind and
analyse the text:

Sources:

Les Voliers Fantomes d'Hitler. Presses de la Cite 1973, Paris, France. Autor Saint-Loup.
German Version, translator Ulrich MOHR!
Titel: Die Geisterschiffe Hitlers, (Saint Loup), Publisher: Verlag Delius Klasing & Co.
Bielefeld 1975.
{Title: Hitler's Ghost Ships............}

Notes

Historic personages mentioned in this report are referenced only to make history clearer.
These people had NOTHING to do with German warships after the end of the war.

Capitulation had brought an end to every activity. The referenced personnel and agents in the OSS/CIA reports are only noted for the indicated wartime period.

All names which are in relation to the escape vessels must be looked up as a rule in the known archives.

In this report are the names until the surrender provided, or rather those missing in the occupation of 1945.

Our Note:

For the translator, Ulrich MOHR may be Dr. Ulrich Mohr, which could be cleared up by certain other information in the German version.
Dr. Ulrich Mohr was stationed on the Tender Ship "Atlantis" as Oberleutnant zur See (d.R), and was promoted in April 1943 to Kapitan Leutnant (d.R) and was since 1942 with the OKM/Skl., Berlin. His mission for "Atlantis" was from November 1939 till January 1942. The fate of "Atlantis" and later also on "Python" and the return of the entire crew by U-boat rescue from the South Atlantic to France is well-known. "Atlantis" also had put into port at the "Kerguelen Islands" U-boat base. The southernmost gravesite of German soldiers still lies to this day near Foundry Bay, [which contains the grave of] the Atlantis-sailor Bernhard Herrmann, who broke his lower leg there and died of an embolism. Dr. Ulrich Mohr published a pictorial documentation in 1944 by John Jahr Verlag, Berlin, which represents a further source after the war in relation to the "Atlantis books."

In the "Atlantis" report to OKM/Berlin, which describes the stay in Kerguelen from December 1940 to January 1941, [it] is referenced here (appendix 1 to 1/Skl. 10284/41 to OKM-AH = Nautical unit under AH-registered under Secret Command Matter 429/1941). Here is also referenced [from] the source: 1. Skl./Berlin, AH-Nautik, from 04 December 1939, secret U-boat base maps.

Before we begin, here's another piece of information on the German agent boats, motor boats:
Sources:

a.) Primary Sources:

--Top Secret Document (Cominch File) F.21..... 75/April 1945/USA
-- OSS Report (CIA) 1945/1946 about the German Abwehr Yolle Operation
-- KTB Abwehr Ausland IV of the OKW 1940-1943
-- KTB of the B.d.U/Doenitz special restricted order/attack ban on sail- and motor-fishing vessels.

b.) Secondary Sources:

--The book of Saint Luop about ghost ships with information on different sail boats and special missions of Garbers.

c.) Seondary Information:

--From Age Nissen in a newspaper article, where he reports about his mission on the motor-boat "Klyoe", after the TWINS cliff near Nolloth/South Africa. (Report of Age Nissen, the painter in the Flensburger Tagblatt: Article: "Ghost Ships, Sugarloaf and Singing Praises of the Fatherland).

Information:

All Abwehr skipper Commanders had orders during ongoing operations not to keep any war diaries. KTB's are therefore not available. Nevertheless, commanders, as a rule Leutnant zur See (S) or Oberleutnant zur See (S) or rather Lt. Z.S.d.R. (S) or OLT z.S.d.R (S) (S=Sonderfuehrer) drew up secret reports about each operation.

This secret report was drafted for the Abwehr Ausland or rather Amt Mil- (Mil-VI.), which in 1944 went directly to the Fuehrer over Chief Kaltenbrunner. The same happened with Garber's report, which reported on his Operation WOLIN to Punta Magates in summer 1944. Garbers received the Knight's Cross for this operation, and in 1943 he received the German Gold Cross for Operation MERCATOR 2 to Cape Frio/Brazil.

Mustering German Motor Boat/Sail Boat Agents:

Operations to:

---South America, Brazil, Argentina, Venezuela, Italy, also OSS-Report for an operation in Chile.
---South Africa, West Africa (Mossamedes/Namibia)
---Ireland
---Planned Canada operation, eventually carried out in 1943
---Planned Panama operation (Reiserte 1945)
---Operations along the Brazilian coast (Operation Reiserte 1 1943/44, postponed to 1944/45, Operation Reiserte 1 = West Coast of Africa).

This had to do with transport trips (freighters), agent transfers back and forth, battle operations i.e. sabotage operations.

The names of hitherto uncovered motor boats/agent ships:

1. Galiana
2. Soizic
3. Maria Magdalena
4. Anni Braz Bihem
5. Carmelita
6. Klyoe
7. Galisan
8. Passim 1
9. KFK-203 verm. Mary
10. KFK-204
11. Ginette 1 (not to be confused with Ginette 2)
12. Santa Barbara -- {rented} Portugese motor boat with ca. 256 BRT (see report in OSS/CIA Report 1945/46)
13. Passim 2 (no longer in service, known as the schooner Prince Adalbert)
14. Vulcano (requisitioned as {Spanish} motor boat in 1945 German fortresses in the Gironde Mouth.
15. Unknown German Abwehr Cutter. September 1943 before Antofagasta/Chile. See the so-called OSS/Antofagasta note with decoded German Abwehr FT to the German Abwehr net LUNA of 30 March 1944 (CG4-4014/913-14) FT.

Thus 15 Abwehr ships are identified up until today (1995), their remainder are still partly unclear to this day.

Because of: German secret base of the Ausland Abwehr
Later: Amt. Mil./Ref. Mil. VI/Ausland Abwehr Berlin 1944/45

Information:
Source: Heinrich Garbers (Lt. (S) z.S) Knight's Cross Holder 1944, received from the hand of the Chief of the SS/SD Abwehr, Dr. Ernst Kaltenbrunner, Obergruppenfuehrer and General of the Waffen SS/Chief of the Rsi Hauptamt Berlin.
While handing over the Knight's Cross to Garbers, Kaltenbrunner spoke of a secret German base. The following is from Garber's book:

"Autumn 1944, probably November. Place: Berlin Fuerstenwalde, Villa in which Kaltenbrunner lived.
Present: Chief of Amt Mil. VI Obergruppenfuehrer Schellenberg, in addition to more officers of the Navy and Kaltenbrunner.
Kaltenbrunner to Garber: "The Fuehrer read your report personally. He admires you. He told me: "These are my kind of men, who are formed in battles on land and in storms on the ocean. They will secure the future of Europe."

---After Garbers offered a short summary of his battle voyages (at the request of Kaltenbrunner), Kaltenbrunner asked Garbers a question---which is of particular interest today:

---Kaltenbrunner asked (according to Garbers notes and {those} laid out in the Saint Loup book) how a small sail boat, as well camouflaged as yours, could have delivered, unnoticed by the enemy, a high-ranking personnel to any given point on the earth?

Garbers answer: "Yes...with a little luck, yes."

Kaltenbrunner: "...and this little sail boat could, for example, even get into a secret area, which is only reachable through a narrow channel?"

Garbers' answer: "Yes, if it had an auxiliary motor."

Kaltenbrunner: "Thank you, Lieutenant, that's all."

Garber left us this enigma of Kaltenbrunner in his Saint Loup book.

Since all the data in the book---after the fact according to the secret OSS/CIC Report of 1944/45, which gives exact information about Passim 1 and Garbers--- will be confirmed, Garbers' testimony ought to be correct.

WHY is this secret base being sought only now, 51 years later, i.e. in 1995?

Presently, a report has appeared in the US, which alludes to a statement of a former German counter-espionage officer. This report refers to a secret German base which served as a refugee point after the war and which was allegedly in existence until 1952. Because of the peculiar agreements found in this report, it could have been alluding to the base described here.

Textual Analysis: Kaltenbrunner/Garbers Discussion November 1944:

1) --Ferrying high-ranking personnel to any point on the globe---
Analysis: The wording indicates escape...

Since the Kaltenbrunner/Garbers meeting in November 1944 in Berlin-Fuerstenwalde took place, that is after the meeting in the Hotel "Maison Rouge" in Strassburg on 10 August 1944, where the heads of the German armaments and supply industries met to secure the existence of a new Fourth Reich after the end of the war. Everyone knew that it was no longer possible to win the war. It is highly probable that the leaders of the Abwehr, perhaps Kaltenbrunner himself, took part in this meeting.

The transfer of assets, licenses, and investments to safe countries was agreed and was, according to the OSS/CIA, set immediately into motion. The countries of refuge for the revival of a Fourth Reich were:

---Switzerland, Portugal, Spain, Turkey
---and South American countries with an emphasis on Argentina

Sources:
--H.G. Richardi, Sueddeutsche Zeitung 22/23.04.95, page 2, Special page (the entire newspaper page) Title: About the Overseas Rat Lines.

--Schwaebische Zeitung. Article about South American correspondent Carl D. Goerdeler of 06 June 1995, page 3. Title: Only Little Fish Get into the Nazi Hunters' Nets.

This article reports on the transfer of money to South America and the discovery of files, which were found in the archives of the Argentinian Foreign Ministry, which attest to the fact that the former military governments and PERON protected top Nazi refugees. Around 1,000 new names of Nazis who after 1945 were transferred to Argentina could be found in these files. Even German Television briefly reported about the discovery of the files, but said no more. The refugees were German, Flemish collaborators and Croatian personalities, who were working for the Third Reich. PERON was supposed to have received 60 million dollars in currency. A further 40 million was to be distributed to the refugees to facilitate their new lives in South America. The capital, so it was noted (Journalist Gaby Weber), originated from Swiss-Lichtenstein Nazi bank accounts. A great deal has already been written about this. Suffice to say that it was widely known that this was a refugee movement--**and a well-organized one at that**. However, the coordination points were never clearly described, and their headquarters is unknown. There are exceptions for Spain or Portugal and for South American residences. The coordinator for the refugee organization was to have been as of April 1945---when the first refugee movement began---a General/Obergruppenfuehrer WAGNER. He wasn't a General of the Waffen SS, there were Obergruppenfuehrer(s) without this rank.
    For the Middle East (Egypt/Syria), the coordinator was Obersturmbannfuehrer (Oberstleutnant) **Franz ROESTEL**. Cover name: **Haddad Said**.
Source: Page 28/114/KTB/1995/Shark.

The refugee organization, known as "ODESSA," was well-known after the war, at the end of the 1940s. Coordination point, Name: **SPINNE** (Spider).
The refugee shelters were in:
---Ostermiething/Salzach (Austria), near the Bavarian village of Tittmoning,
---Zell am See-region and
---Igels (north of Innsbruck).

It is well-known that the refugee organizations ran from Germany through Austria into Italy (with the referenced shelters in Austria) and with further shelters of places, where there were convents. (There are many fabrications and truths in regard to this). Our report only skims the surface.

A total of over 750 ventures were established after the "Maison Rouge" meeting, even through front men in South America. The protocol of secret meetings since 10.08.1944 is, according to information (1995), still in existence.

2) ---without being noticed by the enemy...
Analysis: Points to the fact that the ship must have been underway in enemy-controlled seas and air force zones.

[page 11]

3. ---to any given point on the earth...
Analysis: Shows clearly that the point must have been far from Germany and Europe. Other, better means of refuge are more readily available for all possibilities in Europe or the Middle East. As, for example, even {as far back as the beginning of} May {1945} FW-200 Condor aircraft in the RECHLIN airport north of Berlin could reach the Middle East and Turkey.

The last Condor transports landed, for example, in Barcelona Spain {as late as} **25 April 1945**. (Night flight routes over Salzburg, Alps, Rhonetal, Mittelmeer, Spain). Adolf H{itler's} pilot and General **BAUR** [correct sp = Bauer] had reserved Condor aircraft in Berlin Gatow for flight operations. These were used for overflights to Plattling, south of Passau, and to Salzburg in the middle of April 1945.

Source: Book of pilot Hans Baur [sp]: Mit Maechtigen Zwischen Himmel und Erde {Between Heaven and Earth with the Most Powerful People} Schuetz Verlag, Coburg. Baur [sp] also reports that the leader of Hitler's Private Chancellery, the younger brother of Bormann, Obergruppenfuehrer **Albert Bormann** left Berlin on 15 April 1945 for Munich. According to testimony from the DOCUMENT CENTER from 1995, Albert Bormann was in the Munich Partei-Zentrale [building] until 30 April 1945 and then disappeared. He has been sought after until today (1995).

The location in question was certainly not in Europe, since the Abwehr would not have needed yawls or sail boats. Even the Mediterranean is ruled out. **Fitting out a sailboat thus indicates a considerable traveling distance, since one can reach a given destination even without fuel, for instance the Pacific, Chile, etc.**

Therefore, one can conclude (analysis) that: Kaltenbrunner thought in the first half of the following sentence:

With an auxiliary-motor-equipped sail boat such as the Abwehr sail boat (like Passim 1, Galiana, Carmelitta, Galisan or the earlier Klyoe), he himself could have, or some other person, go, for instance, from Spain into the ocean, with a skipper like Garbers. By November 1944, there were such experienced skippers available as:

Garbers
Oberleutnant zur See z.S.d.R. Christian Nissen
Lt. (S) z.S. Brusgatis or
Oberleutnant zur See z.S. d.R. Horn.

Possibly even **Age Nissen**, who however was no longer at this time sailing for the Abwehr and was only on the Klyoe in Twins/Southaffrica in 1941.

---to go into the ocean and, disguised as a neutral fishing boat i.e. Spanish, Portuguese, etc., to sail the world's oceans to a final Abwehr base!!!

K

And now on to the second half of Kaltenbrunner's question to Garbers:

4.)--**and this little sail boat could, for example, get into a secret base, which is only reachable through a narrow channel.**
Analysis: The most convincing part of the Kaltenbrunner question: The time was November 1944, when a secret base existed somewhere overseas. Only Chile had kept itself neutral or rather silent for the most part. Brasil-Mexico, 1945 even Argentina declared a state of war with Germany. As early as 1941 Peru interned German freighters; and other states like Uruguay refused to help as early as 1939 (the fate of the battleship Graf Spee). Only Chile played fair, and from the many KTB notes of the Abwehr, there are references to the this fair, helpful or neutral, silent behavior.
Therein lies the supposition that the secret base in question is located on Chilean territory.
The development of U-boat places = hideouts, shelters, secret berths, well before the start of the war in Tierra del Fuego, intensifies this supposition.
The altogether established six secret u-boat places in Tierra del Fuego, in addition to four further emergency shelters, isolated anchoring spots in this tangle of islands with thousands of canals and hundreds of large fjords, intensifies this hypothesis.

The reconnaissance and establishment of the U-boat places will be dealt with in the appendixes of this report.

The rumors that surfaced right after the war about a secret German base in the Antarctic, which, based on the German South Pole expedition of January/February 1939, was carried out off Neu-Schwabenland/Antarctica with the "Schwabenland" catapult ship and two Wal-Do J/10 ts seaplanes, arose or rather were spread as part of a worldwide press rumor mill, could have been a well-aimed act of deception.
Someone in South America deliberately spread the Antarctica rumor about a supposed German base in Antarctica, Neu Schwabenland area. (Neu Schwabenland is 70 degrees to 74 degrees South/5 degrees to 16 degrees 30 minutes East. This rumor even made the Americans uneasy, who started the 1946 BYRD expedition "Operation High Jump." The claim was investigated that the "Schwabenland" crew through reconnaissance had left behind. (Thousands of jettisoned arrows/spears, 1.30 meters every 20 kilometers and 1.50 meters to the turning points, all with swastikas, were shot off/thrown out in 1939)
Source: Scientific and aeronautical achievements of the German Antarctic Expedition of 1938/39, published by expedition leader Alfred RITSCHER, captain of the merchant marine and senior civil servant with the Supreme Command of the Berlin Kriegsmarine. Text with maps and sketches appeared in 1943, Koehler & Amelang, Leipzig, Volume 1 with over 300 pages.

The Americans were then in 1946/1947 and 1948 in Neu Schwabenland. The outcome of the additional search is to this day (1995) **off-limits to the public**. Jettisoned arrows were found, with intensive searches from 0 degrees meridian to 20 degrees west, while in reality the German reconnaissance went over 5 degrees west to 16 degrees 30 minutes east. An odd mystery? Why did they search west? Did the whaling boat Suedmeer, which only arrived in Neu Schwabenland in May 1939, perhaps{have} a pair of wooden huts for a West land station there?

www.sharkhunters.com   page 12 of 12

And yet, there was certainly no German station; more likely {it was} a diversionary tactic invented by war's end. A diversion from what?????????????????????????

Chile:
Tierra del Fuego: There could be something here---about which it will now be reported ---to wit two maps, the Marine Grid Chart with three divisions and the copy of a transparent map (published map) with U-boat base accommodations.

Then on to sentence fragment 4.)--- a secret base = the base is not some kind of empty hiding place, by base we mean equipment, personnel on location, supplies, fuel, provisions for a long time, logistics. Bases in comparison were always with crews and with an FT [sic]-station.
---putting in also means to be somewhere, at the end of a distance of travel, the end of a sea canal. Putting in must mean here to be able to put into a bay, canal [channel], shed, small safe anchorage, etc.
---which is only reachable through a narrow channel---This is the clearest indication. The word ONLY, that is, no other possibility, a channel that is narrow, a channel can also be the Tierra del Feugo channel.
The sentence is clear: to put into a secret base, presumably of the German Abwehr... Only through a narrow channel. ---That is, only through a channel [canal], a narrow channel [canal], can the base be reached, and the base is a great distance overseas. It can't be clearer, to be sure it's South America.

The foregoing twelve-page long file was uncovered and sent by S.E.I.G. Agent **TAUCHER**. The next few pages will answer some questions – and will no doubt raise more questions.

On page 171 there is a mention of Heinrich Garbers. He was the Skipper of a sailing vessel, yawl rigged, in various operations including Operation "*Jolle*" which means yawl. He was decorated with the Knights Cross.

On page 171 there is mention of the German agent and our Sharkhunters Member **DON ANGEL ALCAZAR de VELASCO (158-1985)** who was in the "*Spook*" business all through the war and many years thereafter.

Garbers   **DON ANGEL**   Canaris

On page 172 is mention of Canaris. In 1915 he was a young Oberleutnant zur See aboard the light cruiser ***DRESDEN***, the only one of Admiral Graf von Spee's cruiser squadron to survive the Battle of the Falkland Islands. During that ship's escape through the Straits of Magellan to Chile, he made careful notes of the hidden harbors then escaped captivity and went by horseback over the Andes to San Carlos di Bariloche and eventually back to Germany where he went into the "*Spook*" business. He became head of the Abwehr but because he was aware of the plot to kill Hitler at the Wolfsschanze but failed to alert Hitler, he was convicted. He was put into Flossenberg prisoner camp and held there until the Americans were about two days away. He was then stripped naked in the dead of winter, had a thin piece of piano wire wrapped around his neck and left to dangle on a hook while he slowly strangled to death. His naked body was then dumped in a snowbank and used by the soldiers as a makeshift urinal.

On page 176 there is reference to the many secret ships that came and went through the secret places in Argentina. One of the most popular sites

was at the little village of San Antonio Oeste inside the little bay called Calete de los Loros or Parrot Cove. In this village was a large building for the Lahausen Wool Company, a cover for the German spy network all through South America. The sailing ships and *"Black Boats"* came and went unhindered for years.

On page 176 there is mention of *"securing the existence of the Fourth Reich after the war."* Isn't that what this was all about?

On page 180 it speaks of the *"jettisoned arrows"* which were boundary markers dropped from one of the two Dornier flying boats called the *"Do-Wal"* or Dornier Whale. These were part of the 1939 expedition of the Reich to map out & claim Neu Schwabenland on the Antarctic continent. This expeditionary flotilla stopped at the Brazilian island of Trindade on their way south to erect two radio towers. The following pages have more photos and information on this expedition. Every kilometer an *"arrow"* was dropped which was a six foot tall steel spear with a Swastika on the top and every ten kilometers, a two meter tall *"arrow"* was dropped with a Swastika Flag on it; all to mark the boundaries of Neu Schwabenland.

Above – **SCHWABENLAND,** the catapult ship of the expedition

Below – One of the Dornier flying boats taking off

This expeditionary group stopped at Trindade Island for some time in 1939 and 1940. Look at the comparison photos next page. On the left is the plateau where the second radio tower was raised in 1939, official 3rd Reich photo – and on the right is the same place photographed by the author in 2009. It really has not changed.

Taken in 1939   taken in 2009

Above – the base at Neu Schwabenland

Below left – on the ground   below right – an *"arrow"*

Hitler's Suicide?

"To this day, it is speculated if Hitler died in his bunker in Berlin. To this I have to say, probably not. We know that in the last days of April, Hanna Reitsch flew General Ritter von Greim, the last Luftwaffe Commander in Chief, to Berlin. With a Fiesler Storch she landed on the Avus (a race track) and they met with Adolf Hitler. After the meeting, they flew out again.

On May 1st 1945, we were told: *'Hitler died fighting in Berlin, leading his troops against the Russian Army!'*

On May 2nd an Fw 200 landed at our airfield at Königgratz in Czechoslovakia. It was surrounded by special guards. Nobody could approach it as the plane was being refueled. From a distance of 25 meters, I saw everything as by chance, I was on the flight line. I could see some of the passengers in brown uniforms moving around in the plane. Then the Condor took off. Later we heard: *'High-ranking officials from Berlin were en route to Spain!'* I believe Hitler was on that plane."

EDITOR NOTE – This is exactly what was written to us by our Member Baron **GEORG von ZIRK (3290-1993)** in a letter some years ago. **GEORG** was a navigator-bombardier all through the war a Heinkel HE 111 bombers. He survived the war and emigrated to the United States.

Colonia Didnidad

www.sharkhunters.com

THE NAZI SS AND THE NUMBERS
    Bizarre! That was my first and only thought since hearing
of a sinister Nazi enclave and transmitter complex hidden deep
in the foothills of the Chilean Andes just south of Santiago!
    Equally bizarre was the statement from a colleague of the
possibility of some German numbers transmissions originating
from this site! The slight possibility of such a sinister
happening was somewhat reinforced by another source that once
told me that our very own FCC had once stated that some numbers
transmissions (language not identified) originated from this
part of South America!
    This site does exist! Glen B. Infield describes this site
in Secrets of the SS (Stein and Day). According to Infield,
Colonia Dignidad (Noble Colony) has an airstrip and a private
communications system to keep in radio contact with a site in
Sieburg, Germany.
    My own phone calls to sources that would be knowledgeable
of such matters provided vague promises of information to come.
These sources readily admitted to knowledge of this secret
complex but would provide no information on the phone.
    And information did arrive some weeks after my original
phone call. The information, however, was that I should contact
the National Security Agency for information on this noble (?)
colony! And that's the very thing I intend not to do. My
intentions, as soon as time allows, are to pursue this bizarre
tale through other sources.
    Is there any truth, any small amount of truth, in the above
numbers statements?
    Well, maybe so and maybe not. I do know that one source
suddenly became stricken with a severe memory lapse as I pursued
this subject!
    You'll have to agree that this transmitter complex with its
"antenna farm" does not exactly exist to further enhance the
natural beauty of the Chilean foothills.
    I paid scant attention to the words of the man at the FCC
when he suggested I file a Freedom of Information Act Petition
with -- you guessed it -- the NSA to see if they had information
on radio transmissions from this site. The NSA? They're the
"existence or nonexistence" of such information is a duly
classified matter people!

                           "Ende"

                           20535

We had been informed of the existence of Colonia Dignidad some years
ago by our friend & Sharkhunters Member **INGRID SCHARFENBERG
(3308-A/LIFE-1993)**.   She explained that it was a maximum security
village in Chile, founded by some 300 former SS men. The village was
heavily armed and guarded – nobody was allowed inside. The honor,
ethics and education of old Germany were strictly maintained inside.

Colonia Dignidad (continued)

In file photos we see the neatly maintained grounds – typical German lifestyle as we have seen throughout our travels in Germany and Austria. Everything is in order and well maintained.

However, some years ago, during the Chilean coup in which Salvador Allende was overthrown by the military under Augusto Pinochet, a dark cloud of suspicion came over Colonia Dignidad.

Allende

Pinochet

It was rumored that a great many outspoken supporters of Allende were brought into Colonia Dignidad by Pinochet followers – but they never came out........at least not alive.

Towards the end of the 20th Century, the leader of the Colonia Dignidad, Paul Schäfer, was accused of child abuse on about two dozen children at the complex. Some think the charges were accurate while other think they were a convenient way to make him disappear and break up the tightly held community. He was jailed and died in prison at age 89.

Colonia Dignidad was renamed Villa Baviera sometime thereafter.

Now we see files sent to Sharkhunters by S.E.I.G. Agent **REMBRANDT**

www.sharkhunters.com

Secret
CLASSIFICATION

TO   :   Chief, WHD

FROM   :   Acting [IN JOB TITLE] [CIA/LA] WCO/B

SUBJECT: GENERAL— [   ]

         SPECIFIC— Adolph HITLER

DISPATCH NO:

DATE: 3 October 1955

INFO: [CIA/LA]
      [CIA/LA]
      [CIA/LA]

MICROFILMED
JUL 26 1963
DOC. MICRO. SER.

1. On 29 September 1955, [   ] reported the following. Neither [   ] nor this Station is in a position to give an intelligent evaluation of the information and it is being forwarded as of possible interest.

2. [   ] was contacted on 29 September 1955 by a trusted friend who served under his command in Europe and who is presently residing in Maracaibo. [   ] preferred not to reveal the identity of his friend.

3. [   ] friend stated that during the latter part of September 1955, a Phillip CITROEN, former German SS trooper, stated to him confidentially that Adolph HITLER is still alive. CITROEN claimed to have contacted HITLER about once a month in Colombia on his trip from Maracaibo to that country as an employee of the KNSM (Royal Dutch) Shipping Co. in Maracaibo. CITROEN indicated to [   ] friend that he took a picture with HITLER not too long ago, but did not show the photograph. He also stated that HITLER left Colombia for Argentina around January 1955. CITROEN commented that inasmuch as ten years have passed since the end of World War II, the Allies could no longer prosecute HITLER as a criminal of war.

4. On 28 September 1955, [   ] friend surreptitiously obtained the photograph which CITROEN referred to. On 29 September 1955, the photo was shown to [   ] for purposes of getting his reaction to the possible veracity of this fantastic story. Obviously, [   ] was not in any position to make any comments. Nonetheless, he borrowed the photograph long enough so that this Station could take any action deemed advisable. Photostats of this picture were taken, and are being forwarded. The photograph was to be returned to its owner the following day. The person on the left is alleged to be CITROEN and the person on the right is undoubtedly the person which CITROEN claims is HITLER. The back side of the photograph contained the following data: "Adolf SCHRITTELMAYOR, Tunga, Colombia, 1954."

1 Att. w/w

DNB/lac

Attachment: 1 photo
3 October 1955
- Headquarters, w/1 att. in dupl.
- [CIA/LA] w/1 att. 1 copy
- [CIA/LA] w/1 att., 1 copy
1 - [CIA/LA] w/1 att, 1 copy
- [   ] w/1 att., 1 copy

[CIA Employee]

3 oct 55
[@] 2592
201-9393 3

INDEX

CS COPY

Secret
CLASSIFICATION

RI COPY.

EXEMPTIONS Section 3(b)
(2)(A) Privacy
(2)(B) Methods/Sources
(2)(G) Foreign Relations

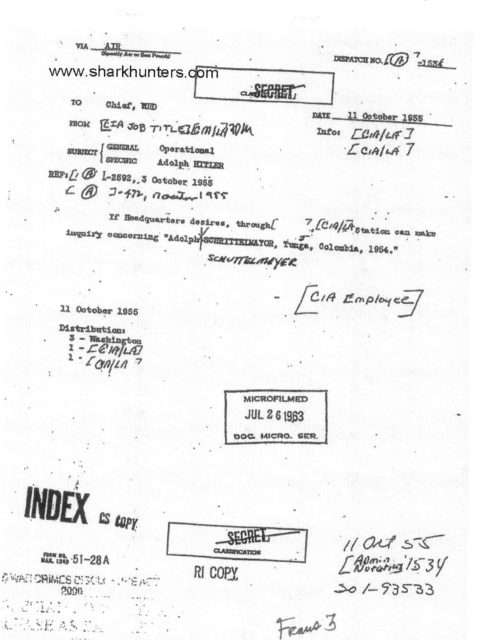

VIA ___AIR___

DISPATCH NO. [(A) 7 -1556

www.sharkhunters.com

SECRET

TO   Chief, WHD

FROM   [CIA JOB TITLE][EMP][A][DM]

DATE ___11 October 1955___

Info: [CIA/LA]
      [CIA/LA]

SUBJECT { GENERAL   Operational
         SPECIFIC   Adolph HITLER

REF: [i (A)' L-2592,.3 October 1955
     [(A) J-472, noah...1955

    If Headquarters desires, through [7 [CIA/LA station can make
inquiry concerning "Adolph SCHRITTEIMAYOR, Tunga, Colombia, 1954."
                       SCHUTTELMEYER

                                                    - [CIA Employee]

    11 October 1955

Distribution:
    3 - Washington
    1 - [CIA/LA]
    1 - [CIA/LA] 7

MICROFILMED

JUL 26 1963

DOC. MICRO. SER.

INDEX CS COPY.

FORM NO. 51-28 A

WAR CRIMES DISCLOSURE ACT
2000

SECRET

CLASSIFICATION

RI COPY

11 Oct 55
[Admin Notating] 1534
So 1-93533

Fraus 3

5

VIA ___AIR POUCH___   DISPATCH NO. [@] 7-472
       (Speedy Air or Sea Pouch)

SECRET
CLASSIFICATION

TO Chief, WH

FROM [CIA JOB TITLE] [CIA/LA]   DATE ___17 October 1955___

INFO: [CIA JOB TITLE], [CIA/LA,
SUBJECT [GENERAL Operational   [CIA JOB TITLE] [CIA/LA]
        [SPECIFIC Adolf Hitler   [CIA JOB TITLE] [CIA/LA]

MICROFILMED
JUL 26 1963
DOC. MICRO. SER.

REF [@] 7-2592, 3 October 1955

1. With reference to the information submitted by Station [CIA/LA] concerning the alleged report that Adolf HITLER is still alive, the files of the [CIA/LA] contain similar information received from the same source, who resides in

2. An undated memorandum, believed to have been written in about mid February 1954, reflects that Phillip CITROEN, who was co-owner of the former Mara-caibo Times, told a former member of this [CIA/LA] that while he was working for a railroad company in Colombia, he had met an individual who strongly resembled and claimed to be Adolf HITLER. CITROEN claimed to have met this individual at a place called "Residencias Coloniales" in Tunja (Boyaca), Colombia, which is, according to the source, overly populated with former German Nazis. According to CITROEN, the Germans residing in Tunja follow this alleged Adolf HITLER with an "idolatry of the Nazi past," addressing him as 'der Fuhrer' and affording him the Nazi salute and storm-trooper adulation.

3. CITROEN also showed the member of this office a photograph which was taken in Colombia of himself standing next to the alleged HITLER. This photograph was borrowed for a few hours to be reproduced, but unfortunately the nega-tives were too poor to make copies from. The original was returned to its owner and could not be easily obtained again. Because of this and the ap-parent fantasy of the report, the information was not submitted at the time it was received.

4. Phillip CITROEN resides in Maracaibo with his brother, Francois and is reported to be employed with a Dutch steamship company. Francois formerly worked for the Maracaibo Herald and about two years ago he went into part-nership with his brother Phillip and Alexander van DOBBEN, the Dutch Consul in Maracaibo as publishers of an English language newspaper, the Maracaibo Times, which is still in circulation. There is no biographical information presently available on Phillip or Francois CITROEN.

INDEX
CS COPY

[@] 472 17 ach COPY SECRET
                CLASSIFICATION   207-93533

NAZI WAR CRIMES DISCLOSURE ACT
2000

SPECIAL COLLECTIONS
RELEASE AS SANITIZED

Frame 4

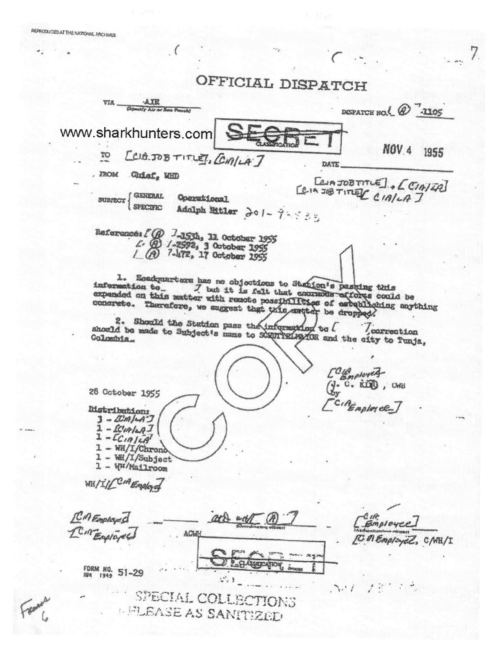

OFFICIAL DISPATCH

VIA ___AIR___
(Specify Air or Sea Pouch)

www.sharkhunters.com ~~SECRET~~
CLASSIFICATION

DISPATCH NO. [@] ⁷-2105

NOV. 4 1955

TO   [CIA JOB TITLE], [CIA/LA]
DATE _____

FROM Chief, WHD

[CIA JOB TITLE] + [CIA/LA]
[CIA JOB TITLE] [CIA/LA]

SUBJECT GENERAL Operational
SPECIFIC Adolph Hitler 201-7-535

References: [@]-1514, 11 October 1955
[@] 1-2592, 3 October 1955
[@] 7-472, 17 October 1955

1. Headquarters has no objections to Station's passing this
information to_ [ ] but it is felt that enormous efforts could be
expended on this matter with remote possibilities of establishing anything
concrete. Therefore, we suggest that this matter be dropped.

2. Should the Station pass the information to [ ] correction
should be made to Subject's name to SCHUTTELMAIER and the city to Tunja,
Colombia.

[CIA Employee]
(J. C. KING), CWH
by
[CIA Employee]

28 October 1955

Distribution:
3 - [CIA/LA]
1 - [CIA/LA]
1 - [CIA/LA]
1 - WH/I/Chrono
1 - WH/I/Subject
1 - WH/Mailroom

WH/I/[CIA Employee]

[CIA Employee]   [and all @]   [CIA Employee]
[CIA Employee]   (coordinating officer)   [CIA Employee], C/WH/I
                        ACWH

~~SECRET~~

FORM NO. 51-29
JUN 1949

SPECIAL COLLECTIONS
RELEASE AS SANITIZED

The foregoing came to us from S.E.I.G. Agent **REMBRANDT**.

We have talked about **DON ANGEL ALCAZAR de VELASCO (158-1985)**, now let's meet him. He was an agent but by all reports, not a very good one. He initially worked for the Japanese *"TO"* spy right. *"TO"* means *"East"* but he soon worked for the German Intelligence groups.

DON ANGEL   Edward VIII

One of his first assignments was to spearhead Operation *"Willi"* in which he was to befriend the former King Edward VIII (then the Duke of Windsor) who was living the high life in Lisbon, Portugal. The Duke, being of German bloodline, was constantly saying in the press that Germany could win the war and that England could be bombed into surrender. He was becoming an embarrassment to the Churchill Government but an unwitting friend to Germany.

DON ANGEL was tasked with befriending the former king and inviting him, as a sportsman, on a hunting trip into Spain. Once in Spain, the waiting SS//SD men would kidnap Edward and using him, they would force the Churchill Government into a peace between Germany and England. In the early days of the war, Hitler made numerous peace proposals to England but all were blocked by Churchill for whatever reason. **DON ANGEL** was not successful in this – Edward did not accept the invitation to go hunting and the entire operation was scrapped. What follows are some of the letters from **DON ANGEL** to Sharkhunters Founder and President **HARRY COOPER (1-LIFE-1983)**.

The following four pages are one of the first letters from **DON ANGEL**.

MEMORIAS DE MIS NAVEGACIONES SUBMARINAS

www.sharkhunters.com   page 1 of 4

No he sido submarinista, aunque por razones de misiones
secretas tuve, en la guerra, que valerme de este medio para
el camino de la travesía del Canal de la Mancha. No puedo pre-
cisar el número de la nave porque en cada viaje le cambiaban el
número.

Confieso haber sentido miedo horas antes de cuantas veces me ~~que~~ embarqué lo que en sí, el acto de embarque constituía
el primero de los misterios en todos los viajes. ~~Viajes entre
las costas francesas y las inglesas~~. Lo primero era esperar en
sitio, también secreto, Al lanchón en el que salvaba la distan-
cia acuática entre la costa y el lugar en el que el sumergible
esperase. . Ya en él, el miedo se convertía en placer. Me sentía liberado de la búsqueda a la que estaba sometido en todas partes.

¿Qué recuerdo me queda (49 años después) del submarino
en los años cuarenta, cuando la guerra comenzaba el auge? Mi
mejor recuerdo es el de la admiración sentida por el submarinista, sea de la bandera que sea. Al submarino de entonces
lo ví como una teoría de circunstancias náutico-sumersivas en
las que se conjugan los factores científicos más esenciales en
cuanto al secreto maravilloso de operar jugando a la zorrería
del ocultismo. Aunque yo en los "U" he navegado únicamente co-

que ver con la navegación, llegué a ser parte de todo sin saber de ello nada.   www.sharkhunters.com

Memorizar sobre mis viajes submarinos, por lógica tiene
porte diferente al de los nautas responsables de su suerte. Mi
recuerdo se reduce a los azares de lo imprevisto. Los efectos
de sumersión eran anímicos. No temía lo que pudiese acontecer,
sentía el acontecimiento. ¡Qué experiencia! Mi condición de a-
gente secreto debía de imponerles a los oficiales cierto res-
peto admirativo en nada menor al que yo sentía hacia ellos. En
tres ocasiones, cedido el periscopio por el comandante, vi
caer cargueros enemigos en los que los torpedos alemanes hacín
blanco. No hay un espectáculo tan bello como ese de partir
(POR LA MITAD) la nave enemiga y ver caer las dos partes lentamente burbu-
jeando perlas de aire.   page 2 of 4

En mi último viaje a bordo de un "U"-el de más rememoran-
za histórico- lo tomé con Martín Borman frente a la ría de Arosa (Pontevedra, España) y acabó en Patagonia (Argentina). Fue
una travesía de la que no esperaba llegar. Hablé de esto varias
veces con Borman cuando la nave, cansada, daba señales de no po-
der seguir. Me aguanté el miedo con apariencia de no sentirlo.
Experimenté diferentes tipos de zozobra, la de la sumersión
inm-ediata violenta ante el vuelo de aviones que rutinariamen-
te salían a husmear avistamientos de cualquier barco sospecho-
so. Zozobra ante las malas noticias originadas por la "salud"
de las pilas del submarino carente de reconocimiento técnico
y reparación desde hacía meses. Y frente a las frías costas
del sur argentino en el que el tráfico de distintos barcos de

guerra buscaban en la Antártida   su última andadura. Fue allí,
en la Antártida donde los cerebros   de la sociedad Tule se fueron a reunir para, con sosiego, estudiar las otras causas de
la derrota, las desconocideas por casi todas las criaturas
de la tierra menos por el almirante Byrd, quien en el año 46,
a bordo de la nave capitana Mount Olympus se encaminó (el 2
de diciembre de 1946) con una copiosa flota de la armada ame-
ricana al continente helado y, según las declaraciones del AL-
MIRANTE en
Santiago de Chile al diario "El Mercurio" (7 de julio del 47)
al almirante Byrd "El Polo se encuentra entre nosotros y nues-
tros enemigos". Todo viene a decirnos que la declaración del
almirante Dönith "El mando está en el paraiso inexpugnable en
algún lugar de la tierra" no cayó en saco roto. Byrd sabía en
donde estaba ese lugar y quienes habían llegado a él. Años más
tarde me forcé por descubrir el informe que Byrd entregó al
Sobre aquel misterio.
Presidente de EE.UU..Y No lo logré. Tampoco supe quien es conociERON
el documento más importante de la guerra.

     Es posible que en COOPER ENTERPRISSE, algún día, en un
libro copioso, demos cuenta detallada   de lo que hoy es pe-
queñísimo "comprimido".

     Ya en el desembarcadero nos recibió mi amigo "Bover",
ALEMAN y del "To" uno de los servicios JAPONESESF
agente del Abwehr en el cono sur y dos señores alemanes a los
que ni Martín ni yo habíamos visto antes. Dieron la consigna
(CONSIGNA que el propio Bover No Conocía)
identificadora. Nos abrazamos. En ellos se reflejaba el temor
VIVIDO en LAS ULTIMAS horas CUANDO)
a lo peor. El contacto radiofónico con nosotros se interrumpía
frecuentemente debido al mal estado de la nave. Se subsanaba
con chapuzas.

     Tras una emocionante despedida de la tripulación (un ofi-

EL Grupo Borman-Bover y...

cial de segundo rango lloró). ▬▬ (partieron hacia no sé dónde y yo continué ▬▬ ▬▬ Buenos Aires por mis propios medios.
Unos días después la prensa bonaerense dió cumplida cuenta de
que un submarino alemán, desvencijado y sin poderse valer, frente al Plata, lo abandonó la tripulación entregándose a las autoridades argentinas.

Now the translation, thanks to **NORBERTO FERADEZ (3796-1994)**:
"I have not been a submariner, although in reason of secret missions in the war I had to use this way for traversing the English Channel. I cannot precise (tell you) the number of the boat because in each voyage the number was changed.

I confess to have been afraid in the hours preceding each of my embarcations, which in itself was the first mystery in all the trips. Trips between the French and English coasts. Firstly I had to wait in the also secret place, for the craft which saved the watery distance between the shore and where the submarine was waiting. Once aboard, fear turned into pleasure. I felt liberated from the shadowing which I was subjected everywhere.

What remembrance do I have after 49 years (he sent this to us in the 1980's) of the U-Boat in the early forties, when the war started to expand? My best remembrance is the admiration I felt for the crew of a submarine, no matter his flag. I regarded the submarine of that time as a theory of circumstances where the scientific factors most essential for the wonderful secret of playing fox-hunting (zorraria) converged. Despite the fact that I have just sailed in the "U" as a '*parcel*' or '*shipment*' to take a carry, I was part of it all, although not knowing a thing about it.

My remembrance of submarine cruisings, are integrally different from those who were responsible of my fate. My memories are reduced to the imprevisible.

The effects of diving were animical. I had no fear for what could arrive to me. I felt the event. What an experience! My condition of secret agent surely did impress the U-Boat officers, who had for me an admiration no smaller than what I had for them. For three times the commander let me control of the periscope, and I saw the enemy cargo vessels fall to the German torpedoes. There is no more beautiful spectacle than this, to see the enemy vessel cut in half and the two parts sliding slowly with air bubbles like pearls.

On my last voyage on an "U", the most historically remarkable, I started with Martin Bormann off the Arosa Estuary (province of Pontevedra, Spain). It was a trip from which I expected no return. I said this to Bormann several times when the boat, tired, seemed unable to carry on. I held my fear without revealing it. I felt different types of distress:

- that of the sudden crash diving in presence of aircraft on routine flights who were out in search of any suspect vessel;
- the distress at the bad news of the '*health*' of the submarine batteries;
- lacking technical service and repairation since some months before;
- and distress off the cold South Argentinean shores where many different warships tried to find in the Antarctic her last trip.

It was here, in the Antarctic, where the minds of the Thule Society reunited in order to study with care the reasons of the defeat, unknown to almost all the creatures on Earth, except to Admiral Byrd, who in 1946 aboard the Flagship **USS MOUNT OLYMPUS** sailed (on 2 December 1946) with a strong task force of the U.S. Navy towards the frozen continent and, following the words of the  Admiral in the newspaper "*El Mercurio*" of Santiago de Chile (7 July 1947) entitled '*The Pole is between us and our enemies*'.

All this means that the declaration of Admiral Dönitz; *'Command is in an impregnable paradise somewhere on Earth'* were no empty words. Byrd knew where this place was and who were in it. Years later I endeavored to find the file in which Byrd handed over to the ███ President about this mystery, but I failed to obtain it. I failed also to ascertain who were the people who knew the content of this document, the most important of the whole war.

It is possible that in Cooper Enterprises some day, in a great book, we could detail what here is strictly forbidden.

When in the landing place we were received by my friend *'Bover'*, agent of the German Abwehr and of the 'TO', one of the Japanese services, and by two Germans whom neither Martin nor me did know. They said the key word (which even *Bover* did not know) and we all embraced. They reflected the fear for the worst, which they had suffered in the last hours. Radio contact with us was lost frequently owing to the bad state of the boat. It was repaired clumsily.

After an emotional farewell from the crew (one petty officer did weep) the group Bormann-Bover departed for a place I do not know, and I followed voyage to Buenos Aires on my own. Some days after, the press of Buenos Aires was given details of how a German submarine, battered and useless, was abandoned by the crew off La Plata and handed themselves to the Argentinean authorities."

EDITOR NOTE – When **DON ANGEL** quoted Großadmiral Karl Dönitz, by "*the command*" he referred to the Government of the Third Reich in exile. Dönitz previously (in 1944) made the statement that the Kriegsmarine had found '*an impregnable fortress for the Führer in Paradise*'. It is believed that he meant the little village of San Carlos di Bariloche and with the help of Juan Peròn, no person or group could possibly approach these people.

Dönitz   Peròn

………more from **DON ANGEL**

ANGEL ALCAZAR DE VELASCO

Madrid - 12 - 11 - 87

Cooper Enterprises
P.O.Box 937
Fox Lake, Il 60020
USA

Querido amigo Cooper:

Gracias por la mención que de mí hace usted en el K T 8 44.

Creo de primordial importancia aclarar que por error de trasducción o mal entendido, ha dicho usted que yo llevé a Argentina a Eichmann. No fue así. No he dicho eso nunca. Al único nazi que llevé a la Argentina, fue a Martin Borman (judío circunciso aunque fuera nazi). Eichmann (igualmente judío) me vino a visitar a Madrid mandado por un cura. Me mostró Eichmann un pasaporte o salvoconducto expedido por el Vaticano. Le atendí durante cuatro días. Después desapareció sin dejar rastro. Un mes más tarde vino Martín Borman y ya le he dicho cómo se desarrolló el viaje.

Los datos que tengo respecto a MENGELE (también judío) coinciden con lo publicado en la prensa. En Asunción (Paraguay) un conocido en el año 63 me dijo que sabía dónde estaba, que si quería verle él me llevaría al lugar en el que se escondía. Me negué porque estaba seguro de que se me seguía. Nunca he visto a Mengele.Aquel año, el servicio de Inteligencia israelí, a través de uno de sus agentes, el señor Casasola, en Madrid -todavía vive- , me propuso que yo le fuese a buscar. No lo acepté.

En cuanto a KLAUS BARBIE lo conocí en París a finales del 42. Fue con motivo de la condecoración que Petain concedió al hoy presidente de la República Francesa, señor Miterrand. La condecoración se llama "Federica" concedida a la "Lealtad acrisolada". Miterrand publicó muchos artículos en un semanario mostrándose gran amigo del Gobierno de Vichi. .

A BARBIE le ví en La Paz, en el año 73. Era entonces Agente del CIA y se movía sin ningún obstáculo.

De otros nazis no recuerdo nada. En el año 65 fui a Gabon porque en la Leprosería de Lambareñé había dos alemanes custodiados por el doctor Albert Schweitzer, Premio Nobel, y comprobé que cuando murió Schweitzer los dos alemanes partieron para la Patagonia chilena, según me informaron.

Repito: yo no llevé a Eichmann a la Patagonia Argentina. Tampoco sé cómo llegó allí.

Me parece muy bien, señor Cooper, que usted venga para julio. Le estoy esperando. Mientras, reciba un fuerte abrazo

www.sharkhunters.com
page 2 of 2

Angel Alcázar de Velasco

The translation, thanks again to **NORBERTO FERADEZ (3796-1994)**:

"Dear Friend Cooper,

Thank you for the mention you made of me in KTB #44. I think it is most important to clarify that by an error of translation or a misunderstanding, you said that I carried Eichmann to Argentina. It is not so. The only Nazi which I brought to Argentina was Martin Bormann (a circumcised Jew although a Nazi). Eichmann (also a Jew) visited me at Madrid sent by a clergyman. Eichmann showed me a passport or safe conduct expended by the Vatican. I attended him for four days. Then he left without a trace. One month later came Martin Bormann and I have already told you how the voyage was.

Bormann   Eichmann   Barbie

The data I have about Mengele (again a Jew) does match with this published by newspapers. At Asuncion (Paraguay) a friend of mine told me in 1963 that he knew where he was and that if I wished to see him he would guide me to where he was hidden. I declined because I was sure that I was being followed. I have never seen Mengele. The same year the Israeli Intelligence Service, through one of its agents in Madrid, Mr. Casasola (he is still alive) proposed me to go looking for him. I said no.

Regarding Klaus Barbie – I knew him at Paris at the end of 1942. It was when Petain decorated who today is President of the French Republic – Mssr. Miterrand. The medal is called 'Faderica' and is conceded to the 'refined loyalty'. Miterrand published many articles on a weekly magazine showing to be a great friend to the Vichy Government. I saw Barbie at La Paz in the year 1973. He was then a CIA agent and moved without obstacles.

I don't remember anything of other Nazis. On 1965 I went to Gabon because there were in the Leprosery of Lambarenè two Germans sheltered by Dr. Albert Schweitzer, holder of the Premium Nobel, and I was informed that when Schweitzer passed away the two Germans left for the Chilean Patagonia.

I repeat: I did not carry Eichmann to the Argentinian Patagonia. I neither know how he arrived there.

It is very well that you will come here in July, Mr. Cooper. I am waiting for you. In the meantime, receive my warmest regards."

EDITOR NOTE – Although it is not a popular thing to "*out*" people in high places, Francois Mitterrand was indeed a collaborator with Germany.

It is reported that Klaus Barbie's CIA handler was Pierre Salinger who later became Press Secretary to President John F. Kennedy.

ANGEL ALCAZAR DE VELASCO

Madrid, 12 - 2 -88

Sr. D. Harry Cooper
SHAKHUNTERS
TAMPA, Florida
USA 33622-1776

Querido amigo:
                    Recibí su carta del 13 - 1 - 88 y me place darle
la enhorabuena por la última interpretación de mis notas en cartas
anteriores respecto a Eigman. Sí, amigo Cooper, la interpretación
que ahora ha hecho es más justa. El viaje de Adolfo Eichman a Argentina nada tuvo que ver con el de Borman ni supe cómo lo hizo.
Tampoco fue mi huésped. Nunca supe en dónde se hospedó en Madrid
ni quise averiguarlo. No obstante, por el análisis que hice de
nuestras conversaciones deduje que estaba hospedado secretamente
en uno de los colegios de una Órden religiosa, sita en el barrio
Salamanca de Madrid (no se lo pregunté por parecerme inelegante
y porque lógicamente desconfiaba de todos). Me llamaba todas las
mañanas sobre las doce de la mañana y nos citábamos en distintos
lugares. Dos veces vino a mi casa y almorzábamos a la hora acos-
tumbrada en España: dos de la tarde en distintos restaurantes.
Una anécdota muy importante: le invité a ver una corrida de toros
y me dijo que no le gustaba ver la muerte de un animal. No quiso
ir.

                    Todo esto sucedió antes de que hiciésemos Borman
y yo la travesía a la Patagonia, a Coig. Durante el viaje no
hablamos una palabra sobre Adolfo que, como le tengo dicho, señor Harry, llevaba documentación vaticana.

                    El tercero y cuarto puntos de su carta 13 - 1-88-
son totalmente correctos.

                    No obstante, el que yo conociera a Klaus Barbie en París, en
el año 42, no quiere decir que todas sus actividades. Me lo pre-
sentó un capitán de SS y me dijo que Barbie se dedicaba a per-
seguir terroristas. La entrevista de mi amigo con Barbie obede-
ció a la voladura de tres partes de conducción eléctrica. Nada más
supe.

                    Barbie ha trabajado en Bolivia y otras países suda-
mericanos con CIA durante treinta años y fue él quien mayor papel
desempeñó en reducir y acabar con "Che" Guevara. Su trato con di-
versos judíos era normal.

                    Borman murió en el año 78 y Menguele en 81. Con el
último nunca tuve contacto. Usted sabe que Menguele era judío de
raza (como Borman) circunciso y que esto le obligó a precauciones
máximas. Yo supe en Paraguay que le protegieron durante un tiempo
judíos de espíritu nacionalsocialista, enemigos del sionismo, co-

CI. IBIZA, 1 - BAJO D
TELF. 273 97 42 - MADRID-9

mo sucede con la palabra "naziñ que es judeo-askernazi y no alemana.
Los judíos se la han aplicado al nacionalsocialismo y es una más
de sus históricas tergiversaciones, con lo que muchos judíos no
están conformes. Borman, que era de origen sefardita, explicaba
así lo de llamarles nazis. Rabiaba escuchando la palabra nazi a-
plicada al nacionalsocialismo.

        No sé si podré unirme a usted y la Comisión de la
próxima Convención.Sin embargo, seguro que en Madrid nos daremos
un buen abrazo y hablaremos, Le presentaré a un joven amigo con
idéntico pensamiento al nuestro, que habla muy bien alemán, in-
glés, francés y por analogía italiano y portugués.

        No, el nombre del submarino que desde la desem-
bocadura de la ría de Aroaa (España) fuimos a la Patagonia (Argentina) nunca supe cual fue realmente. Cuando embarcamos, me
parece recordar -nada cierto porque me bailan los números en la
memoria- que el número era el U-313 pero el comandante me dijo
que era número "clave. Sé sí, que al pasar por la latitud de Dakar, muy al Este mar adentro se cambió la cifra y se volvió a
cambiar nuevamente en aguas de la costa suramericana. Nunca pregunté por los nuevos números. El número con el que se inutilizó
frente al Plata, el último que tuvo, lo publicó toda la prensa,
especialmente la argentina y uruguaya. Es fácil buscarlo en las
hemerotecas de aquellas fechas. Pero, repito: ninguno de los
números se asemejaba al suyo. Recuerdo ahora que el comandante me
dijo que los dos últimos años de la guerra él estuvo con el submarino por aquellos mares. Conocía muy bien las aguas suratlán-
ticas.

        Celebro que ahora viva en Tampa. Pero tenga cuida-
do a quien le da a traducir. En Tampa son muchos los cubanos que
"hablan español" pero poquísimos los que entienden mi prosodia y
sintáxis, son personas de lenguaje casero.

                Un abrazo

                        Angel Alcázar de Velasco

The translation, thanks again to **NORBERTO FERADEZ (3796-1994)**:
"Dear Friend,

I received your letter of the 13th of January, 1988 and I am
pleased to give you the good news. The last interpretation of my
notes was correct of the letters I sent you before with respect to
Eichmann. Yes, my friend Cooper, the interpretation you have
made is not just. The voyage of Adolf Eichmann to Argentina
had nothing to do with the one made by Bormann, and I don't
know how he did it. He was not my tenant (responsibility). I
never knew where he stayed in Madrid, and I never cared to find

out. Nevertheless, in the analogy I made in our conversations, I deduct that he was staying in secret in one of the colleges; in one of the religious orders situated in the neighborhood called Salamanca de Madrid (I never asked him because I thought it was not polite, and by logic he mistrusted everyone). He called me every morning at noontime and we always had a meeting at different places. Twice he called to my house and we had lunch at the accustomed hour of Spain, two in the afternoon in different restaurants.

A very important piece of information – I invited him to a bull fight and he told me he didn't like it because he didn't like to see the death of an animal. All this happened before Bormann and I made the trip to Patagonia. During the trip (**DON ANGEL** and Bormann) we didn't talk a word about Adolf (Eichmann). Like I said to you before, Harry, he was carrying documentation (travel papers) from the Vatican.

The third and fourth points of your letter of the 13th are totally correct.

Nevertheless, the fact that I knew Klaus Barbie in Paris in the year 1942, does not mean that I knew all his activities. He introduced to me a Captain of the SS who told me that Barbie was dedicated to persecute terrorists. The interview of my friend with Barbie resulted in the blowing (dynamiting) of the three parts of the electrical conduction (power lines, towers and ?????). I never knew anything else.

Barbie has worked in Bolivia and other South American countries with the CIA for 30 years and it was him who was one of the major people responsible for the elimination of "*Che*" Guevara. His relationship with different Jews was normal.

Bormann died in the year 1978 and Mengele in 1981. With Mengele I never had a contact. You know that Mengele was Jewish by race (like Bormann). He was circumcised and this made him take maximum precautions. I knew in Paraguay he was protected for some time by Jews with the National Socialist (Nazi??) spirit, enemies of the Zionists. The Jews have applied to the National Socialists and this is one more of history's lies, with which a lot of Jews never agreed. Bormann always got angry when he the word "Nazi" applied as a nationality.

I am not sure if I can meet with you at the next Convention; nevertheless I am sure we will see each other and have a hug and talk in Madrid. I was introduced to a young friend of mine with the same ideology who spoke very good German, English, French and had knowledge of Italian and Portuguese.

No, the number of the submarine that from the entrance of the Ria de Arosas (a bay).......we went to the Patagonian coast of Argentina; I never really knew. When we got into the submarine, I seem to remember the number was U-313. (I am not too certain because numbers are dancing in my memory). But the Commander told me that it was a code number. When we crossed the latitude of Dakar, far to the east, on the high seas, they changed the number...and it was changed again when we got close to the South American waters. I never asked for the new numbers, the number that was used in La Plata, Argentina, the last one was reported in the press especially in Argentina and Uruguay. It is easy to find it in the libraries of that year. But I repeat, none of the numbers is close to yours (Cooper asked him about **U-530** and **U-977**). I remember now that the Captain told me that the last two years of the war he was with the submarine around South American waters. He knew the South American waters.

I'm glad that you live in Tampa. Be careful who is translating this letter. In Tampa there are many Cubans who speak Spanish but only a few who understand the meanings.

A hug,

(signature)

EDITOR NOTE from Cooper – An interesting note actually. Some years ago, I was on the Board of the school my son attended and another of the Board members was a mother from Columbia. When she learned of the research I was doing into the Third Reich in South America, she told me that her father had coffee almost every morning with several friends including a German. One day the German didn't make it for coffee and they heard that he was arrested. When she gave me the dates and details, I informed her that her father's coffee buddy was actually Klaus Barbie.

Domingo 24 de noviembre de 1996 • CLARIN • INFORMACION GENERAL • 39

HABRIAN ENCALLADO EN LA COSTA DE RIO NEGRO DESPUES DE LA GUERRA

Buscan 2 submarinos nazis

La Prefectura Naval comenzó ayer el rastrillaje de dos presuntos submarinos nazis que habrían encallado en un lejano punto del Atlántico sur un mes después de finalizada la Segunda Guerra Mundial. El inicio de la búsqueda coincidió con el testimonio de una testigo, quien dijo que vio a las naves desde la ventana de su casa.

Un guardacostas se ha estacionado en las cercanías de la "Caleta de los Loros", unos 140 kilómetros al sudoeste de Viedma, capital de Río Negro. Dos buzos del Instituto de Biología Marina "Almirante Storni" comenzaron las primeras tareas poco después de las cuatro de la tarde.

Los buzos —Luis "Tony" Brochado y Sandro Acosta— realizarán su trabajo con dos cabos de 30 metros de largo atados a dos botes inflables con poderosos motores fuera de borda. La intención es "peinar" el fondo de la caleta. "Si las condiciones del tiempo nos ayudan, es probable que mañana (por hoy) tengamos alguna pista como para saber si en este lugar hay algo sumergido", pronosticó Brochado.

El piloto civil Mario Chironi, quien dijo que a mediados de la década del cincuenta pudo ver desde el aire los restos de una nave, también participa de la búsqueda, prestando apoyo aéreo a los buzos. "La superficie por rastrillar se puede estimar en unas diez hectáreas, con seis a ocho metros de profundidad en bajamar", apuntó Brochado.

Una mujer de 80 años, Gisella Boche de Paesani, dijo ayer que "al final de la guerra" vio a una nave desde la ventana de su casa, que se encuentra frente a las cos-

tas del Atlántico sur. "Era media mañana, entre las nueve y las diez. Yo estaba tejiendo, pero dejé un momento las agujas para acercarme a la ventana y mirar para afuera, porque tenía la vista cansada. Fue entonces cuando vi al submarino en la Caleta de los Loros", dijo la anciana.

La testigo señaló, también, que relacionó a la nave con el submarino nazi porque había "escuchado por la radio que andaban por aquí barcos alemanes".

La señora de Paesani agregó: "El submarino desapareció y después pasó un avión, así que supuse que lo estaban buscando".

La "Caleta de los Loros" está ubicada dentro del golfo San Matías. En el lugar sólo vive un guardafauna. La zona está considerada "reserva natural", y no existe ninguna comodidad para el turismo. □

Here, thanks to **NORBERTO FERADEZ (3796-1994)** is the translation of the newspaper report on the previous page. This is from the "*Information General*" of Domingo (Sunday) 24 November 1996.

"IN SEARCH OF 2 NAZI SUBMARINES

The Department of the Navy started yesterday the search for two Nazi submarines which some believe had run aground in a far away area in the South Atlantic one month after the end of the Second World War. The beginning of the search coincided with the testimonial of a witness who said she saw the vessels from the window of her home.

A Coast Guard vessel is standing by near the inlet known as '*Caleta de los Loros*' approximately 140 kilometers southwest of Viedma, the capital of Rio Negro. Two scuba divers of the Marine Biology Institute named '*Almitante Storni*' started the diving exercises after four o'clock in the afternoon.

The divers Luis '*Tony*' Brochado and Sandro Acosta will conduct their search using two cables approximately 30 meters long each, secured to two inflatable boats powered by potent outboard motors. The objective of this mission is to carefully '*comb*' the bottom of the inlet.

'If weather conditions remain favorable, it is possible that by tomorrow we may have some clue as to what lies on the ocean floor in this area'.

commented Brochado.

Pilot Mario Chironi, who claims he saw, while flying over the area in the 1950's, the remains of a vessel, is also participating in the search, providing air support to the divers.

'We estimate that the surface of the area to be 'combed' is approximately ten hectares with depths of six to eight meters at low tide',

noted Brochado. An 80 year old woman by the name of Gisella Boche de Paesani, said yesterday that 'At the end of the Second World War' she saw a vessel from the window of her house, which is located in front of the South Atlantic Coast.

'It was mid-morning, between 9:00 and 10:00 a.m. I was knitting; when I put down the needles for a few minutes and went to the window to look outside and the rest my eyes for

a while. It was then that I saw a submarine in the area known as 'La Caleta de los Loros'; the old lady said.

The witness also said she related the vessel with the Nazi submarine because that same morning she had *'heard on the radio that German vessels were patrolling the area'*; Mrs. Paesani added. *'The submarine disappeared and later an airplane went by, so I figured they were looking for the ships.'*

The area known as *'La Caleta de los Loros'* is located in the Gulf of San Matias. Only a forest ranger lives in this area. The region is considered a *'natural reserve'* area, and has no accommodations whatsoever for tourists."

EDITOR NOTE – When this story first broke, I was contacted by a future friend and Sharkhunters Member Lieutenant Commander (of the Argentine Navy) Dr. **EDUARDO GERDING (6895-2004)** called me and gave us all this information. I immediately called an Argentinean Admiral and asked about this. The Admiral constantly said that it was top secret. I explained that there was nothing top secret about what appeared to be a Type VII-C German U-Boat. He would not bend – for an entire week my calls were all received with *"It is all top secret, Senor Cooper!"* but I persisted and after that first week, his answer changed greatly.

"What German U-Boat, Senor Cooper?" is all he said. It was obvious that something was going on and a cover-up was in play but being in the USA and the Admiral in Argentina, it was not possible to meet him face to face or to do any further digging - not then in 1996, but later...........

AMBITO FINANCIERO   1 3 ENE 1997   DIPRE

SECCION
PAGINA /9   SECCION
                      PAGINA   SECCION
                                      PAGINA

Documentos de la fuerza demuestran presencia de buques alemanes en 1945

ARMADA CONFIRMO QUE HUBO SUBMARINOS NAZIS EN EL SUR

Escribe
Abel Basti

San Carlos de Bariloche - Finalmente, el presidente de la Nación, Carlos Menem, cumplió su palabra empeñada hace un mes en El Bolsón y la Armada Argentina comenzó a reconocer que el segundo gobierno de Juan Domingo Perón estuvo al tanto de la presencia de submarinos nazis en aguas jurisdiccionales argentinas.

El Delfín de Adolf Hitler, Martín Bormann, otros jerarcas nazis, así como parte del oro del Tercer Reich habrían arribado a la Argentina en esas naves, según lo sostienen varios investigadores de este apasionante tema.

El sinceramiento del gobierno en realidad aún es tibio y ha consistido en dar a conocer algunos documentos que evidencian un virtual estado de alerta de la Armada ante el avistamiento de submarinos alemanes en costas de este país en 1945. Según esa documentación - que lleva el tradicional sello de "Secreto"- la Armada tenía orden de atacar a los temidos "lobos grises" aún en una época tan tardía como julio del 45, casi tres meses después de que Alemania hubiera firmado el armisticio.

Esta es la primera reacción oficial luego de que el diario patagónico "La Mañana del Sur" realizó una investigación en la que se dio a conocer que dos sumergibles alemanes aún permanecen hundidos en aguas del Golfo de San Matías, a unos escasos 1000 metros de la costa rionegrina.

Esa noticia - difundida hacia fines del año pasado - generó una gran repercusión internacional y motivó que el presidente de la Nación, Carlos Menem, anunciara que "tanto el gobierno como la Armada colaborarían para solucionar este problema. Aunque no sé si es un problema", se autopreguntó el mandatario en un reportaje mantenido con el diario patagónico.

En realidad, el primer movimiento de la Armada fue intentar abrir un sumario al ex

buzo de la Prefectura Naval Argentina, Carlos Massey, convertido en una pieza clave a la hora de hablar de los submarinos hundidos en el Golfo San Matías.

Massey, en agosto de 1978, fue convocado por la Armada, que en aquel entonces evaluaba la posibilidad de un "reflotamiento" de los dos sumergibles que se encuentran en el fondo del Atlántico a solamente unos 14 metros de profundidad.

En la década del '70 un avión Neptune -propiedad de la Armada- detectó las dos siluetas durante un patrullaje efectuado cuando se registraba una "bajamar extraordinaria" en el vasto litoral patagónico.

El episodio generó un gran revuelo oficial que nunca trascendió públicamente, porque inicialmente se pensaba que eran submarinos rusos en actividad que se encontraban merodeando las costas argentinas.

- Clima de nerviosismo

Barcos de guerra y aviones argentinos fueron enviados al sitio en un clima de nerviosismo que finalmente se distendió cuando las autoridades se aseguraron de que en realidad se trataba de los cascos oxidados de dos sumergibles nazis.

A pesar de los peritajes - y de un voluminoso expediente que durante años guardó la Armada en la base General Belgrano- la verdad sobre estas naves hasta ahora nunca fue reconocida oficialmente. Al dar a conocer algunos de los documentos "Secretos" -que hablan de la presencia de las naves en aguas australes- la Armada Argentina reconoció la labor de la prensa patagónica: "Desclasificarse del «Secreto» el presente (documento) por haber transcurrido cincuenta años del acontecimiento relatado y haber pasado la noticia a manejarse públicamente por los periódicos de la zona", indica el texto oficial que deja sin efecto la reserva con que se guardaba la información de los submarinos nazis.

Sugestivos vínculos con el Proceso

Neuquén (especial de "La Mañana del Sur") - Ex oficiales y marinos alemanes que combatieron en la Segunda Guerra Mundial se reunían frecuentemente con jefes de la marina Argentina, y durante el último gobierno militar, en 1978, se ofrecieron para brindarle asesoramiento de combate ante un eventual conflicto armado con Chile. Lo misma ocurrió en 1982, durante la guerra con Inglaterra por las islas Malvinas.

La información a la que tuvo acceso este diario fue revelada ayer por Gustavo Nagel, familiar de Otto Nagel, un submarinista alemán que servía a la

embargo, según los archivos alemanes, Otto Nagel habría servido como capitán del submarino U-640 hasta el 17 de mayo de 1945 -bajo el nombre de Carls II. Nagel-, fecha en que el navío fue dado como desaparecido.

Según la fuente, el marino alemán retornó al país al finalizar la guerra "aunque nunca se pudo reponer de la derrota de Alemania". "Abandonó a su familia para ir a la guerra. Quedó muy mal y siempre recordaba con nostalgia y bronca por la derrota su vida en el submarino".

- Encuentros

Tercer Reich que fue hundida en el Río de la Plata por su propia tripulación.

"En esos encuentros participaban altos jefes militares alemanes que concurrían a las reuniones con sus medallas disimuladas debajo de las solapetadas".

Rubén Nagel recordó que "las reuniones entre los militares argentinos y alemanes me las describió un alto jefe naval de la armada alemana al que le faltaba una pierna y que murió hace algunos años, luego de vivir mucho tiempo a cuatro cuadras de mi casa". Sin embargo, aclaró que no re-

Now thanks to **NORBERTO FERADEZ (3796-1994)** is the translation of the next newspaper report on the previous page. This is the article that beginning "**ARMADA CONFIRMO....**"

"THE DEPARTMENT OF THE NAVY CONFIRMED THAT THERE WERE NAZI SUBMARINES IN THE SOUTH
(Navy documents prove the presence of German vessels in 1945)
San Carlos di Bariloche – Finally, the nation's president Carlos Menem, (photo right) kept his promise given a month ago in '*El Bolson*' and '*The Armada Argentina*'. The Navy started to acknowledge that the government of Juan Domingo Perón was fully aware of the presence of Nazi submarines in the jurisdictional waters of Argentina.

The successor of Adolf Hitler, Martin Bormann, other Nazi officials and some of the gold of the Third Reich had arrived in Argentina in those vessels, according to investigators of this fascinating subject.

The Argentine government has not made too many comments on the subject. They have merely released some documents which add to the fact that the Navy was on a state of watch because German submarines were seen patrolling the Argentinean coast in 1945.

According to these documents which have been labeled 'Top Secret', the Navy back then had orders to attack the fearful 'grey wolves' even as late as July 1945, almost three months after Germany had signed the armistice.

This article is the first official reaction after the Patagonian newspaper '*La Manna del Sur*' conducted an investigation in which it seemed evident that two German submarines still remain beneath the waters of the Gulf of San Matias 1,000 meters off the coast of Rio Negro. The sensational news given at the end of last year reached international proportions and made the Argentinean President Carlos Menem, announce that the

Argentinean Government as well as the Argentinean Navy would collaborate to solve the problem, '*even though it is not a problem*' Menem commented in an interview with the newspaper mentioned above.

In reality the first move of the Navy was to open the file of Carlos Massey, an ex-diver with the Department of the Navy, who played a key role in the investigation of the sunken submarines in the Gulf of San Matias.

In August of 1978, Massey was summoned by the Department of the Navy who at the time was considering refloating the two submarines found at the bottom of the Atlantic at a depth of 14 meters.

In the seventies a class Neptune airplane, property of the Navy, detected two silhouettes during a patrol while a low-tide was taking place in the vast Patagonian coast.

The episode generated great turmoil and uproar, which never transcended publicly, because initially it was thought that these vessels were Russian submarines who were prowling the Argentine coast.

A STATE OF TENSION

Argentinean warships and combat airplanes were sent to the scene in a state of nervousness which finally dissipated when the authorities were convinced that is reality all it amounted to was the rusted hulls of two Nazi submarines.

In spirit of the voluminous file containing all this information kept by the Navy at the General Belgrano Naval Base, the truth about these submarines have never been officially recognized. What the Argentine Navy did recognize was the work of the Patagonian press, after 50 years of top secret information.

PART II – SUGGESTIVE TIES WITH THE PROCESS
Neuquen (special news from '*La Manna del sur*') former German officers and sailors who fought during the Second World War used to meet frequently with top Argentinean Navy officials during the last military government in 1978. These former military men would offer military advice when the conflict with

Chile came about. The same thing occurred in 1982 with the conflict between England and Argentina over the Falklands.

This information given above was obtained by this newspaper through Gustavo Nagel, a relative of Otto Nagel, a German submariner who served in the Kriegsmarine as a volunteer, and who later passed away in the city of Quilmes, Argentina.

According to Ruben Nagel, his father's cousin joined the German Navy as a volunteer and served in various capacities; one of them as a translator. However, according to German files Otto Nagel had served as Captain of U-640 until May 17, 1945 under the name of Carls II Nagel; date in which the submarine was considered lost in action.

According to the source, the German captain returned to this country at the end of the war, even though he never recuperated from the defeat that his country had suffered. He had abandoned his family to go to war and now he was alone and feeling depressed. He would have nostalgic recollections of the life aboard his submarine.

ENCOUNTER

Since his arrival to Argentina until the time he died, Nagal would periodically meet with other comrades in arms in Quilmes and the Federal Capital. In these reunions were men from the GRAF SPEE, the corsair of the Third Reich, which was sunk in 'Rio de la Plata' by her own crew.

In these reunions participated high ranking German officers who attended these reunions with their medals slightly disguised under their overcoats. Ruben Nagel remembered;

'....these reunions among Argentinean and former German military men were described to me by a high ranking German officer who had lost a leg in the war and who died some years ago, after living for a long time only four blocks from my own house.'

Nevertheless Ruben Nagel clarified the fact that he did not remember the German's name, last name or military rank.

Likewise, he pointed out that;

'every year they would meet to celebrate Argentine military men a specific or symbolic date and they would always say *it was a gesture of comradeship and brotherhood which no civilians could join.'*

EDITOR NOTE – It is obvious which *"specific"* or *"symbolic"* date they mean………..Hitler's birthday on 20 April.

As previously indicated, this is a photo of one such birthday celebration in Argentina. Look closely at the photo being held in the center of this shot.

Operation 'MERCATOR'

EDITOR NOTE – Many have asked how anyone could escape Europe in the closing moments of the war with such a huge US Navy and Royal Navy presence across the North Atlantic. **PIZZARRO** solved that problem. Here is his explanation.

As reported in **KTB #222** in 2009, at the end of April 1945, when the Red Army was on the Oder River, the Americans were in Hamburg and the British in Kiel and the war was all but over, why would Großadmiral Karl Dönitz send a total of 103 U-Boats into action in areas where they had virtually no chance of success? We showed the reason – it was to pull every warship off the North Atlantic and to positions on the American coast and to England and the European coast, leaving a wide swath of open Atlantic on the north-south longitude of 30° west. For 500 kilometers on either side of this longitude, from north to south, there were no Allied ships as they were engaged in ASW operations on the eastern and western side of the Atlantic. It was a superhighway, an autobahn as it were for ships, U-Boats etc. to sail south for South America.

Just about anything that could float and submerge was pressed into this operation including Type VII, Type IX and even Type XXIII boats were involved. There were eighteen U-Boats sent to operate off the American and Canadian coast including Type IX-C as well as the very long range Type IX-D2 boats.

Other boats were sent to operate around England and a few into the Arctic Sea, and they included:
U-218, U-242, U-244, U-245, U-246, U-249, U-255, U-260, U-275, U-278, U-285, U-286, U-287, U-293, U-295, U-296, U-299, U-307, U-312, U-313, U-315, U-318, U-320, U-321, U-325, U-326, U-396, U-398, U-399, U-427, U-481, U-483, U-485, U-486, U-636, U-637, U-668, U-681, U-683, U-711, U-714, U-716, U-722, U-739, U-764, U-773, U-774, U-775, U-776, U-778, U-825, U-826, U-901, U-905,

U-907, U-953, U-956, U-963, U-965, U-968, U-977, U-978, U-979, U-992, U-995, U-997, U-1001, U-1002, U-1003, U-1004, U-1005, U-1009, U-1010, U-1017, U-1019, U-1021, U-1022, U-1023, U-1024, U-1055, U-1058, U-1064, U-1105, U-1106, U-1107, U-1109, U-1169, U-1195, U-1202, U-1203, U-1206, U-1272, U-1274, U-1277, U-1302, U-1305, U-2321, U-2322, U-2324, U-2326, U-2329, U-2336* and *U-2511.

Many of our Members rode these boats including:

U-315: **DETLEV ZIMMERMANN (247-LIFE--1987)**
Diving planes operator

U-315: **HERBERT ZOLLER (366-1987)** Commander

U-764: Hans-Kurt von Bremen Commander. He was not a Member, but he always attended our Patrols in Wilhelmshaven.

U-968: **OTTO WESTPHALEN (329-1987)**, Commander

WESTPHALEN   **PULST**

U-978: **WOLDEMAR TRIEBEL (197-LIFE-1986)**, I.W.O.

U-978: GÜNTHER PULST (330-1987), Commander
U-995: HANS-GEORG HESS (125-1985), Commander

HESS   **THOMSEN**

U-1202:   ROLF THOMSEN (6327-2001), Commander

The photo of **THOMSEN** was taken on 29 April 1945 as he was decorated with the *Oak Leaf* to his *Knights Cross*. The war was all but over and the expression on his face tells it all.

A total of 103 U-Boats were sent into action in the closing weeks of the war and look at the U-boat numbers. There were six of the newest boats Type XXIII plus one Type XXI boat sent into this operation. As we know, *U-2511* under Schnee did not have any opportunity to actually engage in combat but the fact that he and all these other boats were near the shores of the United States, Canada, England and the approaches to Russia was enough to pull all the ships out of the middle of the North Atlantic and leave a gaping wide open route to South America.

Many have asked how this could happen – now you know......and if you consult your sea charts in the southern Atlantic, you will find the secret island Trindade just about on the center of the open sea '*highway*', ready to outfit any ships or U-Boats passing by with food and fresh water. Can you see how all the pieces fit together so perfectly......but wait – as the TV commercials always say..........there is more.

Hitler, Mistress Are Reported to Be Safe On Patagonia Estate

CHICAGO, July 16 (UP)—Chicago Times Correspondent Vincent De Pascal reported from Montevideo today that he is "virtually certain" Adolf Hitler and Eva Braun are on a German-owned estate in Patagonia.

His dispatch was carried in today's edition of the Times.

'Friends Are Safe'

"From information just received from Buenos Aires", De Pascal wrote, "I am virtually certain that Adolf Hitler and his 'wife', Eva Braun, the latter dressed in masculine clothes, landed in Argentina and are on an immense German owned estate in Patagonia."

De Pascal said they reportedly landed on a lonely Patagonian shore from a German submarine which "supposedly" returned to surrender to the allies.

He said that according to his information, "received from reliable channels", Hitler and Eva are living on one of a number of estates in Patagonia purchased by Germans to provide sanctuary for Nazi overlords.

"In this connection", De Pascal wrote, "the utmost significance is now attached to the words of Gen. Basilo Pertime at a banquet on June 4: 'I am glad to announce that our friends are safe at last'."

PROBE SUB SURRENDER

BUENOS AIRES, July 16 (UP)— A special investigation commission of the Argentine government proposed tonight that the German sub-

Will Use Idle Govt. Silver For Money

WASHINGTON, July 16 (AP)— Senator Murdock (D-Utah) told the senate today that the treasury and President Truman have agreed that 300,000,000 ounces of idle government silver shall be used for money.

In effect, this "monetization" means the treasury can issue $387,000,000 in silver certificates, holding the 300,000,000 ounces as backing for this currency.

Murdock told reporters the action will "help the prestige of silver money throughout the world."

Murdock also said it would save money in two ways:

1. It would save the interest which would have to be paid if the $387,000,000 were obtained by borrowing. Murdock estimated this interest at $7,740,000 a year.

Comments from Members

An email of 3 December 2013 from **GARY JACKSON (6396-2001)** says: "My mother went with her parents before the war ended in 1945 to Colombia. He father, my grandfather, worked for Standard Oil there. My mother was 18 at the time and got a job in Bogota working as a secretary for the president of Avianca Colombian Airlines. In those days right after the war many of the offices and hangars still had the German language signs posted around the offices and hangars from when the Germans had operated the airline.

Around 1947 she was invited by a good Colombian girlfriend to attend a party one evening, attended by many foreigners and my mother did not know or understand the languages they spoke. Towards the end of the party her friend had arranged for another woman and her male companion to give her a ride back to her place in their car.

My mother had no idea who Martin Bormann was at the time. The only reason my mother remembered this man so well is what happened next, as my mother found it very strange. The man had been very quiet and polite throughout the evening, not really attracting attention to himself. As they were leaving, the man opened the car door for my mother and her friend, the woman in the front seat called out to him, calling him Martin in Spanish.

All of a sudden the man began screaming at the woman in German and in Spanish, yelling that he had told her never to call him that name. My mother never forgot that little incident as that man just exploded in rage and it was so strange as she could not understand why anyone would get upset by being called Martin. After that night, she never saw that man again.

Years later when she saw several photos of Martin Bormann in a book she realized who that man was. Later my mother married and moved to Maracaibo, Venezuela where I was born. Growing up there over the years I saw many German families, who never liked their children to associate with the American oil company family kids, something at the time I could not understand why, but what I remember most was the men or fathers of those German kids, as many seemed to be tall and blond, and always seemed physically fit. So when you write that Hitler and others might have survived in Latin America, I'm sure they did.

Recent email from US Air Force pilot **JIM PRESTON (7168-2007)**:
"I doubted his (Hitler's) death long before I became one of you in Sharkhunters Harry, but after my trip with you to Argentina I was convinced."
JIM was with us on our 2010 Sharkhunters *"Patrol"* to Argentina.

Recent email from **MIKE TORRESON (371-LIFE-1987)**:
"Very good explanation, given the way *'leaders'* of powerful nations act; also given the fact that *'our'* CIA was a 'joint venture' with General Gahlen to bring all those truckloads of Soviet Intel, not to mention other later *'joint ventures'* (General Eisenhower showing up down there). You nailed it =:)"

Why Didn't " *THEY*" Go After Him?

There is no question that Adolf Hitler and many others did indeed escape the crumbled Europe and lived out their lives in relative safety in South America, primarily Argentina – no question at all. However, a listener to the radio show of **JEFF RENSE (7680-2013)** on which I was the guest, asked a question that we have been asked in the past and it is a very valid question – a damn good question indeed. People have frequently asked;
   "Why didn't *THEY* go after Hitler?"

As I said, a very good question – so I immediately ask who is *THEY*?

There is a moment of silence and//or stumbling as they think past their initial question, then they say "*ISRAEL*".

We remind them that there was no such state as Israel at the end of the war and in fact, Israel did not exist until some years later.

They stumble and stammer some more, they then say "*The Mossad*". We remind them that since there was no Israel, there was also no Mossad and even once there was an Israel in 1948, they were a tiny new nation just trying to stay alive in those days so it could not have been Israel and the Mossad.

Then their eyes light up and they ask the really obvious question;
   "What about the USA?"

To fully understand why Adolf Hitler, Eva Braun//Hitler, Martin Bormann and hundreds, perhaps even thousands of men who held high positions in the Third Reich were safe in Argentina we must look at the situation there.

These men came under the protection of Juan Perón and the Argentine military. This *'friendship'* was bought with billions of dollars worth of treasure brought to Argentina and principally under the control of Martin Bormann. In addition to the massive wealth, men of the Reich founded a nuclear research laboratory on an island at the village where Adolf Hitler and so many more lived – Heumel Island on Lake Nahuel Huapi at the town of San Carlos di Bariloche. Perón built his mountain troop training school on the mainland a few hundred yards across the lake from this island. According to some, Dr. Richter and his team achieved the world's first cold fusion at this island laboratory in the early 1950's.

The Argentine Air Force was completely rebuilt and restructured right after the war, thanks to at least three of the Luftwaffe's very best. They were Werner Baumbach, Commander of Kampfgeschwader 200 (KG 200, the bomber squadron that had all the high-tech and secret planes); Hans-Ulrich Rudel, probably the best all-round pilot ever – he sank a battleship, many smaller ships, uncounted trucks and more than 500 Soviet tanks for which he was decorated with the **Knights Cross** with **Oak Leaf, Crossed Swords** and **Diamonds – in** *GOLD*; and there was the *"Fighter General"* **ADOLF GALLAND (2854-1993)**. All this was on top and fairly well known, but there were many, many others of the Third Reich who were needed by Perón as he more or less bought his way to the top in Argentina.

Baumbach												Rudel												**GALLAND**

Further, there were hundreds of former SS men in and around Bariloche. They had heavily armed security both on the land and on the lake, so no small clandestine force would have had any possibility of success. Add to this the large ring of observation points in the mountains all around the lake and in the town. It would have been impossible for anything short of an all-out large scale invasion to get into the area.

Why didn't the USA '*go after Hitler*'? With all this protection from Perón and the unlikelihood that Perón would ever willingly give up any of these men to the USA or to anyone else, nothing short of a full scale invasion could have even begun to accomplish this and the USA was tired of war. But there is another compelling reason.

This now is theory mind you, but based on hard facts. At this point, we look back to 1958 when yours truly was a young punk in the United States Air Force and I spent the first six months of that year in intense weapons training at Lowrey Air Force Base in Denver, Colorado. In the early part of our training, we watched films of the United States early attempts to build a nuclear bomb. The US special weapons project was moving very slowly and in fact, if I remember correctly in the book "*Japan's Secret War*" by **ROBERT WILCOX (25-1984)** released in 1984, **BOB** wrote that Japan test fired their first nuclear device a week before the US did.

German U-Boats were trying to make the dangerous voyage to Japanese held ports in the Indian Ocean and in the Pacific carrying all sorts of high tech weaponry and uranium. The Allies had the codes and knew which boats were carrying what, and they were ambushed by British submarines as they came over Denmark and into the Denmark Straits.

U-234 was under the command of **JOHANN HEINRICH FEHLER (32-1984)** and he was not a young Skipper like the others who walked into the trap. He had been a merchant Skipper before the war and in the early days, was the Demolitions Officer aboard the raider *ATLANTIS*.

Sensing there was something amiss with his ordained course, he changed course and so the Royal Navy submarine waiting in ambush for *U-234* had no target as the wily **FEHLER** had gone a different way. The cease fire order from Großadmiral Karl Dönitz found *U-234* in the North Atlantic so they had a choice where to put in for their surrender. After an officer's conference, they surrendered to the USA – with their 560 kilos of uranium.

Lehmann-Willenbrock   Fehler

Looking back upon my Spec-Weps training, the USA was struggling but right around the time of the German surrender, the US Spec-Weps program took a gigantic leap forward. We were told it was because our brilliant scientists had done magnificent work etc. but as we look back, we must wonder about this.

Photo below – inspecting *U-234* in the US after her surrender

Germany surrendered and suddenly the USA had all manner of brilliant German scientists, fissionable material for weapons building, intercontinental ballistic missiles, jet planes and even rocket powered planes, the first true submarine (the Type XXI and Type XXIII) and God knows what else. Even today we do not know all that came over from Germany after their surrender.

So what if………what if the agreement was made to turn over all this information, material, scientists etc. to the USA and in exchange, nobody would go after Hitler and the others. It was a pretty easy decision to make. On the one hand, the US would receive untold advancements in science, weaponry and other greatly needed areas as already described and Hitler and the others of the Reich would be allowed to live out their lives quietly in Argentina.

On the other hand, if agreement was not reached, how many thousands of the top German scientists would have gone to the Soviet Union? The atomic bomb would not have been ready for Hiroshima or Nagasaki, meaning the deaths of hundreds of thousands of American troops and most likely almost the entire Japanese race who were prepared to fight to the last man if necessary.

The Soviet Union would have been the leader in nuclear armament, would have had the jet fighters, the rockets, the ICBMs etc. much earlier. In other words, if the agreement had not been reached, the war in the Pacific would have gone on much longer, millions more would have died, and the USSR would have been the leader in all phases of weaponry and then the USA would have had to march into Argentina in a full military invasion.

As I already said, this is my theory but I think it is a pretty solid one and, backed up by the thousands of files we have from the various research archives thanks to S.E.I.G. Agents **TAUCHER** and **REMBRANDT**, and our best S.E.I.G. Agent of all – **PIZZARRO**; there is no doubt in my mind that this is what happened. We have files from the US National Archives, from Dutch Intelligence and from various archives abandoned when the STASI moved out.

There is no way anyone else could pull all this together and that is why I am absolutely certain this is the way it actually happened. Sharkhunters is not a part time hobby – I work 12 to 14 hours per day in my office or I am in the field in Argentina, in Germany, in Austria, on forgotten islands, Brazil and so many other places. There is no doubt in my mind that Adolf Hitler, Eva Braun, Martin Bormann and hundreds of others did indeed go to Argentina and other than Adolf Eichmann and Klaus Barbie, lived out their lives in peace and safety thanks to the factors put forth in this book.

What Do Others Think of This Theory?

CARTER MANIERE (6352-2001) emailed:
"I'd venture a guess that since AH had provided the vehicle for untold millions or billions to the Military-Industrial Complex, as well as the various banks and bankers who funded all of the war, he was rewarded with safety for the remaining years of his life. You have most likely read or heard of *'Wall Street and the Rise of Hitler'*. Look at all those tens of thousands of aircraft and ships, tanks etc. built in the US and Britain – how many are left, where did they end up and who paid for them.....and just who got the profits?"

From **BILL KRUSE (6659-2003)**:
"I like your theory about why no one in the US tried to go after Hitler when he escaped to Argentina. It certainly fits for the times we were in and the benefits we got through the acquisition of German scientists like Werner von Braun. It was the perfect get away! Keep up the good work of keeping history straight."

KEITH SANDERS (7035-2006) is with British Military and he says:
"Well done. I agree with you and your summation of the flight in both senses of the word! For me, the disappearance of the 560 kg (of uranium) from the L of C says it all. We have an annotated copy of a document from the TNA where the figure 560 and the annotation 'X' has been added possibly by British Intelligence. We had the elimination of all documentation relating to the German Nuclear Factory on the orders of Harold Wilson in 1966. Harold was a suspected Soviet Agent anyway! You will find on my DVD a reference page from the RAOC Gazette published in 1946 referring to the German Atomic Bomb Factory. Last year the RLC Museum demanded to know which issue I had found the reference. So shortly I will visit again to see if that magazine too has *'disappeared'*. The RAOC, RASC, Pioneers etc. have been merged into the Royal Logistics Corps or the *'Really Large Corps' as we call it*."

From **JAGO SINGH (7159-2007)** in Malaysia;
"Fully agree with your theory. If this agreement had not been reached, not only would the Soviets become the first nuclear power, they also would have had no hesitation to use A-bombs on US forces in Europe if they did not return home immediately.
Consequently – the RED IRON CURTAIN would have begun from the French Coast to the Sea of Japan!!!"

From **BARRY HACKNEY (7659-2012)**:
"As usual, you make perfect sense. Operation '*Paperclip*' brought a large number of German scientists who were known Nazis to the US, which greatly bolstered US advances in many fields, kept them out of Soviet hands and greatly enhanced US advances in weapons, aerospace, medicine and industry. It fueled the US post war economic boom and enabled great strides in military technology. The Congress and the powerful leftist lobby did not want them, but the OSS realized the dire need to get them here rather than to the Soviet Union, so it was done quietly with fake documentation. It is not unreasonable that part of the deal was quietly allowing Argentina to keep some Nazis and Hitler, who was no longer a threat to anyone and not healthy enough to contemplate any kind of a comeback.

EDITOR NOTE – We have in hand, a very large list of the many, many German and Austrian scientists that were brought into the USA. A page or two of such files appear in this book. Some were Members of Sharkhunters including Dr. **HEINZ SCHLICKE (1820-1991)** who worked in Milwaukee on military projects for years after the end of the war.

About the Author

Born and raised in Chicago and the western suburbs, Harry Cooper joined the US Air Force right out of high school. After six months intensive training is special weapons (hydrogen bombs) at Lowry Air Force Base (Denver) he was mis-assigned to Chanute Air Force only 100 miles from his home. To his very good luck, he was assigned to the base swimming pool as a lifeguard, working one day on and one day off, making it easy to go home every second day. When the summer ended, he was transferred to an active base and was assigned to the 98th Bomb Wing at Lincoln Air Force Base just outside Lincoln, Nebraska.

After spending two and a half years working with special weapons and since he always wanted to be a fighter pilot, he applied for Officer Candidate School as he neared his 21st birthday. He was the only one of 30 who passed the tough two-day long battery of tests and he was assigned an OCS class. His pilot's physical gave him a clean slate to fly, but luck was not with him. The Air Force was so overloaded with pilots from World War II and Korea that Air Cadets was shut down. He could be an officer but not a pilot. That is not what he wanted.

He was then honorably discharged from the Air Force and went to college where he earned his BS in Business Administration and began his career in the Chicago area. Since he could not enter aerial combat, he chose the next best thing – he went into auto racing! He first tried his hand at drag

racing and while driving for a friend, he was Class Champion 11 times out of 22 – pretty good. But the following year, he drove his own car and out of the next 26 weeks, he was Class Champion 26 times and Little Stock Eliminator four times, setting some national records along the way.

Then his heart turned to the oval tracks and after three successful years at the short tracks around Chicago, where he was a racing news sportscaster on the *"Motorsports International"* television show, he moved up to the big tracks and raced against A. J. Foyt, the Unser Brothers, Johnny Rutherford and other great racers. He was a Feature Editor at *Stock Car Racing Magazine* during his racing years doing '*behind the wheel*' racing reports as well as monthly columns for major American and Australian racing magazines and was an executive for a Chicago firm.

Things changed drastically for him in 1976. His crew chief left for a job in the normal world, his assistant crew chief quit to open his own auto parts store and his best crew member quit to join the Air Force. While running the 1976 Texas 500 in the lead pack, his engine blew! On the way back to Chicago, the engine in the transporter truck blew. It was not a good sign. The final straw was when he got to the office the next day and found that his superior had left the company and his new boss was a corporate executive for whom Harry had no respect. Time for a change!

1976 Texas 500

It really was time for a major change, so Harry sold everything, bought a 30-foot sailing yacht and went to live the quiet life in the Florida Keys and the Bahamas. This was to change his life and in fact, the history of the War At Sea itself. It was there he became interested in the U-Bootwaffe.

While cruising in the southern Bahamas, Harry stopped at a strange island that had been a working plantation during the war years. There were the ruins of a mansion atop a hill, the remains of a barracks building and a radio shack nearby. The caretaker told him that a few German U-Boats had stopped there for fresh water during the war. That put the hook in Harry and once he returned to Chicago, he began to intensively research the U-Boat portion of WW II and has become the world's preeminent expert on the subject.

Returning to the business world, he became Regional Vice President for a major company in Chicago but founded Sharkhunters in 1983. By mid-1987, he realized that it would be impossible to keep a regular job and then spend all the time necessary to contact the veterans, dig in the files, visit the veterans to interview them and all the other tasks necessary to preserving this history honestly. He made a tough decision.

On a Friday in July, he turned in the keys to his six offices around Illinois and quit his high-paying executive job, just two weeks after getting a nice raise in salary. His wife of just two years was most surprised with this decision and even more surprised (maybe even shocked) to learn that they were moving to Florida to do this research full time and at no salary. She was not convinced at all, since they were to have their first child in less than four months and now there was no insurance, no security - but this had to be done!

Fortunately, it succeeded and Sharkhunters has the great distinction of being the only real source for the history of the WW II U-Bootwaffe.

Harry is a LIFE member of the Adventurer's Club in Chicago (former Editor of the newsletter), member of the Chicago Press Club and the International Press Club of Chicago. He wrote more than a dozen books, helped produce several television productions and escorted dozens of history tours around the world.

Harry is listed in *"Who's Who in America"* as well as in *"Who's Who of American Business Leaders"* and in 2006 was nominated as *"Man of the Year"* by the American Biographical Institute. He spent twelve years with the United States Coast Guard (Aux.) achieving the position of Flotilla Commander with a rank similar to a full Lieutenant. With this research, Harry has met and become friends with most of the surviving Skippers, many of the officers and crewmen from the U-Bootwaffe as well as  American sub vets and world leaders from the US, the former Soviet Union and modern day Russia.

About Sharkhunters

Founded in February 1983, Sharkhunters International is the first, the best and the only accurate and official source of published history on the U-Bootwaffe. The reason is simple; the data not only comes from official files and documents but it also comes from the memories of those who lived this war. The top Skippers, many of the officers and crewmen of the U-Bootwaffe were participating Members as were a great many Allied personnel including the four *Medal of Honor* American submarine Skippers of the war.

Fluckey
(2169-1992)

O'Kane
(1540-1990)

Ramage
(948-1989)

Street
(2448-1992)

Many other great men were Members of Sharkhunters including these;

Kretschmer
(122-1985)

Topp
(118-19985)

Hardegen
(102-1985)

Hess
(125-1985)

RONALD REAGAN (1858-1991) was a Sharkhunters Member from 1991 until his passing.

Let us send a complimentary copy of our **KTB** Magazine for your inspection. Send an email to us at **sharkhunters@earthlink.net**, tell us your name (first & last); by return email, you'll be reading our **KTB** Magazine.

Sharkhunters *'Patrols'* and *'Expeditions'*

In addition to publishing the most historically accurate information on the history of the U-Bootwaffe and the men who fought the war on both sides, Sharkhunters also organizes tours to many historic places for our Members. For instance:

Bunker Patrol from Berlin east to Warsaw.

Destroyed HQ of the OKW

Abandoned fortress in Poland

Gun bunker overlooking the Baltic

Wolfsschanze (Wolf's Lair)

Sharkhunters does not merely use files and documents in our research but we go to the places where this history took place. We videotape, shoot still photos and we walk in the footsteps of history. During this *'Patrol'* we slept in the SS officers' barracks at Hitler's Wolfsschanze, the (Wolf's Lair), where the assassination attempt was made on Hitler in 1944. Sharkhunters was there.

The Southern Redoubt/Fortress Area

The Allies feared the leaders of the Reich would make a desperate last ditch stand in the Bavarian Alps at the Obersalzberg with its bunkers, tunnels and fortifications, some of which are still undiscovered today.

Coal bunkers   **Hitler's tunnel**   **Göring's bunker entrance**

Go to our website www.sharkhunters.com and click Previous Tours

Northern Germany

At the U-Boat Memorial   **The Skipper at the Periscope**

With the veterans   **At the submarine *U-995***

What the Allies Called the "Ratline"

Thousands of important men of the Third Reich escaped Germany in various ways but almost all of them departed from places like Villagarcia in Spain aboard tramp steamers, large wooden sailing ships and in some cases, by U-Boat. To replenish fresh water and food (pigs, goats & turtles) they could stop at Trindade.

Ready to leave the ship by chopper   Northern plateau; radio tower #2

Ruins on the southern plateau where radio tower #1 was built.

Special thanks to the Brazilian Navy for their tremendous help in making this expedition possible. Their ships, their personnel and their Navy was absolutely top notch. We could not have made this exploration to Trindade without them. Obrigado!

The Relocated Third Reich in Argentina

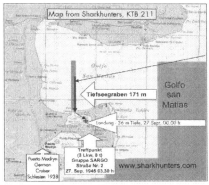

The Reich knew Golfo San Mathias very well before, during and after World War Two

Singing the old German military songs in a quiet restaurant in a little town deep in the Argentine wilderness

Sharkhunters goes where the history was made. We talk to the people who made this history; we talk to those who watched it happen; we talk to children of the people involved and we shoot our own photographs for the most accurate details possible. Much more information is released in the 2nd book in the Hitler Escape Trilogy entitled "*The Secret Alliance*". It is the story of the long relationship between Germany and Argentina.

The Reich Moves to South America
And our Sharkhunters "*Patrols*" follow them.....

.....to an island in the southern Atlantic vacated by Brazil in 1939 for the use of the Kriegsmarine in the early stages of the war then again at the end of the war for two years after, including this radio facility built in 1939.

1939 German photo   2009 photo by the author

Who lived here in Argentina?

In this manor house?   In this eerie hotel?

We know the answers to these questions because our Sharkhunters groups have been here. You may join Sharkhunters for any of our expeditions; check the website for details. You may also read all about the move by the leaders of the Reich to this area in our book "*Hitler in Argentina*" which is also available from Sharkhunters. Check the website for details and click on "*Previous Tours*". Our web address is below on every page.

What Else From Sharkhunters?

We do more here at Sharkhunters – much more. Log onto our website at www.sharkhunters.com and see all that is featured there – such as:

- Books – many more books are listed;
- DVDs – almost 200 different titles covering:
  Combat action on land – tanks, artillery, infantry
  Aerial combat – much from gun cameras
  Submarine warfare of several countries
  Personal interviews with many WW II veterans
  Great films by Sharkhunters Member **LENI RIEFENSTAHL**
  Different looks at life before the war as well as during
  Training films to fly various USAAF fighters and bombers
  Much more………….take a moment to check them out

- Hand signed, limited edition fine art prints
- Hand signed photographs of veterans
- CDs of music of the war years – German, Russian etc
- CDs of interviews with WW II U-Boat Skippers
- History Tours to places of great interest.

Many of the places Sharkhunters visits are not open to the general public.

Naturally you will read all the details on becoming a Member of Sharkhunters – receiving a free hand signed photo of a veteran, our **KTB** Magazine ten times annually, discounts on any items offered by Sharkhunters and you will see all about our:

Sharkhunters 'Patrols'…..you can join us in Germany, France, Austria, Argentina, Chile and any of the other fascinating places we go AND into places off limits to everyone else. Check the website.

Other Great Books from Sharkhunters
"Adolf Hitler In Argentina"

"*Hitler in Argentina*" relates the historically accurate escape of Hitler, Eva Braun, Martin Bormann and many other high ranking figures of the Third Reich with top secret Abwehr and Kriegsmarine charts as well as files from the OSS, FBI and various other Intel organizations.

This book is the faithful transcription of a letter from a man, a Sharkhunters Member, who was a World War Two German agent and a smuggler of "*special*" people. He even had a code name. This was Don Angel Alcazar de Velasco and he told us how he helped Hitler's second in command, Martin Bormann, safely to Argentina - and how he met with Hitler again in 1952.

He reported that the dead "*Hitler*" was a double and that he personally saw the real Hitler forcibly drugged by orders of Martin Bormann and removed from the Führerbunker. We checked him out thoroughly and found him to be exactly who he said he was. This information, combined with hundreds of files from the United States National Archives, from other Intelligence Agencies and from "*Spooks*" of various countries makes this story absolutely factual.

Through our further research and personal visits by Sharkhunters Founder and President Harry Cooper has further proved this to be accurate. Cooper was at the estate where Hitler lived in Patagonia from 1945 until 1955 then to the hotels he frequented in Cordoba until his passing in the early 1960's.

Order this book today and learn real history.

Other Great Books from Sharkhunters

"the Secret Alliance"

"We shall never forget, nor be able to repay, the immense debt of gratitude we owe to our comrades of the German Army."

This was part of a speech made by General Juan Perón – on 4 April 1952! What was the connection between the Third Reich and the Argentine strongman? It's in this book.

The European conflict of World War Two ended in early May 1945, but not all Germans remained to suffer their fate at the hands of the victorious and in many cases, the brutal Allies. There were thousands of high ranking Party members, SS officers, spies, agents, scientists, engineers and all manner of the elite of the Reich who escaped the crumbled Europe in favor of a fresh start in South America, primarily Argentina.

In this book, researcher Michael Ivinheim reveals what his exhaustive researcher has discovered about the *"Black Boats"* that figure prominently into the history – not the **END** of the Third Reich but the ***RELOCATION*** of the Third Reich. This book tears away the veil of secrecy of the history of what really happened to the Third Reich.

The Secret Alliance

MICHAEL IVINHEIM

This book will open your eyes!

Order this book as a companion to *"**Hitler in Argentina**."*

Other Great Books from Sharkhunters

"U-BOAT!" (volume I)

In the *"U-BOAT!"* series, each and every volume is jam-packed with the combat memories of the men who fought the Battle of the Atlantic from all sides. You will read history and see photos available nowhere else.

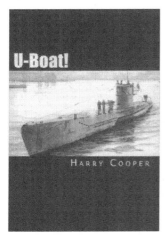

"The pages of "**U-BOAT!**" (vol. I) are fascinating reading. They tell the gripping stories of the war at sea in the words of those who lived and died in submarines and from those who hunted submarines. That old enemies have become friends is the real story of this book. None could have thought that many decades ago that this book could be published or that such mortal enemies would relate the grim stories of the war in a book written together.

I found these stories of great interest and recommend them to those

who would like to know how the war was fought at sea. It should be remembered the life of Britain and Germany depended on the outcome of the U-Boat conflict. This book reveals how this battle took place scene by scene, and the courage and bravery of the men who participated on both sides. I recommend its reading as a reminder never to get enveloped in such a conflict again."

Admiral **Frank Kelso**, CNO and Sharkhunters Member.

Read memories of Kretschmer, Dönitz, Topp, Hardegen and many other Skippers and crews. You won't find this history anywhere else.

Other Great Books from Sharkhunters
"U-BOAT!" (volume II)

"*U-BOAT!*" (vol. II) continues the fascinating tale of the German U-Bootwaffe in World War Two as well as some stories from the American side – and sadly, one of the most barbaric acts of atrocity perpetrated in any war.

These stories come directly from the memories of the men who fought in this greatest of all conflicts and there is no better or more accurate history than that which comes directly from the warriors who made this history. This book is their story and is an extension of "*U-BOAT!*" (vol. I). Come with us on a journey into the greatest conflict the world has ever known.

You'll read wartime memories from:

- Dönitz
- Thäter *U-466*
- Wattenberg *U-162*
- *AVISO GRILLE*
- Italian submarine *FINZI*
- Clandestine supply in the Caribbean to U-Boats?
- *HMS VALIANT*
- The Enemy Below
- The "*Rot Teufelboot*"
- Radiostation Atlantik
- Operation *URSULA*
  Combat long before 1939

- End of *SS SANDEMITRO*
- R-Boats across Europe
- Death of *AWA MARU*
- *SURCOUF* –French giant
- The Type IX U-Boat
- Former Mortal Enemies
- USN "*Armed Guard*"
- *U-DEUTSCHLAND*
- WW I, the Royal Navy and the German Navy
- Pirates - Uncle Sam's Navy
- *SS JEAN NICOLETTE*
  Butchery on the high seas

Other Great Books from Sharkhunters
"U-BOAT!" (volume III)

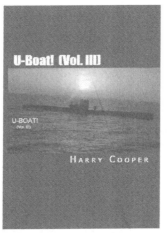

"U-BOAT!" (vol. III) continues the fascinating tale of the German U-Bootwaffe in World War Two as well as some stories from the American side with more first-person memories of the war at sea.

This book is their continuing story and is an extension of *"U-BOAT!"* (vol. I and vol. II). Come with us on a journey into the greatest conflict the world has ever known.

In this book you will read wartime memories from great warriors including:

- The code for Fähnrich
- Erich Topp   *U-552*
- Harry Cooper
- *U-DEUTSCHLAND*
- Werner Hartenstein   *U-156*
- French Submarine History
- American U-Boat Captive
- A Brit in USN Submarines
- Fregettenkapitän Norden
- Paukenschlag off Capetown
- Axis Sally
- Sink the *RIO GRANDE*
- *SS BARKDULL*
- *"Silent"* Otto Kretschmer
- Sinking of the *BERTA*
- Italian Navy Submarines
- Antarctica
- Shinjo Uchino and *I-8*
- The *"Drumbeater"*

- Helmut Schmoeckel   *U-802*
- The mysterious voyage of *U-977* and the so-called 66 days marching submerged
- Cape Fear
- loss of the aircraft carrier *USS BLOCK ISLAND*
- the *"Tethered Goats"* meant to draw kamikaze pilots to a needless death

"With the reminiscences of Topp, Kretschmer, Dönitz, Hardegen and others who fought against us with some who were on our side, we are getting the accurate picture of the men who bore the burden and gave it their all."

Captain **Edward L. Beach**
Sharkhunters Member #**1163-1989**

Other Great Books from Sharkhunters
"U-BOAT!" (volume IV)

"U-BOAT!" (vol. IV) continues the fascinating tale of the German U-Bootwaffe in World War Two as well as some stories from the American side with more first-person memories of the war at sea.

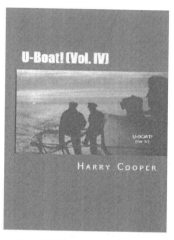

This book is their continuing story and is an extension of *"U-BOAT!"* (vol. I, II and vol. III). Come with us on a journey into the greatest conflict the world has ever known.

In this book you will read wartime memories from great warriors including:

- **U-234** and her living cargo of scientists and high rank Luftwaffe personnel
- Newfoundland as an *"Aircraft carrier"* and **HMCS CARIBOU**
- Reinhard Hardegen **U-123**
- The Golden Gate in '48
- New England's U-Boat War
- Monsunboote
- The 212 Class submarine
- The *"Slender Thread"* of German Japanese cooperation in the war
- Shelling of Lago refinery on the island Aruba by **U-156**
- Werner Hartenstein **U-156**

- Gerhard Thäter and **U-466**; through Gibraltar TWICE!
- Midgets and Chariots – the story of the Italian small boat special operations men
- Was it really a *"Happy Time"*? *"Silent"* Otto Kretschmer gives us his impression of this time

Other Great Books from Sharkhunters
"U-BOAT!" (volume V)

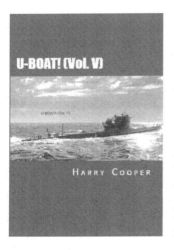

"U-BOAT!" (vol. V) continues the fascinating tale of the German U-Bootwaffe in World War Two as well as some stories from the American side with more first-person memories of the war at sea.

This book is their continuing story and is an extension of *"U-BOAT!"* (vol. I, II, III and vol. IV). Come with us on a journey into the greatest conflict the world has ever known.

In this book you will read wartime memories from great warriors including:

- POW's from *U-66* aboard *USS BLOCK ISLAND*
- Aboard *U-764*; coward?
- Death of *U-654*
- *SS BENJAMIN BOURNE*
- Capture of *HMS SEAL*
- *"Battle of Bowmanville"*
- *U-960* in September 1943
- Helmut Witte *U-159*
- Jürgen Oesten *U-861*
- Art Jacobson, Merchant
- Günther Gräser
- Skipper of *U-81* and *U-513*
- Could the V-2 win the war?
- Eisenhower's Starvation Camps – more than one million starved to death

- More Secrets of *U-234*
- Aboard *USS GRAYLING*
- U-Boat operations off Aruba and Curacao
- *USS QUEENFISH* attacks and sinks *AWA MARU*
- Last Patrol of *U-3030*
- The Type IX U-Boat

Helmut Witte

Other Great Books from Sharkhunters
"Rise and Fall of the U-Bootwaffe"

Germany was designing and building U-Boats in secret long before the outbreak of the Second World War. They had false companies set up in other European countries under cooperation between Krupp's Germania Werft and the German Navy, not yet called the Kriegsmarine. Various world navies placed orders with these shell companies for submarines and the German submarine industry learned.

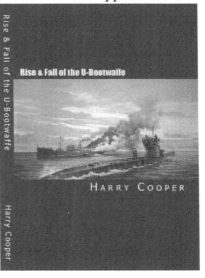

German U-Boats were in combat and sinking ships some three years before World War Two began! In this book you will read the actual oath the U-Bootfahrer swore for these secret missions – and you will walk through the modified *U-234* with her secret cargo of scientists, technicians, a Luftwaffe general with his staff as well as high tech weaponry and uranium.

Insights by Großadmiral Karl Dönitz are in this book as well as Germany's aid to Generalissimo Franco in the Spanish Civil War during the operation named for the daughter of Dönitz.

Why was Germany vigorously involved in building U-Boats in contravention to the edicts of the brutal Treaty of Versailles? How was it kept secret from the rest of the world? Why did Germany enter World War Two so poorly prepared for submarine warfare and what contributed to her loss? The answers are in this book.

Other Great Books from Sharkhunters

"When Eagles Soared!" (vol I)

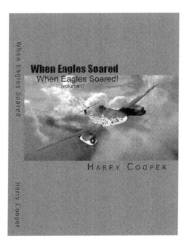

These were the *"Golden Knights"* of the skies in World War Two. They slipped the chains of gravity and soared high above the earth on their wings and dreams. Some returned covered in glory – many did not return at all.

This book contains first person memories of Luftwaffe pilots, American pilots, Royal Air Force and Royal Navy pilots – fliers of many nations are included here as well as some technological insights into the planes, the powerplants and the weaponry they carried.

Some memories will make you ache to turn back the clock to those days of glory – some will bring a tear to your eye for a brave flier who did not return while a few will make you all but collapse with laughter!

There are stories of the war that you've never read; hundreds of photos many of which you have never seen. Stories from the greatest fighter pilots of all time and really funny memories of some very strange planes.

Strap on your parachute and helmet, climb into your P-38, your Me 109, your La-5 or whatever is your favorite warbird and fly along with us on this mission back into military aviation history and memories.

These men will never come our way again; this kind of man vs. man combat in the skies has faded into history forever. Relive it in this book.

Other Great Books from Sharkhunters

"Kassel 1939"
"The First Warrior's Convention of Greater Germany"

Germany and Austria had just reunited during the "Anschluß" forming "Großdeutschland" or Greater Germany and there was great pride in this accomplishment. The city of Kassel hosted the first Greater German Reich Warriors' gathering on the weekend of 2 – 4 June 1939. Hundreds of thousands of soldiers came from all parts of the Reich on more than 120 special trains and hundreds of thousands citizens swelled the group to more than half a million. Kettles of one thousand liters each dished out three hundred sixty thousand meals daily – this was a demonstration of power!

Germany was destroyed – devastated, broken and helpless under the victorious Allied powers after World War One and Germany was allowed only a token military. By 1939 however, Germans held their head up proudly – they had their dignity back!

Return with us now to a time when national pride and patriotism was at its zenith in Germany as well as in many other nations. The Reich was forged in a fire never before witnessed in the civilized world.

This book is a compilation of 100 rare photos of this massive event that haven't been seen since the end of World War Two. One of our European Members found these extremely rare photos and sent them to us for this book. It is pure history!

Other Great Books from Sharkhunters
"Rare U-BOAT Types"

The U-Bootwaffe of the Kriegsmarine had the largest submarine Force ever in history, before or since World War Two.

The Type VII and Type IX with all of their variants are well known, and there were hundreds of these Types built. They cruised the world's oceans with great success and will be the subject of other books in the near future.

In this book we look at U-Boats that were produced in limited numbers as well as boats that the Kriegsmarine thought about, planned, built, experimented with including some that were far advanced for their time. They were quickly scooped up by the victorious Allies and went to the USA, to England and to the Soviet Union for testing and evaluation.

This book tells about those rare Types and included photos of the boats and the Skippers, some never seen before, as well as Turmabzeichen (conning tower emblems) along with the dates of launch, commissioning, their final fates as well as any ships they sank during their career.

This book gives details of the rare U-Boats Types like no other before. We know of no other book that gives all this history.

Keep checking our website www.sharkhunters.com as we are coming out with a few new books each year............facts and history that you can't get anywhere else. This all came from the veterans themselves.

Send an email to *sharkhunters@earthink.net* with your name and we will send the current issue of our **KTB** Magazine to you by return email at no charge or obligation.

DVDs of History

In addition to great books of history, Sharkhunters has also made available DVDs of history. Many of our DVDs come from the veterans themselves. Go to **www.sharkhunters.com** then click **DVDs** for full information and in many cases, for short clips of the DVD.

DVD-4   DVD-5   DVD-6

DVD-8   DVD-11   DVD-12   DVD-14

DVD-15   DVD-16   DVD-17   DVD-18

More Great DVDs of History

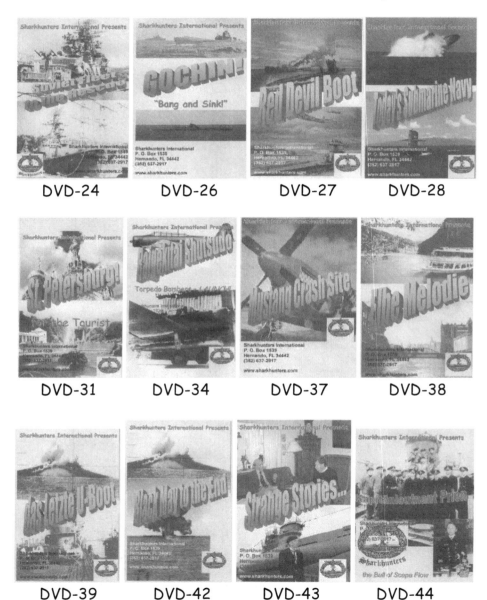

DVD-24   DVD-26   DVD-27   DVD-28

DVD-31   DVD-34   DVD-37   DVD-38

DVD-39   DVD-42   DVD-43   DVD-44

More Great DVDs of History
You Can't Find Anywhere Else

DVD-4   The story of *U-995* in the Kriegsmarine and Norwegian Navy
DVD-5   The lost bunker with three Type XXI boats still inside
DVD-6   Günther Prien and his triumphant entry into Berlin
DVD-8   **KARL-FRIEDERICH MERTEN** and *U-68*
DVD-11 Castles of the SS
DVD-12 Tunnels of the Third Reich
DVD-14 Triumph of the Will
DVD-15 U-Boats in Combat
DVD-16 Combat at Sea
DVD-17 Dive and Discovery of "*U-WHO*"?
DVD-18 Visit the Soviet Union 1991
DVD-24 Soviet Fleet to the Rescue
DVD-26 *GOCHIN!* Ride along aboard *I.10* on her 4th war patrol
DVD-27 Red Devil Boot – Ride along with **ERICH TOPP** and *U-552*
DVD-28 Today's Submarine Navy; run to the recruiter
DVD-31 St. Petersburg for the Tourist; magnificent city
DVD-34 Raigekitai Shutsudo
DVD-37 Mustang Crash Site. The war ends in a Florida swamp
DVD-38 Elbe Melodie – beautiful German tourism film
DVD-39 Das Letzte U-Boot; the story of *U-234*
DVD-42 Black May to the End; Hans-Georg Hess tells of the end
DVD-43 Strange Stories; more from Hans-Georg Hess
DVD-44 Kapitänleutnant Prien; story of the "*Bull of Scapa Flow*"
DVD-46 Interview with **HANS GÖBELER** of the crew of *U-505*
DVD-47 Interview with **GERD RICHTER** of the crew of *U-81*
DVD-48 Interview with **DETLEV ZIMMERMANN** of *U-315*
DVD-49 Champagne in the Combat Boot; riotously funny!
DVD-50 1994 Interview with **ERICH TOPP** (*U-57, U-552*)
DVD-52 1994 Interview **REINHARD HARDEGEN** (*U-147, U-123*)
DVD-53 Secrets of the Third Reich
DVD-54 1994 Interview with **GERD THÄTER** (*U-466, U-3506*)
DVD-56 1994 Interview with **OTTO KRETSCHMER** (*U-23, U-99*)
DVD-58 1994 Interview with **HANS-GEORG HESS** (*U-995*)

More Great DVDs of History
Check the website for full details

DVD-46

DVD-47

DVD-48

DVD-49

DVD-50

DVD-52

DVD-53

DVD-54

DVD-56

DVD-58

DVD-59

DVD-60

More Great DVDs of History
Rare – and Full of Action

DVD-63

DVD-64

DVD-65

DVD-66

DVD-68

DVD-69

DVD-70

DVD-72

DVD-73

DVD-74

DVD-76

DVD-78

More Great DVDs of History
And Your Satisfaction is Guaranteed!

DVD-59   The Red Baron; story of von Richtofen

DVD-60   Interview with **JÜRGEN OESTEN**

DVD-63   Wreck of "*U-WHO?*" Revisited

DVD-64   2000 Interview with **WILHELM GRAP (*U-506*)**

DVD-65   Germany Special

DVD-66   2000 Interview with **JÜRGEN OESTEN**

DVD-68   2000 Interview with **GÜNTHER HEINRICH (*U-960*)**

DVD-69   Katoh Hayabusa Sentatoi

DVD-70   2000 Interview **HELMUT SCHMOECKEL (*U-802*)**

DVD-72   2000 Interview **GERD THÄTER (*U-466, U-3506*)**

DVD-73   Capture of *U-505* on the high seas

DVD-74   2000 Interview with **HANS-GEORG HESS (*U-995*)**

DVD-76   2000 Interview **HORST von SCHROETER (*U-123*)**

DVD-78   2000 Interview with **KURT DIGGINS (*U-458*)**

DVD-80   2000 Interview with **VOLKMAR KÖNIG (*U-99*)**

DVD-81   Rover Boys Express; shot down over Japan

DVD-82   2000 Interview with **HARRY COOPER**

DVD-85   Germany by Rail; a wonderful touristic trip

DVD-86   Westernfront! Pure combat action

DVD-87   Corregidor Sogogeki; All our assault on Corregidor

DVD-88   Sensuikan Ito Go

DVD-89   die Grauen Wolfe; More combat at sea

DVD-92   Rhine Cruise; another great touristic look to Germany

DVD-93   Song of My Comrades; Japanese submariners

DVD-94   Eva Braun Home Movies – in color

DVD-98   der Rote Faden; the Red Thread Around Hamburg

DVD-100 Wehrmacht in Combat – 1; pure combat action

DVD-101 Wehrmacht in Combat – 2; more incredible combat

More Great DVDs of History
Check the website for special prices

DVD-80   DVD-81   DVD-82   DVD-85

DVD-86   DVD-87   DVD-88   DVD-89

DVD-92   DVD-93   DVD-94   DVD-98

More Great DVDs of History
Check the website for special prices

| DVD-100 | DVD-101 | DVD-103 | DVD-104 |

| DVD-105 | DVD-106 | DVD-107 | DVD-108 |

The next four are from **LENI RIEFENSTAHL (3157-1993)**

| DVD-110 | DVD-111 | DVD-112 | DVD-113 |

More Great DVDs of History
You may view short clips on the website

DVD-114

DVD-115

DVD-116

DVD-117

DVD-118

DVD-120

DVD-121

DVD-122

DVD-123

DVD-126

DVD-127

DVD-129

Go to www.sharkhunters.com to short clips of these DVDs

More Great DVDs of History
Pure History Available Nowhere Else

DVD-103   WW II, the Beginning (1939 – 1941)
DVD-104   Barbarossa; the Invasion of the Soviet Union
DVD-105   Kampf in Sewastopol! The Crimean Campaign
DVD-106   Only the Elders; Soviet Fighter Pilots
DVD-107   Soviet Dive Bombers
DVD-108   Soviet Torpedo Bombers
DVD-110   das Blaue Licht; from **LENI RIEFENSTAHL**
DVD-111   SOS Iceberg; in English from **LENI RIEFENSTAHL**
DVD-112   Victory of Faith; from **LENI RIEFENSTAHL**
DVD-113   Olympia I; from **LENI RIEFENSTAHL**
DVD-114   Day of Freedom; from **LENI RIEFENSTAHL**
DVD-115   Olympia II; from **LENI RIEFENSTAHL**
DVD-116   History of the Reich; great history
DVD-117   Vlassov; the Soviet general with the Reich
DVD-118   the Winter War; Finland turns back the Red Army
DVD-120   Vichy; many French hated the British & Americans
DVD-121   Interview with SS Soldier; right to the point
DVD-122   Tiefland; from **LENI RIEFENSTAHL**
DVD-123   Prelude to War
DVD-126   die Goldene Stadt; Prague was beautiful
DVD-127   Doctor of Stalingrad; post-war Prison Camp
DVD-129   Firebombing of Dresden; an atrocity
DVD-130   Geburtstag der Führer; Hitler's Birthdays
DVD-131   Interview with Wolf Hess
DVD-132   SS Division Viking; how it was formed and fought
DVD-133   History of the SS
DVD-135   Blitzkrieg; STUKA dive bombers and tanks in action
DVD-136   Birth of a Nation; birth of the Klu Klux Klan

More Great DVDs of History
Check the website for special prices

DVD-130

DVD-131

DVD-132

DVD-133

DVD-135

DVD-136

DVD-137

DVD-138

DVD-139

DVD-140

DVD-141

DVD-142

Check the website for complete description of each DVD

More Great DVDs of History
Pure History Available Nowhere Else

DVD-143

DVD-144

DVD-145

DVD-146

DVD-147

DVD-148

DVD-149

DVD-150

DVD-151

DVD-152

DVD-153

DVD-154

More Great DVDs of History
Satisfaction Guaranteed or Full Refund

DVD-156

DVD-157

DVD-158

DVD-159

DVD-161

DVD-162

DVD-163

DVD-164

DVD-165

DVD-166

DVD-167

DVD-168

More Great DVDs of History
So real you hear the guns; smell the powder

DVD-137   German Folk Life; how it was in the early war years

DVD-138   Hitler Junge Quex; Early Reich History

DVD-139   Fortress Europe; hard fought combat

DVD-140   Nürnberg! The Beginning

DVD-141   Advances in Russia I; Barbarossa

DVD-142   Advance in Russia II; Barbarossa

DVD-143   Third Reich in Color; great color films of the time

DVD-144   Despair! German civilians were not well treated

DVD-145   Shattered Dreams; the end of the war was bitter

DVD-146   Personal Wars; personal films from various soldiers

DVD-147   Legion Condor; the famed fighting force in Spain

DVD-148   Reich Classics; German orchestras

DVD-149   Krieg in Farben I; the war in color

DVD-150   Krieg in Farben II; more of the war in color

DVD-151   Hitler's First Speech

DVD-152   Franco's Italians; more soldiers in Spain

DVD-153   Italian Air Force; combat not usually seen

DVD-154   Operation Drumbeat

DVD-156   Top Secret 212 Class; film taken out of Germany

DVD-157   Weltfeind; the enemy of the world – the USSR

DVD-158   Adolf Hitler – Dead or Alive; propaganda

DVD-159   Party Rally Nürnberg; a very early rally

DVD-161   Learn to Fly the P 47; USAAF film

DVD-162   Learn to Fly the B 25 and the B 26; USAAF film

DVD-163   Learn to Fly the P 40 and the P 38; USAAF film

DVD-164   Fly with the Nickel Air Force

DVD-165   Battle for Seeloh Heights; at doorsteps of Berlin

DVD-166   Starvation Camp Lager X; an Eisenhower Camp

More Great DVDs of History
Pure History Available Nowhere Else

DVD-169   DVD-170   DVD-172   DVD-173

DVD-167   Battle of the River plate; GRAF SPEE
DVD-168   Kamikaze
DVD-169   *USS BARB*; last patrols
DVD-170   Anti-Communist Russians in WW II
DVD-172   92nd Bomb Group I; actual combat films
DVD-173   92nd Bomb Group II; actual combat films

We are constantly adding great historical DVDs to our list – combat footage, interviews with veterans and much more. Please keep checking back to our website and check out our unique DVDs.

Sharkhunters offers almost 200 great CDs as well. Some are music of marching bands, others are speeches and yet others are – interesting. Go to our website and click on CDs to see them all.

Check our website www.sharkhunters.com often. We are constantly adding new DVDs and CDs. Don't miss seeing our new additions.

We are constantly adding more books to our list as well. Look at the website to see when new books are released.

NOTES

Use this page for your notes and observations.

Made in the USA
Charleston, SC
14 June 2014